A WORD IN SEASON

A WORD IN SEASON

Readings for the Liturgy of the Hours

VII

Ordinary Time, Year II
(Weeks 1-17)

AUGUSTINIAN PRESS
1999

ISBN: 0-941491-11-0 (Series)
ISBN: 0-941491-85-4 (paper)
ISBN: 0-941491-86-2 (cloth)

Augustinian Press
P.O. Box 476
Villanova, PA 19085 USA

Cover design: Dame Joanna Jamieson, O.S.B., of Stanbrook Abbey.
Printed in the United States of America.

Contents

FIRST WEEK IN ORDINARY TIME

MONDAY
Origen of Alexandria 1
Gregory Palamas 2
Hildegard of Bingen 4
Abhishiktananda 5

TUESDAY
Hilary of Poitiers 7
Julian of Norwich 8
Pierre de Bérulle 9

WEDNESDAY
John Henry Newman 10
Catherine of Siena 12

THURSDAY
Abhishiktananda 14
Ambrose of Milan 15
Chromatius of Aquileia 17

FRIDAY
Ephrem of Syria 18

SATURDAY
Jean Daniélou 20
Augustine of Hippo 22

SECOND WEEK IN ORDINARY TIME

SUNDAY
Jean Daniélou 24
Augustine of Hippo 25

MONDAY
John Chrysostom 28

TUESDAY
Gregory of Nyssa 29
Bede Griffiths 31

WEDNESDAY
Jean Daniélou 32

THURSDAY
Irenaeus of Lyons 34
Hildegard of Bingen 35

FRIDAY
John Henry Newman 37

SATURDAY
Jean Daniélou 39
Clement of Rome 40

THIRD WEEK IN ORDINARY TIME

SUNDAY
John Chrysostom 43
John Henry Newman 45

MONDAY
Clement of Rome 46
Jean Daniélou 48

TUESDAY
Origen of Alexandria 49

WEDNESDAY
John Chrysostom 51
Augustine of Hippo 53

THURSDAY
Jacob of Sarugh 54
Origen of Alexandria 55
Theodoret of Cyrus 56

FRIDAY
Francis of Sales 58
Jean Daniélou 60

SATURDAY
Philoxenus of Mabbug 61
Rupert of Deutz 62
Origen of Alexandria 63

FOURTH WEEK IN ORDINARY TIME

SUNDAY
Bernard of Clairvaux 66

MONDAY
Hilary of Poitiers 68

TUESDAY
Augustine of Hippo 69
Meister Eckhart 72
Aphraates of Persia 73

WEDNESDAY
Rupert of Deutz 75

John Climacus 76

THURSDAY
Gregory the Great 78
Guerric of Igny 80

FRIDAY
Bede of England 82

SATURDAY
Cyril of Alexandria 83
Caesarius of Arles 85

FIFTH WEEK IN ORDINARY TIME

SUNDAY
Chromatius of Aquileia 87
Novatian 88

MONDAY
Quodvultdeus of Carthage 89
Procopius of Gaza 91

TUESDAY
Quodvultdeus of Carthage 92

WEDNESDAY
Cyril of Alexandria 94

THURSDAY
Quodvultdeus of Carthage 95

FRIDAY
John Henry Newman 97

SATURDAY
Rupert of Deutz 98

SIXTH WEEK IN ORDINARY TIME

SUNDAY
John Chrysostom 100

MONDAY
John Chrysostom 102

TUESDAY
Cyprian of Carthage 103
Fulgentius of Ruspe 104

WEDNESDAY
Symeon the New Theologian 106
Augustine of Hippo 107

THURSDAY
Jean de Caussade 109

FRIDAY
John Henry Newman 111

SATURDAY
Pierre Teilhard de Chardin 112

SEVENTH WEEK IN ORDINARY TIME

SUNDAY
Leander of Seville 115
John Henry Newman 116

MONDAY
Cyril of Alexandria 118

TUESDAY
Ralph the Fervent 119

WEDNESDAY
John Chrysostom 121
John Henry Newman 122

THURSDAY
Symeon the New Theologian 124
Augustine of Hippo 125

FRIDAY
Augustine of Hippo 127
Primasius of Hadrumetum 128

SATURDAY
Ralph the Fervent 130

EIGHTH WEEK IN ORDINARY TIME

SUNDAY
John Henry Newman 132
Paul VI 133

MONDAY
Paulinus of Nola 135
Henry of Friemar 136

TUESDAY
Leo the Great 138

WEDNESDAY
John Chrysostom 140

THURSDAY
Ralph the Fervent 142
Walter of Saint Victor 143

FRIDAY
Thomas More 145
John Henry Newman 147
SATURDAY
Jean Daniélou 148

NINTH WEEK IN ORDINARY TIME

SUNDAY
John Chrysostom 151
MONDAY
Tertullian of Carthage 152
John Chrysostom 155
TUESDAY
Thomas Merton 156
Columban 158
Ildefonsus of Toledo 160
WEDNESDAY
Theodoret of Cyrus 162
Meister Eckhart 163
Jerome of Jerusalem 164
THURSDAY
John the Solitary 166
Letter to Diognetus 167
FRIDAY
Gregory Nazianzen 169
Thomas Merton 170
SATURDAY
Augustine of Hippo 172
Isaac of Stella 174

TENTH WEEK IN ORDINARY TIME

SUNDAY
John Chrysostom 176
MONDAY
Columban 177
John Chrysostom 178
Richard Rolle 180
TUESDAY
Guerric of Igny 181
WEDNESDAY
Augustine of Hippo 183

THURSDAY
Augustine of Hippo 184
Augustine of Hippo 186

FRIDAY
John Henry Newman 188

SATURDAY
Meister Eckhart 190

ELEVENTH WEEK IN ORDINARY TIME

SUNDAY
John Chrysostom 192

MONDAY
Bede of England 193

TUESDAY
Hilary of Poitiers 195

WEDNESDAY
Jacques Bossuet 197

THURSDAY
Jean Daniélou 198

FRIDAY
Gregory the Great 200
Carroll Stuhlmueller 202

SATURDAY
Cyril of Alexandria 203

TWELFTH WEEK IN ORDINARY TIME

SUNDAY
Cyril of Alexandria 205

MONDAY
Walter Hilton 207
Cyril of Alexandria 208

TUESDAY
Bede of England 210

WEDNESDAY
Gregory of Nyssa 211
Bede of England 212

THURSDAY
Leo the Great 214

FRIDAY
Augustine of Hippo 216

SATURDAY

Bede of England 217

Cyril of Alexandria 219

THIRTEENTH WEEK IN ORDINARY TIME

SUNDAY

Guerric of Igny 221

MONDAY

Cyprian of Carthage 223

TUESDAY

Augustine of Hippo 224

WEDNESDAY

Nicolas Cabasilas 226

THURSDAY

Clement of Alexandria 228

FRIDAY

John Chrysostom 230

SATURDAY

Julian of Norwich 231

FOURTEENTH WEEK IN ORDINARY TIME

SUNDAY

Angela of Foligno 234

MONDAY

John Henry Newman 236

TUESDAY

Guerric of Igny 238

Athanasius of Alexandria 239

Augustine of Hippo 240

WEDNESDAY

Prosper Guéranger 242

THURSDAY

John Justus Landsberg 244

Max Picard 245

FRIDAY

Julian of Norwich 247

SATURDAY

Adam of Perseigne 249

Luis de León 250

FIFTEENTH WEEK IN ORDINARY TIME

SUNDAY
Gregory the Great 252

MONDAY
John Chrysostom 254
Jean Daniélou 255

TUESDAY
John of the Cross 257

WEDNESDAY
Meister Eckhart 258

THURSDAY
Ogerius of Locedio 260

FRIDAY
Gregory the Great 262

SATURDAY
John of the Cross 263

SIXTEENTH WEEK IN ORDINARY TIME

SUNDAY
Jean-Pierre de Caussade 266

MONDAY
Jean Daniélou 268

TUESDAY
Thomas Merton 269

WEDNESDAY
Fulgentius of Ruspe 271

THURSDAY
Jean Daniélou 273

FRIDAY
Meister Eckhart 274

SATURDAY
John Henry Newman 276
Yves Congar 277

SEVENTEENTH WEEK IN ORDINARY TIME

SUNDAY
Hilary of Poitiers 280

MONDAY
Zeno of Verona 282

TUESDAY
Gregory the Great 283

WEDNESDAY
Bernard of Clairvaux 285

THURSDAY
Gregory the Great 287

FRIDAY
Hilary of Poitiers 289

SATURDAY
Gregory the Great 290
Origen of Alexandria 291

BIOGRAPHICAL SKETCHES 295

BIBLICAL CURSUS 311

INDEX OF AUTHORS 315

FIRST WEEK IN ORDINARY TIME

MONDAY Year II

First Reading   Genesis 1:1—2:4

Responsory   *Gn 1:1.31; Jn 1:1.3*
In the beginning God created the heavens and the earth, † and God
saw everything that he had made, and it was very good.
V. In the beginning was the Word, and the Word was with God and
the Word was God. All things were made through him. † And God
saw . . .

Second Reading   From a homily on Genesis by Origen of
                     Alexandria (In Gen. Hom 13, 4: PG 12, 234-245)

God will make his heavenly likeness shine out in us

Let us make man in our own image and likeness. The work of so
great and skilled an artist as the Son of God, the creator of this
image, can never be destroyed by malice, though it can be obscured
through negligence. God's image remains within you always, even
though you yourself superimpose upon it the earthly likeness of
the man of dust. This earthly likeness is not produced in you by
God. You paint it yourself, using various kinds of sins as if they
were a palette of assorted colors. In view of this the only remedy
is to invoke the help of him who tells us through his prophet: *I have
wiped out your transgressions like a cloud and swept away your sins
like a mist.* When God has eradicated those multi-colored stains of
sin, the beautiful image which God created in you will appear in
all its radiance. You can see from this how holy scripture makes
use of forms and figures to teach the soul how to recognize and
purify itself.

Perhaps you might like to consider this image under yet another aspect. In the register of our lives there are some entries that
God makes and some that we make ourselves; the latter are the
record of our sins. Mark the apostle's words: *God,* he says, *has
canceled the legal bond which stood against us; God has set it aside,
nailing it to the cross.* What Saint Paul here calls a bond is the
obligation we put ourselves under on account of our sins. Each and

every one of us is answerable for the sins he or she commits; we write our own record. When Daniel describes the court of God sitting in judgment, he says that the books were opened. There is no doubt that these were the books containing the record of people's sins. When we sin, we ourselves write our own case record. From this it is clear that our side of the register is made up of sins, while God's side consists of acts of virtue. Saint Paul bears me out when he says: *You yourselves are a letter written not with ink but with the Spirit of the living God, a letter written not on stone tablets but on human hearts.* So then, you have within yourself God's record written by the Holy Spirit; but if you sin, you draw up a legal bond against yourself.

Observe, however, that once you have come to the cross of Christ and the grace of baptism, that bond of yours is nailed to the cross and canceled in the baptismal font. Do not rewrite what has been canceled; do not renew what has been abolished. Keep within you God's record only; let what the Holy Spirit has written be all that remains in your heart.

Responsory   Sir 42:15-16; 43:28

By the words of the Lord his works come into being, and all creation obeys his will. † As the sun as it shines looks upon all things, so the work of the Lord is full of his glory.

V. Where can we find the power to praise him, since he is greater than all his works? † As the sun . . .

Alternative Reading

From a homily by Gregory Palamas (Hom. 3, 35: PG 151, 35)

What has our creator not done to improve us?

Before creating us our creator first brought this whole universe into being from nothing for the maintenance of our bodily existence. But as for improving our ways and guiding us toward virtue, what has our Lord in his love of goodness not done for us? He has made the whole of this perceptible universe as a kind of mirror of heaven, so that in spiritual contemplation of the world around us we may reach up to heaven as if by some wonderful ladder. God has implanted in our minds an innate law, as it were an inflexible rule, an infallible judge or an unerring teacher, that is our own conscience. And so if we look deep within ourselves we shall need no other teacher to instruct us in the knowledge of good. And if we look outside ourselves we shall find the invisible God visible to us in his created world, as the apostle says.

And so having opened a way for teaching us the virtues through our own nature and through the created world, God gave us angels to protect us, and raised up the patriarchs and prophets to be our guides, and showed us signs and miracles to lead us into faith. God also gave us the written law, as a help to the law innate in our minds and the teaching of the creation. And at last, when we had scorned everything in our apathy — how different from his own continuing love and care of us! — God gave himself to us for our salvation. He poured out the wealth of his divinity into our humble state; he took our nature and became a human being like ourselves, and was called our teacher. He teaches us the greatest of his own love for us, proving it in word and deed. At the same time he urges those who obey him to imitate his compassion, and breaks down the hardness of their hearts.

Although there is love involved in the management of worldly affairs, just as there is in the relation of shepherds to their flocks and even in the devotion of owners to their personal possessions, it hardly compares with the love that unites families in close relationship, especially the love that parents feel for their children. It is based on this relationship that our Lord proves his own love for humanity, since he speaks of himself as the human Father of us all. For our sake he became human, and has given us a new life through holy baptism and through the grace of the Holy Spirit which we receive in baptism.

Responsory   *Sir 42:15-16; 43:28*

By the words of the Lord his works come into being, and all creation obeys his will. † As the sun as it shines looks upon all things, so the work of the Lord is full of his glory.

V. Where can we find the power to praise him, since he is greater than all his works? † As the sun . . .

Alternative Reading

From the writings of Saint Hildegard of Bingen
(Works of God I, visio 1, VII, X: PL 197, 746.747)

Let there be

Everything that God created in fact existed in him before the beginning of time. For all visible and invisible things were evident in the pure and holy divinity without movement and without time from eternity, just as trees or anything else that is near water appear in the water, and although they are not in it physically yet they appear there exactly as they really are. So when God said: *Let there be*, all created things immediately assumed the form which they had had when physically non-existent but observed from eternity in the foreknowledge of God. For just as everything in front of a mirror is reflected in it, so all God's creation appeared in its timeless state in the holy divinity. For how should God exist without having prior knowledge of the divine works? After assuming physical reality all his creation exists fully in the office it shares with him, which the holy divinity knew beforehand it would share with him, knowing, understanding, and ministering. For just as even a ray of light shows up a form in shadow, so the pure foreknowledge of God observed the form of all creation before it received actuality, since God knew what he was going to create before it was given a body, when it shone out according to that likeness; just as we ourselves see the splendor of the sun points to the sun itself, so too the angels show us God in their praise; and as there can be no sun without its light, so there is no divinity without the praise of angels.

For when God said: *Let there be light*, rational light arose, that is, the angels, those who remained true to him as well as those who fell into outer darkness where there was no light, because they denied that God was the true light shining before eternity and without beginning, and because they wanted to make someone like him which was impossible. Then God called another life into existence which he clothed with a body, humanity, to whom he gave both the place and the glory of the lost angel, to achieve in praise of God what the other had refused to do. So angels are shown with a human form because they are devoted to the world in body, yet serve God continually in the spirit, nor, just because they are detained physically in the physical world, do they forget that they are spirits in the service of God. And their faces are turned to the east because being both spiritual and worldly, and as servants of God desiring to preserve their souls in life, they must turn toward the source of holy living and happiness.

Responsory   *Sir 42:15-16; 43:28*
By the words of the Lord his works come into being, and all creation obeys his will. † As the sun as it shines looks upon all things, so the work of the Lord is full of his glory.
V. Where can we find the power to praise him, since he is greater than all his works? † As the sun . . .

Alternative Reading

From the writings of Abhishiktananda (*Saccidananda*, 165-166)

The true image of God

The words of Genesis could only be understood fully by the human mind when the Spirit had let human beings into the secret that the true image of God is only to be found in the bosom of God himself. Only the divine consubstantial Word, who proceeds from the Father in unity of majesty and holiness, is the one who reflects the glory of God and bears the very stamp of his nature.

It is in this eternal image, and indeed as the image of this image, that humankind has been created. This is rightly understood only by those who have learned from the Spirit the secret that they are born of God. Human nature is not an image of the divine located in some inconceivable manner outside God. Its existence springs from the very heart of the Trinitarian mystery. In the eternal Word it is a true word of God. In the eternal image it is a genuine image of God. In God's Holy One it is itself holy. In God's glory it is glorious, a living song of praise to God, a true *doxology*. In the mutual presence to each other of the Father and the Son it is itself present to the Father's presence within it.

Creation's call to exist is included within the procession of the Son. The call to be could not have come about either within the mystery of the Father, the absolute beginning, or within the mystery of the Spirit, the absolute finality, the ultimate consummation of Being. Only in the mystery of the second person could the manifestation of the divine mercy be located. The entire Trinity is certainly present in the mystery of the Son, yet it is as the image of the Father that the Son manifests the glory of the Trinity. It is also as the image of the Father within the Son, the eternal image, that humankind reflects the same glory. Only in the Son does it realize its calling to be *in the image and likeness of God*.

This is why it was the Son who became incarnate. It is in Christ, the incarnate Word, that the world has its being, so that all creation is a Christophany. By virtue of being a Christophany, and for no other reason, the world and all that it contains is a Theophany, a manifestation of God. This it is within the eternal manifestation of the glory which the Son possessed before the world was.

All of us who have been called in Christ pre-exist in an ineffable manner from all eternity in the person of the Son. Our call is to share in his own glory at its very source in the heart of God. Creation is not a supplement, an after-thought, something as it were added on to God after the Trinity had come to perfect expression in the procession of the Spirit. There is but one indivisible and unique divine act of trinitarian expansion, in which Christ — and with him the whole universe, his pleroma — comes to be.

Responsory   *Col 1:15-16*
He is the image of the invisible God, the first-born of all creation.
† In him everything in heaven and on earth was created.
V. The whole universe was created through him and for him. † In him everything . . .

TUESDAY   Year II

First Reading   Genesis 2:4-9.15-25

Responsory   *Gn 2:24; Eph 5:32*
A man leaves his father and mother to be united to his wife, † and the two become one.
V. This is a great mystery, which I take to refer to Christ and the Church. † And the two . . .

Second Reading   From the writings of Saint Hilary of Poitiers
(Tract. Mysteriorum: SC19bis, 83-85)

Revelation of the mystery hidden in Christ

In Adam's sleep and the creation of Eve we should see a revelation of the mystery hidden in Christ and the Church, since it contains an analogy pointing to faith in the resurrection of the body. For in the creation of woman dust is not taken from the ground as before; a body is not formed from earth; inanimate matter is not transformed by the breath of God into a living soul. Instead flesh grows upon bone, a complete body is given to the flesh, and the power of the spirit is added to the complete body. That this is the way the resurrection will take place God proclaimed through the prophet Ezekiel to teach us what his power would accomplish in time to come. Then everything will happen at once: the body will be there, the spirit will fly towards it, none of his works will be lost to God, for whom, to give life to the body he had made, things that did not previously exist were present.

Now this, according to the Apostle, is *the mystery hidden for long ages* in God, namely, that *the Gentiles are joint heirs with the Jews, part of the same body, having a share in his promise in Christ,* who is able, as the same Apostle says, to *transform our humble bodies into the likeness of his own glorious body.* Therefore when the heavenly Adam rose again after the sleep of his passion, he recognized the Church as his bone, its flesh not now created from dust or given life by breath, but growing upon bone it became a body made from a body and was perfected by the coming of the Spirit.

For those who are in Christ will rise again like Christ, in whom the resurrection of all flesh has already taken place, since he himself was born in our flesh with the power of God by which the Father begot him before the world began. And since Jew and Greek, barbarian and Scythian, the slave and the free, men and women, are all one in Christ, since flesh is recognized as proceeding from flesh, and the Church is the body of Christ, and the mystery which is in Adam and Eve is a prophecy concerning Christ and the Church, all that has been prepared by Christ and the Church for the end of time was already accomplished in Adam and Eve at the beginning of time.

Responsory   *1 Cor 15:47.49.53*

The first man was from the earth, made of dust; the second man is from heaven. † As we have borne the image of the man of dust, so we shall bear the image of the heavenly man.

V. This perishable body must put on imperishability, and this mortal body must put on immortality. † As we have . . .

Alternative Reading

From the writings of Julian of Norwich *(Revelations of Divine Love* 58)

Being, growth, and perfection

When he made us God almighty was our kindly Father, and God all-wise our kindly Mother, and the Holy Spirit their love and goodness; all one God, one Lord. In this uniting together he is our real, true husband, and we his loved wife and sweetheart. He is never displeased with his wife! "I love you and you love me," he says, "and our love will never be broken."

I saw the blessed Trinity working. I saw that there were these three attributes: fatherhood, motherhood, and lordship — all in one God. In the almighty Father we have been sustained and blessed with regard to our created natural being from before all time. By the skill and wisdom of the second person we are sustained, restored, and saved with regard to our sensual nature, for he is our mother, brother, and savior. In our good Lord the Holy Spirit we have, after our life and hardship is over, that reward and rest which surpasses for ever any and everything we can possibly desire — such is his abounding grace and magnificent courtesy.

Our life too is threefold. In the first stage we have our being, in the second our growth, and in the third our perfection. The first is nature, the second mercy, and the third grace. For the first I realized that the great power of the trinity is our Father, the deep wisdom our Mother, and the great love our Lord.

Thus in our Father, God almighty, we have our being. In our merciful Mother we have reformation and renewal, and our separate parts are integrated into perfect man. In yielding to the gracious impulse of the Holy Spirit we are made perfect. Our essence is in our Father, God almighty, and in our Mother, God all-wise, and in our Lord the Holy Spirit, God all-good. Our essential nature is entire in each person of the Trinity, who is one God. Our sensual nature is in the second person alone, Jesus Christ. In him is the Father too, and the Holy Spirit. In and by him have we been taken out of hell with a strong arm, and out of earth's wretchedness have been wonderfully raised to heaven, and united, most blessedly, to him who is our true being. And we have developed in spiritual wealth and character through all Christ's virtues, and by the gracious work of the Holy Spirit.

Responsory   *Ps 18:7-8; 118:105*

The law of the Lord is perfect; it revives the soul. † The precepts of the Lord are right; they gladden the heart.

V. Your work is a lamp for my feet, and a light for my path. † The precepts . . .

Alternative Reading

From the writings of Cardinal Pierre de Bérulle (Discours de l'Estat et des Grandeurs de Jesus, 499-501)

An epitome of God's works

The ancients used all their eloquence to the full in extolling the grandeur and perfection of humanity, and rightly, since the human being is really a great miracle. For in its substance we see two very different natures united in an admirable fashion. One of these natures is entirely spiritual, which sets many things in motion without itself moving. It can ascend to heaven and descend into the abyss without changing its place. It has room for the whole world in its memory, without the physical presence of the world. It can unite the whole of the past into one, without succession in time. It is entirely enclosed in this body, and in every part of it, as in its own universe. It is an image of God, and the divine sovereignty and the working of God on earth. The other nature is material, animal, and sensitive, by which the human being lives, feels, and imagines; and in its structure and composition it is an epitome of this universe. And the uniting of these two natures together results in an excellent compound, which has existence like the elements, life like plants, feeling like animals, and intelligence like the angels.

It is the most perfect and admirable mixture existing in nature. It seems that God wanted to make it an epitome of his works and to reproduce in it the grandeur of his universe in miniature, or rather to create a new universe and a small world. It is a small world enclosing all the perfection of the great universe with added wonders; a small world in the midst of the universe, bearing within itself a kind of epitome of God in the human spirit, an epitome of the world in the composition and admirable structure of the human body. And in this mixture, perfect though it is, there is no confusion of natures: for each remains different in its essence, its powers, and its working; but they are admirably united in substance, and in the unity of the same person composed of two such different natures.

In the light of these thoughts it seems to me that humanity in the image of God, by whom we are created, is also an image of the God-man, by whom we are recreated, and that in creating humanity God foreshadowed the mystery of the incarnation.

Responsory   *Ps 18:7-8; 118:105*
The law of the Lord is perfect; it revives the soul. † The precepts of the Lord are right; they gladden the heart.
V. Your work is a lamp for my feet, and a light for my path. † The precepts . . .

WEDNESDAY   Year II

First Reading   Genesis 3:1-24

Responsory   *Gn 3:14.15; 1 Jn 3:8*
The Lord God said to the serpent: I shall put enmity between you and the woman, and between your offspring and hers. † He shall crush your head and you will strike at his heel.
V. The reason the Son of God appeared was to undo the work of the devil. † He shall crush . . .

Second Reading   From a sermon by Cardinal John Henry
                       Newman (*Parochial and Plain Sermons* VIII, 64-67.74-75)

Our great security against sin lies in being shocked at it

One chief cause of the wickedness which is everywhere seen in the world, and in which, alas! each of us has more or less of a share, is our curiosity to have some fellowship with darkness, some experience of sin, to know what the pleasures of sin are like. Not to know sin by experience brings upon us the laughter and jests of our companions: nor is it wonderful this should be the case in the descendants of that guilty pair to whom Satan in the beginning held out admittance into a strange world of knowledge and enjoyment, as the reward of disobedience to God's commandment. A discontent with the abundance of blessings which were given, because something was withheld, was the sin of our first parents: in like manner, a wanton roving after things forbidden, a curiosity to know what it was to be as the heathen, was one chief source of the idolatries of the Jews; and we at this day inherit with them a like nature from Adam.

I say, curiosity strangely moves us to disobedience, in order that we may have experience of the pleasure of disobedience. We indulge our reason, we indulge our passions, we indulge our ambition, our vanity, our love of power; we throw ourselves into the society of bad, worldly, or careless companions; and all the while we think that, after having acquired this miserable knowledge of good and evil, we can return to our duty and continue where we left off, merely going aside a moment to shake ourselves, as Samson did, and with an ignorance like his that our true heavenly strength is departed from us.

Now this delusion arises from Satan's craft, the father of lies, who knows well that if he can get us once to sin, he can easily make us sin twice and thrice, till at length we are taken captive by his will. Our great security against sin lies in being shocked at it. Eve gazed and reflected when she should have fled. For sin is like the serpent, which seduced our first parents. We know that some serpents have the power of what is called "fascinating." Their eye has the power of subduing — nay, in a strange way, of alluring — their victim, who is reduced to utter helplessness. What a dreadful figure this is of the power of sin and the devil over our hearts! At first our conscience tells us, in a plain straightforward way, what is right and what is wrong; but when we trifle with this warning, our reason becomes perverted, and comes in aid of our wishes, and deceives us to our ruin.

Sinners think that in the devil's service there are secrets worthy of our inquiry, which you share not: yes, there are secrets, and such that it is a shame even to speak of them; and in like manner you have a secret which they have not, and which far surpasses theirs.

The secret of the Lord is with them that fear him. Those who obey God and follow Christ have secret gains, so great that as well might we say heaven were like hell, as that these are like the gain which sinners have.

Let us not then be seduced by the tempter and his promises. He can show us no good. He has no good to give us. Rather let us listen to the gracious words of our Maker and Redeemer, *Call unto me, and I will answer you, and show you great and mighty things, which you do not know.*

Responsory   Ps 36:1.3

Sin speaks to the sinner deep in his heart; † there is no fear of God before his eyes.
V. He has lost all understanding of what is right. † There is no . . .

Alternative Reading

From the writings of Saint Catherine of Siena (*Dialogues* 21-22)

I gave you a bridge

By Adam's sinful disobedience the road was so broken up that no one could reach everlasting life. Since they had no share in the good for which I had created them, they did not give me the return of glory they owed me, and so my truth was not fulfilled. What is this truth? That I had created them in my image and likeness so that they might have eternal life, sharing in my being and enjoying my supreme eternal tenderness and goodness. But because of their sin they never reached this goal and never fulfilled my truth, for sin closed heaven and the door of my mercy.

This sin sprouted thorns and troublesome vexations. My creatures found rebellion within themselves, for as soon as they rebelled against me, they became rebels against themselves. Their innocence lost, the flesh rebelled against the spirit and they became filthy beasts. All created things rebelled against them, whereas they would have been submissive if all had been kept as I had established it in the beginning. But they stepped outside my obedience and so deserved eternal death in both soul and body.

With sin there came at once the flood of a stormy river that beat against them constantly with its waves, bringing weariness and troubles from themselves as well as from the devil and the world.

You were all drowning, because not one of you, for all your righteousness, could reach eternal life.

But I wanted to undo these great troubles of yours. So I gave you a bridge, my Son, so that you could cross over the river, the stormy sea of this darksome life, without being drowned.

I want you to look at the bridge of my only-begotten Son, and notice its greatness. Look! It stretches from heaven to earth, joining the earth of your humanity with the greatness of the Godhead. This is what I mean when I say it stretches from heaven to earth — through my union with humanity.

This was necessary if I wanted to remake the road that had been broken up, so that you might pass over the bitterness of the world and reach life. From earth alone I could not have made it great enough to cross the river and bring you to eternal life. The earth of human nature by itself, as I have told you, was incapable of atoning for sin and draining off the pus from Adam's sin, for that stinking pus had infected the whole human race. Your nature had to be joined with the height of humanity. Then human nature could endure the suffering, and the divine nature, joined with that humanity, would accept my Son's sacrifice on your behalf to release you from death and give you life.

So the height stooped to the earth of your humanity, bridging the chasm between us and rebuilding the road. And why should he have made of himself a roadway? So that you might in truth come to the same joy as the angels. But my Son's having made of himself a bridge for you cannot bring you to life unless you make your way along that bridge.

Responsory   *Ps 118:33.34; Ps 18:8*

Teach me the demands of your statutes and I will keep them to the end. † Train me to observe your law, to keep it with my whole heart.
V. The precepts of the Lord are right, they gladden the heart. † Train me . . .

THURSDAY   Year II

First Reading   Genesis 4:1-24

Responsory   *Heb 11:4; Gn 4:4-5*
Because of his faith Abel offered a better sacrifice than Cain, and for
that God accepted his offerings and bore witness to his righteous-
ness. † Although he is dead he still speaks by his faith.
V. The Lord looked with favor on Abel and his offering, but not on
Cain and his offering. † Although he is . . .

Second Reading   From the writings of Abhishiktananda
                        (*Saccidananda*, 140-142)

Human "koinonia" is the manifestation of the divine

The tiger which preys upon the deer has no hatred for the deer.
Its action is instinctive and of the same order as the plant's assimi-
lation of nutritive elements absorbed by its roots and leaves from
soil and atmosphere. But when a man deliberately kills his brother
— the age-old drama of Cain and Abel — he is of set purpose
destroying the material frame which supports another consciousness. His desire and intention is to obliterate that consciousness,
which he feels is standing in his way and preventing the full
expansion of his own personality. We must go further and recognize that whatever mutilates human beings or impedes their
proper development, whether physical, mental or spiritual, is
equivalent to homicide. No one has the right to impede or divert
to his or her exclusive use the onward march of the universe. To
make use of things or to claim the service of other people is only
legitimate when that contributes directly or indirectly to the development of the whole, and — in the case of humans — when it does
not obstruct their personal growth but rather assists it. Sin means
to appropriate things merely for one's own satisfaction, to hold on
to them selfishly, and thus, at least by intention, to impede their
natural progress towards the end which God has determined for
the whole universe. When a human being is made the object of such
selfish use, that is, when one person is sacrificed to another, this is
to sin against love, and comes near to being the sin against the Holy
Spirit, since the Spirit is love.

To sin against one's fellow men and women is to sin against God, and to refuse communion with other people is to refuse communion with God, since human "koinonia" is the manifestation of the divine. Sin is the refusal of one "absolute" to enter into communion with other "absolutes," and therefore with the supreme Absolute, God himself.

Sin causes multiplicity to become monstrous. In origin multiplicity is no more than a fact of nature and a silent invitation of "koinonia," the ultimate communion of all spirits in the One Spirit. But through sin it becomes the very stuff of opposition and division between conscious beings. Human sin affects the whole universe, including matter itself, as the Christian doctrine of original sin vividly suggests. Because humans have sinned the flesh rebels against the spirit, and material nature itself, as if wronged and outraged, is also in revolt against them. The fall of the human race entails the debasement and derangement of things as well as division among humans.

Responsory   *1 Jn 3:12.11; Ps 133:1*
We must not be like Cain, who belonged to the evil one, and murdered his brother. † The message you have heard from the beginning is that we should love one another.
V. How good and how pleasant it is for brothers and sisters to live in unity! † The message . . .

Alternative Reading

From a commentary by Saint Ambrose of Milan (In Ps. 39, 11-14: PL 14, 1061-1062)

Christ's love for his Church

At the beginning of the book scripture speaks of me. In the opening chapters of Genesis it was foretold that Christ would come to fulfill his Father's will for the redemption of mankind. This was when the sacred writer described how in creating Eve to be man's helpmate God made her a type of the Church. Where indeed can we find help for our bodily weakness and protection against the upheavals of the world around us, except in the grace of salvation which comes to us through the Church and the faith by which we live?

In the first pages of the Bible we read: *Bone of my bone and flesh of my flesh! Because of this a man will leave father and mother and cleave to his wife, and they will be two in one flesh.* If you wish to know the real speaker of these words, listen to the following: *this is a great sacramental mystery; I tell you it refers to Christ and the Church.* The meaning is that the love that should exist between man and wife can be compared with Christ's love for his Church. We are members of Christ's body, sharers of his flesh and bone. What greater well-being can we have than to be so close to Christ, to cleave to him in a kind of bodily oneness, in a union with that body of his which is without blemish or stain of sin?

We are told in the early pages of the same book that righteous Abel's sacrifice was acceptable to God while his murderous brother's was rejected. This, surely, is a clear sign that the Lord Jesus was to offer himself up for us, and that in and through his passion he would hallow a new sacrifice to supersede a rite proper to a parricidal people. It is even more clearly expressed in the holy patriarch Abraham's offering of his son Isaac, in whose stead a ram was ultimately immolated. And this showed that it was man's flesh, the flesh he has in common with the animals and not the divinity of the only Son of God, that was destined to endure the rigors of the passion.

At the beginning of the book it is written that in due time there would come a man who held command over the powers of heaven. This prophecy was fulfilled when the Lord Jesus arrived on earth and angels ministered to him, according to his own prediction: *You will see the heavens opened and God's angels ascending and descending around the Son of Man.*

Again at the beginning of the book it is said that *you must choose out for yourselves a full-grown yearling lamb, a male without blemish, which the whole assembly shall then ceremonially slay.* The identity of that lamb you know already: *Behold the Lamb of God who is to bear away the sin of all the world!* He is the one that was slain by the entire Jewish people. It was indeed necessary that he should die for all men, so that through his cross every sin might find forgiveness and in his blood the stains of all the world be washed away.

Responsory   *Ps 68:3; 1 Cor 2:9*
  The righteous shall rejoice before God, † they shall exult and dance
  for joy.
  V. Eye has not seen, nor ear heard, nor human heart conceived what
  God has prepared for those who love him. † They shall . . .

Alternative Reading

From a sermon by Saint Chromatius of Aquileia (Sermo 23, 3: SC 164, 64-66)

Christ the royal lamb

Let us turn our thoughts to a great mystery. Although our
Savior is called a shepherd, he is also referred to as a sheep or a
lamb. So it is not without reference to the mystery of the Lord's
passion that in today's reading we are told that Abel made an
offering to the Lord God from the sheep of his flock.

Because of their innocence the holy patriarchs and prophets are
called rams and sheep. Without doubt it is of them that we read in
scripture: *The meadows are clothed with flocks, and the valleys
abound with corn.* And again: *We are his people and the sheep of his
flock.* It was from this holy flock that there came a spotless and
undefiled ewe, namely holy Mary — she who, contrary to nature's
ordinary course, brought forth for us that royal lamb, Christ the
King.

Now Christ the Lord is quite rightly known as the royal lamb,
for he was not made a king — he was born one. Not every king is
born to royal estate. A man may become a king some time after his
birth, be clothed in purple vesture of a king, and thus acquire the
eminence of kingship. Our Lord and Savior, however, came forth
from the virgin's womb itself invested with kingly power; he was
already a king before he was born. Listen to what this same Lord
says in the gospel. When Pilate asked him, *Are you a king?* he
replied: *For this I was born, and for this I came into the world.* Even
those wise men from the east acknowledged his royal dignity, and
this at the very beginning of his incarnate life, when they asked the
Jews: *Where is he that has been born king of the Jews? We have seen
his star out in the east, and we have come to worship him.*

The offering Abel made to God was the more acceptable because it was made from the firstborn of his flock. In the same way

the dedication of the Christian people — that is, ourselves — is more in accord with true religious sentiment when God enables us to offer him the gift of upright and honest lives. We offer the Lord a gift from the firstborn of our flock when we live lives of blameless innocence in the sight of God. Moreover, we offer the Lord a gift from the fatlings of our sheep if we present to God, as a rich sacrifice, our works of mercy and love.

Responsory   *Ps 68:3; 1 Cor 2:9*

The righteous shall rejoice before God, † they shall exult and dance for joy.

V. Eye has not seen, nor ear heard, nor human heart conceived what God has prepared for those who love him. † They shall . . .

FRIDAY   Year II

First Reading   Genesis 6:5-22; 7:17-24

Responsory   *Ps 14:2-3; Jer 18:10*

The Lord looks down from heaven upon the whole human race to see if any act wisely, if any seek God, but all have gone astray, † all alike are corrupt.

V. If a nation does evil in my sight by disobeying me, then I will think again about the good I had in mind for it. † All alike . . .

Second Reading   From a hymn by Saint Ephrem of Syria
(Hymns on Faith, 49: Brock, *A Garland of Hymns from the Early Church*, 77-79)

Praise to your coming

How splendid was Noah, whose example surpassed
all his contemporaries':
they were weighed in the scales of justice
and were found wanting;
a single soul,
with its armor of chastity
outbalanced them all.
They were drowned in the flood
having proved too light in the scales,
while in the ark
the chaste and weighty Noah was lifted up.
Glory be to God who took pleasure in Noah.

Noah extended his ministry either side of the flood,
depicting two types, sealing up the one that had passed,
opening up that which followed.
Between these two generations
God ministered to two symbols,
dismissing the former,
making preparation for the latter.
God buried the generation grown old,
and nurtured the youthful one.
Praises be to him who chose him

Over the flood the ship of the Lord of all flew,
it left the east, rested in the west,
flew off to the south, and measured out the north;
its flight over the water served as a prophecy for the dry land,
preaching how its progeny would be
fruitful in every quarter,
abounding in every region.
Praises to his Savior.

The ark marked out by its course the sign of its preserver,
the cross of its steersman, and the wood of its sailor
who has come to fashion for us
a Church in the waters of baptism:
with the threefold name
he rescues those who reside in her,
and in place of the dove, the Spirit administers her anointing
and the mystery of her salvation.
Praises to her Savior.

His symbols are in the law, his types are in the ark,
each bears testimony to the other;
just as the ark's recesses
were emptied out, so too the types in scripture
were emptied out; for by his coming he embraced
the symbol of the law,
and in his churches he brought to completion
the types of the Ark.
Praise to your coming.
My mind wanders, having fallen into the flood
of our Savior's power. Blessed is Noah, who,
though his ship, the ark, floated around over the flood,
yet his soul was recollected. May my faith, Lord,
be a ship for my weakness, for the foolish are drowned

in the depths of their prying into you.
Praises be to him who begot you.

Responsory   *Ps 113:1.3.5*
When Israel came forth from Egypt the house of Jacob from an alien
people, † the sea fled at the sight; the Jordan turned back on its
course.
V. Why was it, sea, that you fled, that you turned back, Jordan, on
your course? † The sea fled . . .

SATURDAY   Year II

First Reading   Genesis 8:1-22

Responsory   *Gn 8:20-21; Sir 35:7*
Noah built an altar to the Lord, and sacrificed burnt offerings upon
it. When the Lord smelled the pleasing odor he said: † Never again
will I put the earth under a curse.
V. The sacrifice of the righteous is acceptable, and its memory will
not be forgotten. † Never again . . .

Second Reading   From the writings of Cardinal Jean Daniélou
                      (Holy Pagans of the Old Testament, 130-132)

Sanctity consists in a heroic love of God

Sacrifice is the characteristic note of humanity in the religious
sphere, as the tool is in the secular sphere. By the one humans
affirm that they are masters of the world, by the other that God is
the master of humankind. The time for the tool is the period of the
six days, the time for the sacrifice is that of the seventh day. The
hebdomadal liturgy is the first sign of the covenant between God
and the human race.

Now the pagan saints are priests of this cosmic religion which
is common to all humanity. Abel, the first of them, offers in sacrifice
the first-born of his flock. After the flood *Noah built an altar to the
Lord and chose out beasts that were clean and birds that were clean,
and made burnt offerings there.* Job rose early and offered a burnt
sacrifice for his children. Finally Melchizedek, the priest of the
Most High, brings bread and wine. By showing us sacrifice in its
primary essential, as the spontaneous act of humankind, as the

very expression of its creaturely nature, they remind us that humans are not made merely to have mastery over the world by means of the tool, but that they may refer the world back to God by means of sacrifice.

That is perhaps a message that the world today has need of. Being entirely engrossed in their effort to control the universe by technical science, modern men and women have lost the other half of themselves which expresses itself in sacrifice. For them the world has lost its sacred character; they see it only as the field for their experiments. They no longer grasp its symbolic aspect, its mystic side. They no longer see anything in it but the reflection of themselves which it offers them; they fail to see the imprints of God whose likeness they mirror.

How could a more lofty revelation take hold of a person or a world of this sort, so wholly unspiritual, when the very sense of the mystical, the very sense of the sacred is dead in them? How can one talk about a new creation to people who no longer recognize that they are creatures, or of the incarnation to those who no longer see the action of God in the world, or of contemplation to those whose knowledge of things is limited to their practical utility? What has to be restored to the world is the primary, original, universal basis of religion in the soul, and this is what the saints of paganism stand for, together with the problems they had to meet.

Granted there is a cosmic liturgy, it is proper that it should have its saints just as the liturgy of Israel and the Christian liturgy have had theirs, and the veneration paid to its saints, Saint Abel, Saint Job, and Saint Lot, duly accords with the calendar of this cosmic liturgy which persists beneath the successive liturgies that have superseded it. Sanctity consists in a heroic love of God, and this existed in the cosmic religion. We are here touching on a grand theme, one well known since Augustine, that namely of the virtues of the pagans, and it is one which still remains a great mystery.

Responsory   *Sir 35:10; 2 Cor 9:7*

Give to the Most High as he has given to you, † as generously as your means allow.

V. God loves a cheerful giver. † As generously as . . .

Alternative Reading

From a sermon by Saint Augustine of Hippo (Sermo 361, 20.22: PL 39, 1610-1611)

Christ is building his Church, the ark of which he has made himself the foundation

Watch yourselves: this world is passing away. Remember how the Lord foretells in the gospel that it will be the same on the last day as it was in the days of Noah: *People ate and drank, bought and sold and married right up to the day when Noah entered the ark; then the flood came and destroyed them all.*

The reason the ark took so long to build was to make unbelievers wake up. Noah worked on it for a hundred years, yet people were not awake enough to say: "The man of God must have good reason for building this ark: it must mean that the human race will soon be destroyed."

Once again the ark is being built, and those hundred years represent the days in which we live: this whole period of time was prefigured by that number of years. If those, then, who paid no heed when Noah was building the ark deserved to die, what do they deserve who are careless about their salvation while Christ is building his Church? There is as much difference between Noah and Christ as between servant and lord, or rather as between humans and God, for the servant and his master are both human beings. And yet the people of those days have become a fearful example for their descendants because they did not believe the man who was building the ark.

Christ, who is God become man for us, is building his Church, the ark of which he has made himself the foundation. Every day incorruptible timber, that is, believers renouncing this world, is added to the structure of this ark, and still people say: *Let us eat and drink for tomorrow we shall die.* Answer them back, then, and say: "Let us fast and pray for tomorrow we shall die." Those who say *Let us eat and drink for tomorrow we shall die* have no hope of rising again, but we who, thanks to the words of the prophets and the preaching of Christ and the apostles, believe in and proclaim the resurrection, we who hope for a life after death, must not lose courage or let our minds be dulled by dissipation and drunkenness. Let us rather be dressed for action with our lamps alight as we await the Lord's coming with all sobriety; let us fast and pray, not because tomorrow we shall die, but so that we may die without fear.

Responsory   *Lk 17:27; Mt 24:42*

As it was in the days of Noah, so will it be in the days of the Son of Man. People ate and drank and married until the day when Noah entered the ark and † the flood came and destroyed them all.
V. Stay awake, then, because you do not know on what day the Lord will come. † The flood . . .

SECOND WEEK IN ORDINARY TIME

SUNDAY   Year II

First Reading   Genesis 9:1-17

Responsory   *Rm 13:9-10*

All the commandments: You shall not commit adultery, you shall
not kill, you shall not steal, you shall not covet, and any other
commandment there may be are summed up in this single command: † You shall love your neighbor as yourself.
V. Love cannot wrong a neighbor; therefore love is the fulfillment
of the law. † You shall love . . .

Second Reading   From the writings of Cardinal Jean Daniélou
(Holy Pagans of the Old Testament, 78-80.83)

The fidelity of the living God

It is in connection with Noah that the momentous notion of a
covenant appears for the first time in holy scripture. The covenant
is one of the essential characteristics, the most characteristic quality
perhaps, of the God of the Bible. It signifies that God communicates
certain good things to humankind and that this is in the nature of
an irrevocable settlement. Thus it allows us to depend upon these
benefits, not in virtue of any right we have to them but by reason
of God's fidelity to his word.

The covenant made with Noah is connected with the cosmic
religion and bears essentially upon God's fidelity in the order of
the world. It is first of all a question of a covenant not with a
particular people but with humanity as a whole and even with the
whole cosmos. By this covenant God pledges himself not to destroy life upon the earth, whatever may be the sins of the human
race. God's fidelity will be expressed particularly in the regularity
of the laws of the cosmos, in the recurrent seasons: *All the days of
the earth seed time and harvest, cold and heat, summer and winter,
night and day, shall not cease.* This text is of prime importance. It
establishes the right to see in the recurrent seasons the revelation
of the fidelity of the living God. And this revelation, says Saint
Paul, is given to all people among whom God has not left himself

without testimony, giving them rain and fruitful seasons. This revelation constitutes the authentic basis of the pagan religions for which the recurrent seasons are the foundations of their worship.

By this covenant, God gives, as it were, an official document which bears witness to his pledge for all the generations to come. This document is the rainbow: as the paschal lamb is to be the memorial of the Mosaic covenant, as the holy eucharist is the sacrament of the new eternal covenant replacing the ancient, so the rainbow is the memorial and sacred sign of the cosmic covenant which persists throughout the establishment of new and more perfect covenants.

The order of the world is no longer at the mercy of human sin. In the economy now beginning God will give temporal goods to sinners as well as to saints. The God of the covenant is not a God who will rain upon the just and will refuse rain to the unjust, but, in line with the very words of Christ, *he makes the sun to rise upon the good and bad, and rains upon the just and unjust.*

By the covenant with Noah a break is made in the connection between sin and punishment whereby salvation can be brought in. Thus the covenant is a manifestation of love. It reveals something new about God, for it is the first manifestation of redemptive love, while the former divine economy showed only creative love. What now appears is that long-suffering mercy with which God endures in order to save the sinner.

Responsory   Acts 14:16-17; Mt 5:45

In the past God allowed each nation to go its own way, and yet he did not leave you without evidence of himself in the benefits he bestows. † He sends you rain from heaven and the crops in their seasons.

V. The Father causes his sun to rise on good and bad alike, and his rain to fall on both the honest and dishonest. † He sends you . . .

Alternative Reading

From a sermon by Saint Augustine of Hippo (Sermo 19, 3: CCL 41, 253-254)

The sacramental signs have changed, but not the faith

If you wish to please God, you know what you must do. Turn to the fiftieth psalm, and you will see that it is written: *Had you desired a sacrifice, I would certainly have offered one, but you take no pleasure in burnt offerings.* Does this mean that one must be empty-handed, without any sacrifice that can please God? No; read on, and see what the next verse says. Now complete the quotation: *A sacrifice acceptable to God is a contrite spirit; a broken and contrite heart God will not despise.* The offerings of the past may no longer be welcome, but you can still find something to offer.

In the days of the patriarchs you used to offer animal victims, and they were called sacrifices. This is the significance of *Had you desired a sacrifice, I would have offered one.* But, my God, though you do indeed demand a sacrifice, it is not of this kind. Your people want to know what they should offer you, if not the victims offered in the past. For these people of yours are still the same people, though generations have come and gone. And the faith is the same, though the sacramental signs have been modified. Changes in the outward signs of faith have not affected the underlying truth. Ram, lamb, calf, or goat, whatever the victim once offered, Christ was foreshadowed in them all.

He is the ram, because he leads his flock. It was he who was discovered in the thicket when Abraham the patriarch, on being told to spare his son, was not permitted to depart without making an oblation. Both Isaac and the ram were types of Christ. Isaac carried the wood for his own holocaust; Christ carried his own cross. But whereas the ram was sacrificed on behalf of Isaac, there was no substitute for Christ. He took the part of both Isaac and the ram. The ram was held by its horns in a thornbush. Ask the Jews what they used to crown the Lord Jesus.

Christ is also the lamb. *Behold the Lamb of God, who takes away the sins of the world.* And he is the bull; see how the arms of the cross are his horns. He is the goat, for he took upon himself the likeness of sinful flesh. But these things were all shrouded in mystery, *until the day broke and the shadows fled away.*

The patriarchs of old, then, believed in Christ, their Lord and ours. Not only did they believe him to be the Word of God, but they also believed that *the man Christ Jesus is the mediator between God and humanity,* and by word and prophecy they handed on that faith to us. This is what the apostle means by saying: *We have the same spirit of faith, and therefore it is written, "I believed, and I have spoken accordingly."*

So when the holy king David said: *Had you desired a sacrifice, I would certainly have offered one, but you take no pleasure in burnt offerings,* he was speaking of sacrifices which are no longer offered to God. However he showed the vision of a prophet in this psalm. Setting aside the practices of his own day, he looked into the future and declared: *You take no pleasure in burnt offerings.* Yet, my God, when you no longer take pleasure in burnt offerings, will you be content with no sacrifice at all? By no means. *The sacrifice acceptable to God is a contrite spirit; a broken and contrite heart God does not despise.*

Well then, my friends, you have a sacrifice to offer. No need to go in search of a flock of sheep, nor sail to distant lands to bring back spices. Search your own heart that is broken and contrite. Are you afraid that such breaking will be the death of it? Do not fear; in this psalm you have the words: *A pure heart create in me, O God.* Create a pure heart in me, and to that end let the unclean heart within me be broken.

Responsory

In the past God allowed each nation to go its own way, and yet he did not leave you without evidence of himself in the benefits he bestows. † He sends you rain from heaven and the crops in their seasons.

V. The Father causes his sun to rise on good and bad alike, and his rain to fall on both the honest and dishonest. † He sends you . . .

MONDAY   Year II

First Reading   Genesis 11:1-26

Responsory   See Is 14:13.14; Gn 11:7; Prv 16:18

You said in your heart, I will ascend to heaven above the stars of God, above the clouds; I will make myself like the Most High. The Lord said: † Come, let us go down and confuse their language so that they will not understand one another.

V. Pride goes before destruction, and arrogance before a fall. † Come, let us . . .

Second Reading   From a homily by Saint John Chrysostom

(Deuxième homélie sur la Pentecôte, 2: Bareille V, 123-124)

The cultivator of human nature came
and poured out on it the fire of the Spirit

When the apostles had heard the Lord's words: *Go and make disciples of all nations* and were perplexed, not knowing where each of them should go or in what part of the world they should preach the word, the Holy Spirit came upon them in the form of tongues and assigned to each of them the place where he was to teach. By means of the language given to each, he made known, as though by a letter of credence, the boundaries of the region in which he was to have authority and give instruction.

That was one reason for the Spirit's coming in the form of tongues, but not the only one. It was also to remind us of something that happened in ancient times. When long ago people fell into such madness that they decided to build a tower reaching the sky, God thwarted their evil design by confusing their language. By alighting on them now in the form of tongues of fire the Holy Spirit united the divided world. Something happened that was new and contrary to all expectation: for as in the past languages had divided the world and frustrated an evil plan, so now languages unite the world and bring discord into harmony.

This then is why the Holy Spirit appeared in the form of tongues; but the reason they were tongues of fire was to destroy the thorns of sin running riot within us. For just as rich and fertile land that is not cultivated produces an abundant crop of thistles, so was it also with human nature. Created good by God, it was capable of producing the fruits of virtue, but because it had not been plowed by faith or sown with the knowledge of God it brought forth thistles and the other weeds of wickedness. And as the ground is often completely overgrown by thistles and other weeds, so also the nobility and purity of our souls was quite invisible until the cultivator of human nature came and poured out on it the fire of the Spirit to cleanse it and make it capable of receiving the heavenly seed.

Responsory   *Acts 2:1-4*
When the day of Pentecost had come the apostles were all together
in one place. † What seemed like tongues of fire came to rest on
each one of them.
V. They were all filled with the Holy Spirit and began to speak in
other languages. † What seemed like . . .

TUESDAY   Year II

First Reading   Genesis 12:1-9; 13:2-18

Responsory   *Gn 12:1; Heb 11:8.10*
The Lord said to Abram, Leave your own country, your family and
your father's house, and go to a land that I will show you. † By faith
Abraham set out, not knowing where he was to go.
V. He looked forward to a city with firm foundations, whose archi-
tect and builder is God. † By faith . . .

Second Reading   From the writings of Saint Gregory of Nyssa
                       (Contra Eunomium III, II: Jacger II, 67-70)

Intermediary of faith

Let us, if we may, interpret the meaning of the sacred history,
according to the profound insight of the apostle, by transposing
the story of Abraham to an allegorical level, even though we allow
the validity of the literal meaning. Abraham at the divine command went forth from his own country and from his own kin, but
his migration was such as befitted a prophet in quest of the
knowledge of God. Indeed, there is no physical migration, I think,
that can prepare us for the knowledge of those things which are
discovered by the spirit. But by going out of his native land, that
is, out of himself, out of the realm of base and earthly thoughts,
Abraham raised his mind as far as possible above the common
limits of our human nature and abandoned the association which
the soul has with the senses. Thus, unhindered by sense data, his
mind was clear for the apprehension of the invisible, and neither
the operation of his sight nor hearing could cause his mind to err
because of appearances. And so, as the Apostle says, walking *by
faith and not by sight*, Abraham was so raised in the grandeur of

his knowledge that he understood the limitation of human perfection; he knew God insofar as it was possible for his weak and mortal faculties to attain him when strained to their capacity.

Hence the Lord of all creation is called the God of Abraham, almost as though he had been discovered by the patriarch himself. And yet, what does the text say of him? That *he went out, not knowing whither he went.* He was not even allowed to know the name of him whom he loved; yet he was not ashamed or disturbed by this ignorance. Here, at any rate, was the sure path to his goal, in that he was not guided in his knowledge of God by anything merely on the surface; nor was his mind ever overwhelmed by what he had already learned so as to stop in its progress towards that which transcends all knowledge.

Abraham surpassed in understanding his native wisdom, that is, the philosophy of Chaldea, which rested merely in appearances; he went far beyond that which can be perceived by the senses, and from the beauty that he saw around him and from the harmony of the heavenly phenomena he gained a yearning to gaze upon the archetypal Beauty. So too, all the other qualities which are attributed to the divine nature, such as goodness, omnipresence, necessity, infinity and the like, Abraham understood them all as he advanced in thought; and he took all these as his provisions on his journey to heaven, using them as steps; and relying on what he had already found he stretched himself forth to the things that were ahead.

Abraham passed through all the reasoning that is possible to human nature about the divine attributes, and after he had purified his mind of all such concepts, he took hold of a faith that was unmixed and pure of any concept, and he fashioned for himself this token of knowledge of God that is completely clear and free of error, namely the belief that God completely transcends any knowable symbol. Thus this became the norm of faith for all that followed; for in his life we are taught that for those who are advancing in the divine paths there is no other way of drawing near to God than by the intermediary of faith; it is only through faith that the questing soul can unite itself with the incomprehensible Godhead.

Abandoning, then, the curiosity of the mind, Abraham, says the text, *believed God, and it was reckoned to him as righteousness.*

Responsory   *See Rm 4:3.16; Heb 11.1*

Abraham believed God, and this was counted as justifying him.
† He became the father of all believers.
V. Faith is the assurance of things hoped for, convincing us of
realities beyond our vision. † He became . . .

Alternative Reading

From the writings of Bede Griffiths *(The Marriage of East and West, 123-125)*

Israel was a pastoral people

Go from your country, it is said, *and from your kindred and your
father's house, to the land that I will show you.* Man had been cast
out of the garden of Eden and an angel with a flaming sword was
set to bar the way to the tree of life. There was no way of return to
lost innocence; the way lay forward through the trials and conflicts
of this world to another land. We must never forget that the Bible
represents the story of humankind in its relation with God. It
begins with the first man, Adam, and ends with the second Adam,
the new man. Adam is the representative of humankind. Saint Paul
calls him the figure or type of him who was to come, and human
history is the story of the passage of human beings from their
primordial state of innocence to their final state of perfection, of
"mature human beings."

This passage is represented as a journey to a promised land,
and it is significant that Israel was a pastoral people, a nomadic
tribe, always going from place to place in search of pasture. This is
indicated at the beginning in the story of Cain and Abel, when the
first effect of sin is seen as a conflict between the pastoral and the
agricultural peoples. For Abel, it is said, *was a keeper of sheep,* but
Cain was a *tiller of the ground.*

The agricultural peoples represent the great settled civilizations of antiquity, in particular Babylon and Egypt, who settled in
the river valleys and built up great civilizations. To them we owe
not only agriculture, but also pottery and weaving, metal work and
engineering, commerce and banking, as well as mathematics and
astronomy. Depending on the earth and their own industry for
their prosperity, they turned to the worship of the earth, the great
powers of the modern world. But Israel was a pastoral people,
living in tents and journeying from place to place. Depending on

the rain from heaven for their livelihood, they worshiped the God of heaven and learned their radical dependence on him.

In this way the Hebrews were led to see their status as a pastoral people *dwelling in tents* as symbolic of their position as the *people of God*, having no *abiding city* in this world but living as *pilgrims and strangers* on earth because they were seeking the city of God. Thus the great division of humankind was begun between those who make their home in this world and seek salvation through the powers of nature, that is, through science and technology, and those who are in search of another country, another world, to which the Spirit is leading us, where above all human fulfillment is to be found. This is the significance of the promise made to Abraham. He is to leave his country and his father's house and go in search of a land, and there he will become a great people and in him *all the races of the world will be blessed.*

Responsory   *Ps 88:2.9; Ps 5:2*
Let my prayer come into your presence; incline your ear to my cry.
† I call to you, Lord, all the day long; to you I stretch out my hands.
V. Hearken to the sound of my cries, my king and my God. † I call . . .

WEDNESDAY   Year II

First Reading   Genesis 14:1-24

Responsory   *Heb 7:1; Ps 110:4; Heb 7:3*
Melchizedek, King of Salem, priest of God Most High, met Abraham returning from the defeat of the kings and blessed him. † You are a priest forever after the order of Melchizedek.
V. Melchizedek has no father or mother or genealogy; his life has neither beginning nor end, but like the Son of God he remains for ever. † You are a priest . . .

Second Reading   From the writings of Cardinal Jean Daniélou
                            (*Holy Pagans of the Old Testament*, 104-106. 109-110)

God's glory is the very purpose of creation

Melchizedek is the high priest of the cosmic religion. Gathered in him is all the religious worth of the sacrifices offered from the beginning of the world until Abraham and he is witness to its acceptance by God. He is a priest of that primitive religion of humankind, which was not to be limited to Israel but to embrace all peoples. He does not offer sacrifice in the Temple at Jerusalem, but the whole world is the temple whence rises the incense of prayer.

He does not offer the blood of goats or bulls, the sacrifice of expiation. He offers the pure oblation of bread and wine, the sacrifice of thanksgiving; it is certainly the sacrifice of thanksgiving he offers for the victory gained by Abraham, to whom God had sent him. He receives the tithe from Abraham, that is, the portion exacted upon all possessions for use in the service of God. Though Abraham is to enter into a new and loftier covenant, he first of all renders homage to the validity of the first covenant. In like manner, on the banks of the same river Jordan, at another turning point in history, Jesus received the baptism of John the Baptist before seeing the latter bow down before him. Melchizedek is a king and priest, receiving in his one person the two anointings which will be divided between David and Aaron and will not be again united except in Jesus.

Sacrifice is the supreme act of religion, the act whereby humans acknowledge the sovereign dominion of God over them and over all things by offering to him the first fruits of all their possessions. It remains always the expression of our most urgent need, namely to maintain our link with God, our creator, which is the very justification of our existence. Melchizedek is the most authentic expression of this basic human need.

But Melchizedek's greatness does not derive only from his being the most perfect pattern of his particular human category, but from his being the prefiguration of the eternal high priest who is to offer the one perfect sacrifice. In the fullness of time, the Son of God, united to human nature by an indestructible bond, was made obedient unto death, even to the death of the cross, manifesting by his obedience the infinite lovableness of the divine will and so rendering perfect glory to God. But God's glory is the very purpose of creation, so that in Christ's priestly action God was perfectly glorified in such fashion that no further glory could be given to him. Thus all other sacrifices were eliminated and we could no longer offer to the Father any but the one sacrifice of Jesus Christ.

But in thus eliminating all the sacrifices of old, Jesus Christ did not destroy them: he completed them. Through him all the sacrifices of all the peoples, every human endeavor to glorify God, all are borne to the Father and reach him: "through him, with him, in him all glory and honor is yours almighty Father." And the mention of Melchizedek's sacrifice in the canon of the Mass bears witness to the fact that it is not only the sacrifices of the temple of Israel, but also those of the pagan world which are thus taken and included in the sacrifice of the eternal high priest.

Responsory   *Acts 10:34-35; Mal 1:11*

God shows no partiality: † in every nation those who are God-fearing and do what is right are acceptable to him.
V. From the rising of the sun to its setting my name is great among the nations, and everywhere incense and pure offerings are presented to my name. † In every nation . . .

THURSDAY   Year II

First Reading   Genesis 15:1-21

Responsory   *Rm 4:18; Gn 15:5; Rm 4:3*

Hoping against hope, Abraham believed that he would become the father of many nations, for he had been told: Look up at the sky and count the stars, if you can. † So many will your descendants be.
V. Because of his faith Abraham was regarded as righteous. † So many . . .

Second Reading   From the writings of Saint Irenaeus of Lyons
                         (Adv. Haer. IV, 5, 3-5:SC 100, 432-436)

We are justified by faith in God

Your father Abraham rejoiced to think that he would see my day; he saw it and was glad. What does this mean? *Abraham believed God, and his faith was regarded as righteousness.* He believed first that God, the only God, was the Creator of heaven and earth, and then that he would make his descendants as numerous as the stars in the sky, or as Paul says, *as lights in the world.* Rightly then did he renounce all his earthly relations to follow God's Word, and go into exile with the Word, in order to live with the Word.

The apostles also, who were of Abraham's race, rightly abandoned their boat and their father to follow the Word. And we too, who share Abraham's faith, rightly take up the cross, like Isaac laden with the firewood, and follow him. For in Abraham we have already learned and become accustomed to following the Word of God. It was Abraham's faith that made him obey the command given by the Word of God, and willingly deliver up his only son whom he loved as a sacrifice to God, so that on behalf of all his descendants God too might be willing to offer his only Son whom he loved as a sacrifice for our redemption.

Abraham therefore greatly rejoiced because, being a prophet, he saw through the Spirit the day of the Lord's coming and the dispensation of the passion, by which he and all who believed in God as he did would be saved. The Lord, then, was not unknown to Abraham, since he longed to see his day, for through the Word he had learned about God and believed in him, and the Lord regarded this as righteousness, since it is by faith in God that humankind is justified.

Responsory   Gal 3:8.6

Scripture, foreseeing that God would justify the Gentiles through faith, preached the gospel beforehand to Abraham, saying: † In you all nations shall be blessed.

V. Abraham believed God, and his faith was regarded as righteousness. † In you all . . .

Alternative Reading

From the writings of Saint Hildegard of Bingen (The Works of God I, visio 1, XVI, XVII: PL 197, 750-751)

Worship God in the simple longing of your hearts

Just as Adam is the father of the whole human race, so too through the Son of God, who became incarnate in virgin nature, a spiritual people arose who will ascend to the heights. This was God's promise to Abraham through an angel, that his descendants would be as numerous as the stars in the sky, as it is written: *Look up at the sky and count the stars if you can. And he said to him: so will your descendants be. Abraham believed God, and it was counted to him as righteousness.* The meaning of this is clear. You who worship and revere God with good will must look into the secrets of God, and examine the reward earned by those who shine before God day and night, if indeed this is possible for a human being burdened with a material body, because as long as our knowledge is restricted to earthly things we cannot fully understand those of the spirit. And it is said with true revelation to all who strive to worship God in the simple longing of their hearts. In this way your heart's seed will be multiplied and illuminated: if you have sown it in a good field watered by the grace of the holy Spirit, it will rise up and shine out in manifold blessed virtues even in the presence of the supreme God, as the stars shine in the sky. Therefore all who faithfully believe in the divine promise, having the height of true faith in God, which makes them despise all earthly things and strive upwards towards heavenly things, will be reckoned as righteous among the children of God, because they loved truth and their hearts were guileless.

For God also knew there was none of the serpent's guile in Abraham's mind, since nothing he did was done to anyone's harm. Therefore it was even from his descendants that God chose the unawakened earth, which was completely ignorant of the fruit with which that same ancient serpent deceived the first woman. For that earth, foreshadowed by Aaron's staff, was the Virgin Mary, who in great humility became the closed sanctuary for the king; for when she received the message from the throne that the supreme King wished to dwell in the sanctuary within her she examined the earth out of which she had been created, and answered she was God's servant. The first woman in her deception failed to do this, since she desired something forbidden. It was also Abraham's obedience, by which God tested his faith at the time when he showed him the ram caught among thorns, that foreshadowed the obedience of the blessed Virgin. Believing the words of God's messenger she chose to comply with all he had said; and therefore it was also the Son of God, clothing himself in flesh within her, whom the ram caught among thorns had prefigured. But also because God said that Abraham's descendants would be multiplied to become as numerous as the stars in the sky, he foresaw that among these descendants those of the heavenly community would be included in the total reckoning. And since Abraham believed God faithfully in everything, he was therefore also called the father of those who will be the heirs of the kingdom of heaven.

Responsory   *Ps 5:7; Is 6:3*
   Through the greatness of your love I have access to your house. † I bow down before your holy temple, filled with awe.
   V. Holy, holy, holy is the Lord of hosts; the whole earth is full of his glory. † I bow down . . .

FRIDAY   Year II

First Reading   Genesis 16:1-16

Responsory   *Gal 4:22-23.28*
   It is written that Abraham had two sons, one by a slave and the other by a free-born woman. The son of the slave was born in the ordinary course of nature, but † the son of the free woman was born through God's promise.
   V. We, like Isaac, are children of God's promise. † The son of . . .

Second Reading   From a sermon by Cardinal John Henry
                            Newman *(Parochial and Plain Sermons III, 114-115.124-125)*

You are a God who sees me

When Hagar fled into the wilderness from the face of her mistress, she was visited by an angel, who sent her back; but together with this implied reproof of her impatience, he gave her a word of promise to encourage and console her. In the mixture of humbling and cheerful thoughts thus wrought in her, she recognized the presence of her Maker and Lord, who ever comes to his servants in a two-fold aspect, severe because he is holy, yet soothing as abounding in mercy. In consequence, she called the name of the Lord who spoke to her, *You are a God who sees me.*

Such was the human condition before Christ came, favored with some occasional notices of God's regard for individuals, but for the most part instructed merely in his general providence, as seen in the course of human affairs. In this respect even the Law was deficient, though it abounded in proofs that God was a living, all-seeing, all recompensing God. It was deficient, in comparison with the gospel, in evidence of the really existing relation between each human soul and its Maker, independently of everything else in the world. Of Moses, indeed, it is said that *the Lord spoke to him face to face, as a man speaks to his friend*. But this was a special privilege vouchsafed to him only and some others, as to Hagar, who records it in the text, not to all the people, but, under the New Covenant, this distinct regard, vouchsafed by almighty God to every one of us, is clearly revealed. It was foretold of the Christian Church: *All your children shall be taught by the Lord, and great shall be the peace of your children*. When the eternal Son came on earth in our flesh, people saw their invisible Maker and Judge. He showed himself no longer through the mere powers of nature, or the maze of human affairs, but in our own likeness to him. *God, who commanded the light to shine out of darkness, has shone in our hearts, to give the light of the knowledge of the glory of God in the face of Jesus Christ*, that is, in a sensible form, as a really existing individual being. And, at the same time, he forthwith began to speak to us as individuals.

God beholds you individually, whoever you are. He *calls you by your name*. He sees you and understands you, as he made you. He knows what is in you, all your own peculiar feelings and thoughts, your dispositions and likings, your strength and your weakness. You were one of those for whom Christ offered up his last prayer, and sealed it with his precious blood.

Responsory   *Ps 139:2.3.4*

Lord, you know when I sit down and when I rise up, you discern my thoughts from afar. † All my ways lie open to you.
V. Even before a word is on my tongue, you know it, Lord, through and through. † All my ways . . .

SATURDAY   Year II

First Reading   Genesis 17:1-27

Responsory   *Gn 17:1-2*

The Lord said to Abram: I am God Almighty. † Live always in my presence and be blameless.
V. I will make a covenant with you and give you many descendants.
† Live always . . .

Second Reading   From the writings of Cardinal Jean Daniélou
(*Advent*, 10-12)

The story of the flood

There is one notion of capital importance in the Bible — the absolute center of all its meaning — which all too often we do not understand: the idea of covenant. The word is not well chosen: it is a translation of the Hebrew "berith," which means pact or engagement. What was this covenant, this testament? It was God's promise to Abraham of three things: first to lead his people into the promised land, the land of Canaan; second, that of his race he should be born who would save the world; and lastly, that all the nations of the earth should be blessed in his seed. But note that this was not the first covenant to be made. We have in the Bible one passage which is extremely curious for the light it throws on the whole thought of scripture, the story of the flood. In this story we see God after the flood telling Noah that henceforward he would make a covenant with him not to upset the natural order of things again, and that the sign of this promise was to be the rainbow: for whenever God saw it he would remember his covenant and stop the rain.

Whenever, later, the Jews wanted to remind God of his covenant, that is, of the promises he had made them, they always began with this: "You who by your faithfulness maintain the order of the world, and who are therefore faithful to the promise you have made to Noah, be faithful also to the promise you have made to your people, to the promise you have made to Abraham." This meant that, just as God is faithful in the natural order — this was the Jewish idea: if the sun rose every day, it was not because of some physical determinism, but because of God's faithfulness, for there was nothing impersonal about creation — so in the same way — and this is the more important thing — God is faithful to the plan he has made in the order of grace: nothing will stop its being carried out, and nothing will ever change it.

Human beings can do nothing to stop the plan. Human freedom has no part here, for the plan is carried out independently of human fidelity. Had it been a contract between ourselves and God — which some of the words given for it suggest — and if, therefore, one contracting party could be freed from his obligations insofar as the other did not fulfill his, then the alliance would have been broken long ago. Since humans have not carried out their obligations, God would not have been bound by his word. Now, Saint Paul tells us, what it is most important for us to realize is that what joins us to God is not a bilateral contract, as the Pharisees thought, but a unilateral promise. God's promise, that is to say, is not at the mercy of our infidelities; it is at the mercy of our infidelities insofar as our infidelities prevent us from getting the fruits of the promise, but not insofar as the promise could ever be revoked. By sin we can place ourselves in a position where we cannot gain anything from it, but the promise itself can never be taken back: it is as irrevocable as the natural order which God has bound himself to preserve. And it is because it sees things in this light that Christian thought has such deep-rooted optimism.

Responsory   *Ps 105:8; Gn 17:5; Ps 145:13*
God is mindful of his covenant for a thousand generations: the covenant which he made with Abraham, the oath which he swore to Isaac. † You will become the father of many nations.
V. The Lord is faithful in all his words, and loving in all his deeds.
† You will become . . .

Alternative Reading

From a letter by Saint Clement of Rome (Ad. Cor. 40-43: SC 167, 167-171)

Let each of us abide in his own rank with dignity

Our of reverence for the deep wisdom of God, we should discharge in an orderly way the duties which the Master has instructed us to carry out at regular times. For it is he who has commanded that the sacrifices and other rites should be celebrated, and this not at random or in a haphazard manner but on specific occasions and at fixed hours. By his sublime will he has determined where and by whom these sacred rites are to be conducted, so that all of them may be devoutly performed in accordance with his good pleasure and thus be acceptable to him. Those who present their offerings at the times enjoined find favor with him and are blessed, for by conforming to the usages the Master has established they do not go astray. Moreover, upon the high priest special functions devolve, to the priests their proper place is assigned and on the levites particular services are imposed. The lay person, however, is subject to the rules appropriate to the laity.

Let each of us, my sisters and brothers, try to be pleasing to God through a good conscience, by abiding in his own rank with dignity and not deviating from the rule laid down for his worship. Among the Jews it is not everywhere that the perpetual sacrifices are presented, or the votive offerings, or the sacrifices for sin or inadvertent offenses; it is only in Jerusalem, and even there not indiscriminately in any place. Only on the altar before the inner sanctuary is the victim offered, after scrutiny by the high priest and the aforesaid ministers. Those who in any way infringe the custom willed by God incur the death penalty. So you see, my brothers and sisters: the nobler the knowledge of which we have been deemed worthy, the greater the danger to which we are exposed.

The apostles received the good news on our behalf from the Lord Jesus Christ. Jesus Christ was sent from God. So Christ is from God and the apostles from Christ; both missions were effected in due order and in accordance with God's will. Instructed, fully assured through the resurrection of our Lord Jesus Christ and confident in God's word through the conviction of the Holy Spirit, the apostles went out to preach the good news of the coming kingdom of God. They proclaimed it in countryside and cities, and among the firstfruits of their converts they tested the spirits of some and ordained these men bishops and deacons for those who would come to believe. And this was no innovation, for overseers and deacons had been mentioned in scripture long since; there is a text which says: *I will appoint their overseers in righteousness, and their deacons in faithfulness.*

Is there anything remarkable about the fact that the apostles, who in Christ had been entrusted with this work from God, should have ordained these men? No indeed: the blessed Moses, *faithful servant in God's whole house,* noted down in the sacred books all that was committed to him, and the rest of the prophets followed him in this, jointly attesting to the legal provisions made by Moses. Now when jealousy had been stirred up about the priesthood and there was sedition among the tribes as to which of them should be adorned with the priestly prerogative of the glorious name, Moses ordered the twelve tribe leaders to bring him twelve rods, with the name of one tribe inscribed on each. He took them, tied them into a bundle, sealed them with the signet rings of the chiefs and put them into the tent of the testimony on God's table. Closing the tent he sealed its fastenings in the same way as the rods. Then he said to them, "The tribe whose rod shall bud is the one God has chosen to exercise the priestly office and offer him worship." Next morning he assembled all Israel, some six hundred thousand men, and offered the seals to the tribal leaders for inspection; he then opened the tent of the testimony and brought out the rods. And it was found that Aaron's rod had not merely budded but even borne fruit.

What do you think of that, beloved? Did Moses not know beforehand that such would be the case? He certainly did! But he acted in this way so that anarchy should not prevail in Israel, and that the name of the true and only God should be honored. To God be glory for ever and ever. Amen.

Responsory   *Ps 105:8; Gn 17:5; Ps 145:13*

God is mindful of his covenant for a thousand generations: the covenant which he made with Abraham, the oath which he swore to Isaac. † You will become the father of many nations.
V. The Lord is faithful in all his words, and loving in all his deeds.
† You will become . . .

THIRD WEEK IN ORDINARY TIME

SUNDAY

Year II

First Reading   Genesis 18:1-33

Responsory   *Mt 25:34-35; Heb 13:2*
Come, you whom my Father has blessed, take possession of the
kingdom prepared for you from the foundation of the world, for I
was hungry and you gave me food; I was thirsty and you gave me
a drink; † I was a stranger and you made me welcome.
V. Do not neglect to show hospitality, for by receiving guests some
have entertained angels unawares. † I was a . . .

Second Reading   From a sermon attributed to Saint John
Chrysostom (Contra theatra: PG 56, 545-546)

You had no hesitation in believing the promise

How, blessed Abraham, shall I describe the hospitality of your
tent? How shall I not admire the oak called Mambre which you
cultivated so well? The tent was a common dwelling-place for
travelers, with abundant feasting for every stranger, a free inn for
the whole world. It was not hidden away so that no one should
know the benefit of rest, but though in the desert it was right on
the route through it, which was also the common gateway to
almost the whole of Palestine.

You passed your whole day under the oak, and travelers found
you the good angel of rest. Christ appeared to you, excellent man,
in the company of two angels, and so your hospitality led you to
share your tent with God and angels. How blessed that tent which
received God with angels through the incarnation! Christ appeared to you in human form, showing you the mysteries of his
divine coming for our salvation; yet the glory of your guest was
not hidden from you by his servile form, for you had other eyes
with which to perceive the Lord. And so you recognized the
mediator of God, the son destined to be made known standing
between two living beings. I admire, blessed man, your personal
care for those who appeared before you; for you could have
ordered a servant to deal with their needs as you wished, but

instead of that you yourself, though an old man, ran to your herd, youthful eagerness supporting your aged body. Your wife, too, eagerly shared the work with you, loading the table with unleavened bread (for zealous hospitality could not wait for fermentation). But all was done in fear and reverence, not as for the entertainment of a human guest but like the offering of a sacrifice to God. So the fruit of your hospitality was good, blessed man, and the reward for your devotion was also good.

For beyond all hope fertility was restored to a barren womb, and the near-dead body of an old man was revived for the begetting of a legitimate child, and you received from the only God the promise of an only son. *At this time I shall return*, God said, *and Sarah will have a son*. Truly blessed man, how shall I praise you enough for your faith? For you had no hesitation in believing the promise, and you were not perturbed by it. You did not consider how dead your body had become, being as you were about a hundred years old, nor think of the barrenness of Sarah's womb, but your faith was strengthened because you knew that God was able to fulfill whatever he promised. For nature's creator is not a slave to nature's passions, since God as all nature's creator is subject to no constraint of nature in any of his works; but nature obeys the free will of its creator in every kind of change. Therefore, blessed man, you were not disappointed in your hopes, but at the appointed time and in your near-dead age you were called a father.

Responsory   *Ps 37:1-3.16*

    Do not fret because of the wicked, or envy those who do evil, for soon they will fade like the grass, and wither like green pasture.
    † Trust in the Lord and do good, and you will live in the land and be secure.
    V. The few possessions of the righteous are better than the wealth of the wicked. † Trust in the . . .

Alternative Reading

From a sermon by Cardinal John Henry Newman *(Parochial and Plain Sermons* III, 24.364-366)

Oh that we may labor in the power of God the Holy Spirit

The privilege of intercession is a trust committed to all Christians who have a clear conscience, and are in full communion with the Church. We leave secret things to God — what each person's real advancement is in holy things, and what his real power is in the unseen world. Two things alone concern us, to exercise our gift and make ourselves more and more worthy of it. The slothful and unprofitable servant hid his Lord's talent in a napkin. This sin be far from us as regards one of the greatest of our gifts! By words and works we can but teach or influence a few; by our prayers we may benefit the whole world, and every individual of it, high and low, friend, stranger, and enemy. Is it not fearful then to look back on our past lives even in this one respect! How can we tell but that our king, our country, our Church, our institutions, and our own respective circles, would be in far happier circumstances than they are, had we been in the practice of more earnest and serious prayer for them! How can we complain of difficulties, national or personal, how can we justly blame and denounce evil-minded and powerful people if we have but lightly used the intercessions offered up in the litany, the psalms, and in holy communion! How can we answer to ourselves for the souls who have, in our time, lived and died in sin; the souls that have been lost and are now waiting for judgment, the infidel, the blasphemer, the profligate, the covetous, the extortioner; or those again who have died with but doubtful signs of faith, the death-bed penitent, the worldly, the double-minded, the ambitious, the unruly, the trifling, the self-willed, seeing that, for what we know, we were ordained to influence or reverse their present destiny and have not done it!

Secondly and lastly, if so much depends on us, *What manner of persons ought we to be, in all holy conversation and godliness.* Oh that we may henceforth be more diligent than heretofore in keeping the mirror of our hearts unsullied and bright, so as to reflect the image of the Son of God in the Father's presence, clean from the dust and stains of this world, from envies and jealousies, strife and debate, bitterness and harshness, indolence and impurity, care and discontent, deceit and meanness, arrogance and boasting! Oh that we may labor, not in our own strength, but in the power of God the Holy Spirit, to be sober, chaste, temperate, meek, affectionate, good, faithful, firm, humble, patient, cheerful, resigned, under all circumstances, at all times, among all people, amid all trials and sorrows of this mortal life! May God grant us the power, according to his promise, through his Son our Savior Jesus Christ!

Responsory   *1 Tm 2:1; Jas 5:16; 1 Tm 4:14*
I urge that petitions, prayers, intercessions and thanksgivings be offered for everyone. † A good person's prayer is very powerful.
V. Do not neglect the gift you have. † A good person's . . .

MONDAY   Year II

First Reading   Genesis 19:1-17.23-29

Responsory   *Wis 10:6-8*
Wisdom saved a good man when the godless were being destroyed, and he escaped the fire that rained down on the Five Cities. † Evidence of their wickedness is still visible in a pillar of salt that stands as a monument to a disbelieving soul.
V. Because they neglected the path of wisdom they not only lost the ability to recognize the good, but also left the world a reminder of their folly. † Evidence of their . . .

Second Reading   From the letter to the Corinthians by Saint Clement of Rome (Ad. Cor. 9:1-4; 10:1-7; 11:1-2: SC 167, 114-118)

Abraham proved his loyalty by his obedience to God's orders

Dear friends, let us obey the sovereign, glorious will of God. Let us cast ourselves in entreaty upon his mercy and kindness, and turn back once more to his compassion. Let us have done with our vain struggles, our discords and the jealousy which leads to death, and direct our gaze instead towards the men who perfectly served his glorious majesty.

Look at Enoch, for example: he was found righteous in his obedience and was taken away from God, so that no trace was ever found of his death. Noah too was found faithful. His ministry was to be the herald of rebirth, for through him the Lord saved all the living creatures which agreed to enter the ark together. Abraham, whom God called his "friend," proved his loyalty by his obedience to God's orders. He forsook his country, his kindred and his father's house out of obedience, so that leaving behind a restricted homeland, an obscure family and a little house he might inherit the promises of God. For God had said to him, *Come away from your land, your kindred and your father's house into a land which I am going to show you. I will make you into a mighty nation, and I will bless you and make your name great, and you shall be blessed. I will bless those who bless you and curse those who curse you, and all the races of the earth will be blessed in you.* And again at the time of his separation from Lot God said to him: *Lift up your eyes and look from the place where you are standing toward the north and the south, to the sunrise and to the sea, for I am going to give all the land you can see to you and to your descendants forever. I will make your descendants as many as the earth's grains of sand; if anyone is able to number the grains of sand on the ground, then he will be able to count your descendants too.* Elsewhere scripture tells us, *God took Abraham outside and said to him, "Look up to heaven and count the stars, if it is in your power to reckon them. That is what your posterity will be like." Abraham believed God, and this was accounted to him as righteousness.* In view of his faith and his hospitality a son was granted to him in his old age, and in obedience he offered the boy as a sacrifice to God on one of the mountains that he had shown him.

Lot was rescued from Sodom because of his hospitality and his piety, when the whole surrounding countryside was punished by fire and brimstone. In this way the Lord made it clear that he does not abandon those who hope in him. But he does consign the rebellious to chastisement and torment; a sign of this was given when Lot's wife, who had indeed left Sodom with her husband but was inconstant in mind and out of harmony with him, was turned into a pillar of salt. So she remains to this day, as a reminder to all of us that wavers who doubt God's power are condemned to stand as a warning sign for all generations.

Responsory   *1 Cor 10:11-12; Is 48:15*

These things happened as warnings and were written down for our
instruction. Therefore † let those who think they are standing firm
be careful or they may fall.
V. I myself have spoken and called him, brought him and prospered
his plans. † Let those who . . .

Alternative Reading

From the writings of Cardinal Jean Daniélou (*Holy Pagans of the Old Testament,* 115-117)

Lot's dutifulness

Holy Scripture and the Fathers speak of Lot's dutifulness.
When the angel appears to him and invites him to rise up and leave
Sodom with his family, he at once obeys, in spite of the incredulity
of his sons-in-law. He sets forth without a backward glance, his
eyes fixed upon God's will. His wife, on the contrary, cannot tear
herself away from her former way of life. She turns back, and for
that she is turned into a statue of salt. Our Lord himself gives the
episode its full meaning: *On that day, if anyone is on the housetop,
with his goods in the house, let him not go down to take them away . . .
Remember Lot's wife. Whoever seeks to save his life will lose it, and
whoever loses his life will save it.*

Lot represents the person who consents at the call of God to
leave the circle of familiar things and to move towards unknown
lands. He does not shut himself up in the world of his own
experience, but allows himself to be guided towards those foreign
shores of which we can know nothing from our previous experience, for it is only to the extent that we have trust in God that he
will lead us in this way. Such people can escape from imprisonment within themselves, from the unending cycle of biological life,
from the alternation of desires and satiety in which the men of
Sodom lived enclosed. Lot comes out from Sodom, that is, from
the slavery of the senses; he emerges into the freedom of the spirit.

Only those who thus leave without hope of return, without a
backward glance, burning their boats, only those who thus lose
their lives, have found in very truth the way of life, the living way,
upon which they will never cease to go forward. But those who
turn to look back, who will not agree to let themselves be dispos-

sessed, who keep a tight hold on their riches, such people, like Lot's wife, are fixed in the immobility of spiritual death and, thinking to save their lives, lose them and themselves as well. What gives particular value to the example of Lot is that in his case, unlike that of Melchizedek or Enoch, it is not a question of some eminent personage, some priest or sage of ancient days. Lot appears as a simple man, as representing ordinary everyday life. He is thus the epitome of all the virtues which are woven into so many ordinary lives, lives of those numberless men and women who have known only the interior light of conscience but have obeyed it because they recognize it as a revelation from God. In him holy scripture acknowledges the authenticity of virtues to be found in pagans and the salvation to which they lead.

Responsory   *Mt 16:24-25; Lk 9:62*
Jesus said to his disciples: Anyone who wants to be a follower of mine must renounce self. Whoever seeks to save his life will lose it, but † whoever loses his life for my sake will find it.
V. No one who puts his hand to the plough and looks back is fit for the kingdom of God. † Whoever loses his . . .

TUESDAY   Year II

First Reading   Genesis 21:1-21

Responsory   *Gal 4:22-23.28*
It is written that Abraham had two sons, one by a slave and the other by a free-born woman. The son of the slave was born in the ordinary course of nature, but † the son of the free woman was born through God's promise.
V. We, like Isaac, are children of God's promise. † The son of . . .

Second Reading   From a homily by Origen of Alexandria
(In Gen. Hom. VII, 2: SC 7bis, 196-202)

Joy, love, peace, and patience

Abraham rejoiced and *gave a great banquet on the day that Isaac was weaned.* Some time later Isaac was playing, playing with Ishmael. Sarah was indignant at the son of a slave playing with the son of a free woman. Thinking that the sport would be her ruin, she gave Abraham this advice: *Throw out the slave and her son, she said. The son of a slave shall not share the inheritance with my son Isaac.*

There is no need for me to explain how this is to be understood, for this was done by the Apostle when he said: *You who read the law, do not hear the law? For it is written that Abraham had two sons, one by a slave and the other by a free woman. The son of the slave was born in the ordinary course of nature; the son of the free woman was born as the result of a promise.* What do I mean? Was Isaac not born in the ordinary course of nature? Did Sarah not give birth to him? Was he not circumcised? When he played with Ishmael, did he not play like any other boy? Indeed, this is what is marvelous in the Apostle's interpretation. Events which undoubtedly took place in the ordinary way he called allegories, in order to teach us how to understand other passages, especially those in which the historical narrative seems to reveal nothing worthy of the divine law.

Ishmael, then, was born the son of a slave, in the ordinary course of nature, but Isaac's birth of the free woman was not an ordinary birth, but the result of a promise. The Apostle says of the two women that *Hagar bore children into slavery,* a carnal people, but Sarah, who was free, brought forth a people which is not carnal but which has been called in freedom, the freedom whereby Christ has made it free.

But let us see what the Apostle adds to this by way of explanation. *But as the son who was born according to nature persecuted the son born through the Spirit, so it is now.* For you also, if you live a worldly life, are a child of Hagar and therefore an enemy of those who live by the promptings of the Spirit. If you have within you the fruits of the Spirit, which are joy, love, peace, and patience, you can be Isaac, the child of the free woman, born not in the course of nature but in fulfillment of the promise. If the words of the Apostle, *but you are not carnal but spiritual, if the Spirit of God dwells in you,* can fittingly be applied to you, then you also have been born not in the ordinary way but in a spiritual way in fulfillment of the promise, and you will be heir to the promises according to the text: *heirs indeed of God and co-heirs of Christ.* You will not be the co-heir of the son born in the course of nature, but the co-heir of Christ, for *even if we once knew Christ in the flesh, that is not how we know him now.*

Responsory   *Jn 8:31-32.34.33*

If you abide by my teaching, you are my disciples. You will know the truth, and the truth will make you free. † Everyone who commits sin is a slave.

V. They answered him, We are descendants of Abraham and have never been slaves of anyone. † Everyone who commits . . .

WEDNESDAY   Year II

First Reading   Genesis 22:1-19

Responsory   *Gn 22:15-17; Sir 44:20-21*

The angel of the Lord called to Abraham and said: Because you have not withheld your son, your only son, † I will make your descendants as many as the stars in the sky or the grains of sand on the seashore.

V. When put to the test Abraham was found faithful. Therefore the Lord promised him on oath that the nations should be blessed through his descendants. † I will make . . .

Second Reading   From a homily by Saint John Chrysostom
                        (Hom. in Gen. 47, 3-4: PG 54, 432-434)

The light of truth has illumined the whole world

Abraham stretched out his hand and took the knife to kill his son. What love for God he had! What strength of mind! What intense devotion that enabled him to overcome his natural human feelings! *He took the knife to kill his son.* Which should amaze me, astonish me more — the steadfastness of the father or the obedience of the son? For the boy made no resistance or objection, but submitting to whatever his father did, he lay like a lamb on the altar, silently waiting for his father to strike.

However, once the interior sacrifice had been made, without any omission, the good Lord showed that his command was given not from any desire for the boy's death, but only to reveal the holy patriarch's virtue. Therefore, accepting the patriarch's intention of making the complete sacrifice, he rewarded the holy man for his resolve by showing his own goodness.

The angel of the Lord called to him from heaven and said: "Abraham, Abraham! Do not lay your hand on the boy or do him any harm." Then Abraham looked up and saw a ram caught by his horns in a thicket. He went and took the ram, and offered it up as a burnt offering in place of Isaac his son.

All this was a foreshadowing of the cross, which is why Christ said to the Jews: *Your father Abraham rejoiced to think that he would see my day. He saw it and was glad.* How did he see it when he lived so long before? Through a symbol and foreshadowing. As the sheep was then offered for Isaac, so the spiritual lamb was offered for the whole world. It was only fitting for the reality to be portrayed beforehand by a symbol — see how faithfully everything was prefigured. Then there was an only son; now there is an only Son. Then there was a beloved and legitimate son; now too there is a beloved and legitimate Son, for God says in the gospel: *This is my beloved Son in whom I am well pleased.* Isaac was delivered up by his father as a burnt offering; Jesus too was delivered up by his Father, as Paul declares when he says: *He did not spare his own Son, but gave him up for us all. How then can he fail to give us every other gift as well?*

So much for the foreshadowing: the reality far surpasses it. For this spiritual lamb that was offered for the whole world has cleansed the whole world. He has freed us from error and brought us back to the truth. He has made earth heaven, not by changing its physical composition, but simply by showing us how to lead a heavenly life here on earth. Thanks to him the worship of demons has come to an end. Human beings no longer adore sticks and stones; creatures endowed with reason do not bow down before senseless objects. On the contrary, all error has taken flight, and the light of truth has illumined the whole world.

Responsory   *Jn 5:39; 8:56*

Jesus said: You study the scriptures because you think that in having them you have eternal life. † Now these scriptures bear witness to me.

V. Your father Abraham rejoiced to think that he would see my day. He saw it and was glad. † Now these scriptures . . .

Alternative Reading

From a sermon by Saint Augustine of Hippo (Sermo 2, 3-4 : CCL 41, 12-13)

God tries us in order to teach us

When God puts someone to the test, it is not to learn something he had not known before. He tests, questions a man, so that his hidden qualities may be brought out into the open. The psalmist prays: From hidden faults acquit me — for there are in man things hidden from himself and they do not come out, they are not opened up and discovered except he be put to the test. A man does not know himself in the way his Creator knows him, just as a sick man does not know himself in the way that a doctor knows him. A man falls ill — it is he who is suffering, not the doctor; the patient is the one who awaits the diagnosis from one who is not a patient. If God were to give up putting us to the test, he would give up teaching us.

God tries us in order to teach us, the devil in order to deceive us. Temptation coming from the devil is paltry and ridiculous — unless the person tempted yields. Saint Paul says: Do not give way to the devil. Men give way to him because of their concupiscence. They do not see him whom they battle with, but they have a simple remedy: Let them overcome themselves interiorly and they will triumph over the devil exteriorly. Why do we say this? Because a man does not know himself except he be put to the test. When he learns to know himself, he is no longer negligent. He may neglect his hidden self, he does not neglect the self he has come to know.

What shall we say then, brethren? Even if Abraham knew himself, we did not know him. His character had to be uncovered either for his own sake or, more certainly, for ours — for his sake, so that he might know why he should be grateful; for ours, so that we might know what we must ask of the Lord and what we must imitate in this man.

What then does Abraham teach us? To put it briefly: that we should not put God's gifts above God: that we should not take it amiss if he would withdraw those gifts, for God is to be loved without thought of remuneration — and what sweeter reward is there from God than God himself?

Responsory   *Ps 55:22; 37:5*
Entrust your cares to the Lord and he will support you. † He will
never allow the righteous to stumble.
V. Commit your life to the Lord; trust in him and he will act. † He
will never . . .

THURSDAY   Year II

First Reading   Genesis 24:1-27

Responsory   *Jn 4:13-14*
Jesus said to the Samaritan woman: Those who drink this water will
be thirsty again, but † those who drink the water that I shall give
them will never be thirsty again.
V. The water that I shall give will be within them a spring welling
up to eternal life. † Those who drink . . .

Second Reading   From a homily by Jacob of Sarugh
(Hom. sur les fiancailles de Rébecca: *L'Orient Syrien* 3 [1958] 324-326)

The wedding of Rebecca prefigures
the spiritual wedding of the Church

There are symbols hidden in the scriptures for those who know
how to interpret them, and great wealth to be found by those who
immerse themselves in these texts. The inspired prophets were
artists who drew portraits of the Son of God, and they used
symbolism to veil his beauty in their writings. Let those who would
see the Son spiritually open the Bible: there, in his splendor, they
will find him.

Thus the fiancée whom the old servant Eliezer presented to
Isaac as his bride represents the church of the nations. Isaac himself
is a symbol of the Son of God, our Lord, the incorruptible Victim.
For anyone who seeks to understand, Eliezer symbolizes John the
Baptist, who also brought about the wedding of his Master through
water. Rebecca's wells represent and foretell the baptism that
prepares the bride for her marriage with the Son of God. Abraham
is the symbol of the true Father who gave his Son a mysterious
bride, chosen from far off among the nations, to make her heir of
his wealth.

You who have understanding, take the book, study it, and recognize the image of the Son hidden in these texts. When one goes over the broad outlines of this history, it is the path of our Lord that stands out. When you listen to the Bible being read, open your ears to the two ways of understanding it; develop the art of distinguishing the two levels of meaning. When the history of Isaac is related literally, learn how to see in it another figurative meaning.

Thus the Son of God used water to celebrate his marriage. By water he wedded the Church and made her his own. By baptism the Bridegroom and the bride were united; they were two and they became only one in the one Spirit, as it is written. It is toward these symbols that Eliezer speeds when he unites the daughter of pagans to the son of promise. The way he travels is a foreshadowing of the true and definitive way opened by John the Baptist. The wedding of Rebecca, a virgin of dazzling beauty, prefigures the spiritual wedding of the Church.

Responsory   *Lk 24:44-45.27*
Jesus said to his disciples: Everything written about me in the law of Moses and the prophets and the psalms must be fulfilled. † Then he opened their minds to understand the scriptures.
V. Beginning with Moses and going through all the prophets, he explained to them the passages throughout scripture that refer to him. † Then he opened . . .

Alternative Reading

From a homily by Origen of Alexandria (In. Gen. Hom. X, 2-3: SC 7bis, 258-264)

Christ wishes to betroth you to himself

Every day Rebecca went to the wells, every day she drew water. And it was because she spent some time by the wells every day that Abraham's servant was able to find her and betroth her to Isaac.

Do you suppose the Holy Spirit means simply to recount fables and legends in Holy Scripture? On the contrary, it is imparting spiritual instruction to teach you to come daily to the well of the scriptures. The waters of the Holy Spirit, every day draw from them continually and take home a full pitcher, as the holy Rebecca did. She could never have been betrothed to the great patriarch

Isaac, who was born as the result of a promise, if she had not drawn water, and drawn so much that she had enough to give not only to those at home, but to Abraham's servant as well — and not only to his servant, for she drew so much water from the wells that there was ample for the camels as well.

Everything in scripture is symbolic. Christ wishes to betroth you to himself, for it is to you that he is speaking when he says through the prophet: *I will betroth you to myself for ever. I will betroth you to myself in faithfulness and mercy and you shall know the Lord.* And so because he wishes to wed you, he sends you his servant, in advance. This servant is the message of the prophets, which you must receive before you can become the bride of Christ.

But, you may object, if the servant stands for the message of the prophets, how can he be given a drink by Rebecca? Should he not rather give her a drink?

There is no problem. Even the Lord Jesus, though he is the bread of life that feeds the faith of hungry souls, admits that he too feels hunger, where he says: *I was hungry and you gave me food;* and again, although he is *the living water,* and gives drink to all who are thirsty, he still asks the Samaritan to give him a drink. It is the same with the message of the prophets: like the Lord himself it gives drink to the thirsty but is said nonetheless to have its own thirst quenched by those who devote themselves to studying it.

Responsory   Ps 149:2-4

Let Israel rejoice in its Maker; let the people of Zion exult in their king. † Let them praise his name with dancing, and sing psalms to him with timbrel and lyre.

V. For the Lord accepts the service of his people; he crowns the humble with victory. † Let them praise . . .

Alternative Reading

From the writings of Theodoret of Cyrus (De Divina Providentia 8-13)

The Character of Rebecca

Before Abraham's servant had finished his prayer, Rebecca showed signs of hospitality. She was asked for a little water and was eager to give drink to all the camels. With an effort she drew the water and relived the thirst of humans and beasts, showing both courage and kindness, and appearing as the archetype of the maiden depicted in the words of the prayer, worthy of the house of Abraham in that she had a hospitable disposition resembling that of her future father-in-law.

This was the object of the trusty servant's quest, not beauty, nor poise, nor a fresh complexion, nor lovely eyes, nor well-lined eyebrows, nor illustrious parentage, nor a big dowry, but a hospitable disposition, a gentle manner, a calm, measured voice, a capable, generous character, worthy of the master's house where there was an open door for visitors of all sorts, and everyone got what he wanted. That was the object of his quest, and that is what he got.

He did not take her without examination, but he went over everything that had happened to see whether the Lord had really blessed his way. When he discovered all the signs he sought, he thought of thanksgiving before producing the tokens of a suitor and did not in his delight forget his benefactor. Looking at the gift, he saw, with the eyes of faith, the benefactor, and he accepted the gift after praising him with all his might. He learned on inquiry about her and her family, that she was the daughter of Bethuel, and he got a stable and fodder for his camels.

He bowed down and adored, saying: Blessed be the Lord God of my master Abraham who has not taken away his mercy and truth from my master and has brought me the straight way into the house of my master's brother. When he had received more than he sought—for the maiden not only gave him water but freely promised to give him lodging and food for himself and his camels—when he had received friendship unsought in addition to what he did seek, he returned thanks to the best of his ability and bore testimony to the truth of the divine promises: *Blessed be the Lord God of my master Abraham who has not taken away his mercy and truth from my master,* Abraham. You are just, he means, in being more than provident to those who reverence you and in regarding your well-disposed servant — my good master — as worthy of every attention. Events prove the truth of your words. You confirm in children the promises you gave my master.

Praising the beneficent God in these terms, he gave the suitor's tokens to the maiden, and she adorned her ears with golden rings to show that she had favorably and readily understood the requests of the strangers. Likewise she adorned her hands, too, in perfect submission to the generous impulse of her heart. When he entered the house and saw her parents, and revealed his master's wishes, did he, recognizing the assistance of God in this, and conscious of all the help he had received, forget his master, or overlook him in his preoccupation with his own thoughts, or put his own pleasure before duty? By no means. When her father and mother, and he who had brought the sorrows on them, were prevailing on her to stay that they might have the pleasure of her company, at least for a few days, the slave said: *Stay me not, because the Lord has prospered my way. Send me away that I may go to my master.*

He embellished his speech with frequent mention of the name of God, attributing the abundance of blessings he received to him, and gave the credit to providence for what he had done himself.

Responsory   *Ps 149:2-4*
   Let Israel rejoice in its Maker; let the people of Zion exult in their king. † Let them praise his name with dancing, and sing psalms to him with timbrel and lyre.
   V. For the Lord accepts the service of his people; he crowns the humble with victory. † Let them praise . . .

FRIDAY   Year II

First Reading   Genesis 24:33-41.49-67

Responsory   *Ps 45:10-11*
   Listen, my daughter, give ear to my words: forget your own people and your father's house. † Then will the king desire your beauty.
   V. He is your lord now, pay homage to him. † Then will the . . .

Second Reading   From the writings of Saint Francis of Sales
                     (*Treatise on the Love of God* II, 15.88-89)

We have a natural tendency toward the supreme good

Under the rays of the noonday sun we are no sooner aware of its brightness than we feel its heat. So it is with the light of faith: no sooner has it shed the splendor of its truth on the mind than straightway the will feels the glowing warmth of charity. With infallible certitude faith gives us knowledge of God's existence, shows us that he is infinite in goodness, that he is capable of sharing his life with us . . . indeed, not merely that he can do this, but that he wants to. With this in view, he has provided — with indescribable tenderness — all that we need to attain the bliss of eternal glory.

We have a natural tendency towards the supreme good. As a result the human heart knows an innermost eagerness, a constant restlessness, which it has no way of quietening; it has no way of hiding its lack of perfect satisfaction, of utter contentment. Once faith has pictured to the mind the beauty of the goal of its natural tendency, God alone knows how we thrill through and through with joy and happiness! As though caught off balance by the sight of such superlative beauty, we cry out with love: *How fair thou art, my true love, how fair!*

Abraham's servant, Eliezer, went in search of a wife for his master's son. He was uncertain of finding anyone as fair and gracious as he wished. But when he did discover her by the well, when he saw her outstanding beauty, her exquisite charm of manner — most of all when she had been given to him — he fell to worshiping and praising God with a joyful gratitude that knew no bounds. The human heart is drawn to God by a natural tendency, even though a man has no clear knowledge of who God is. When we discover him at the well of faith, however, when we see how good he is, how beautiful, how kind, how gracious toward everyone, how ready to give himself as the supreme good to all who want him — heaven knows the gratification we feel, the inspirations we have to unite ourselves forever with a goodness so supremely lovable! "I have found him at last," cries a soul moved in this way; "I have found the one I have been looking for, and now I am satisfied." But just as Jacob wept for joy after he had seen the fair Rachel, after he had greeted her with a kiss, so the human heart melts with love when it has found God, when it has received from him the first kiss of faith — when it has had its first sight of the infinite treasures of supreme beauty.

Responsory   *Ps 91:11-12; Heb 12:1*

He will charge his angels to guard you wherever you go; † they will bear you upon their hands that you may not strike your foot against a stone.

V. Since we are surrounded by so great a cloud of witnesses, let us run with resolution the race that lies before us, our eyes fixed on Jesus, the pioneer and perfecter of our faith. † They will bear . . .

Alternative Reading

From the writings of Cardinal Jean Daniélou *(Advent,* 45-46)

The marriage of Isaac and Rebecca

The Fathers saw in the marriage of Isaac and Rebecca a figure of the marriage of the Word, first with the Jewish people, and later with all humankind; to them this marriage was the greatest of all mysteries — the fact that God has called us to some sort of sharing in his life, to an intercourse of which the figure is that between husband and wife. The Canticle of Canticles is not a love poem that found its way into the Bible by mistake; it is the very heart of the Bible, it is the marriage song of the covenant between God and his people, between our soul and the Word. It is at once the great ecclesiological and cosmic poem of the marriage of humankind with the Word of God, and the inner poem singing the union of the Word with each soul, with all its changing pattern of infidelities and fidelities, which reaches its culmination in the perfect union we find in the great mystics.

The Fathers of the Church saw this already in figure with the patriarchs. Isaac, who was the son of the promise, and therefore a figure of Christ, married Rebecca, who had been found for him beside a well, which was, Origen tells us, a figure of the waters of baptism. Remember how the Epistle to the Ephesians says that the bridegroom must first cleanse the bride so as to present her holy and without blemish to God; that is to say, that before he joins himself to human beings Christ must first wash them in the waters of baptism that they may become completely pure and holy, and able to celebrate their virginal marriage with him.

When Isaac married the pagan Rebecca primitive humanity was betrothed; it was a far-off anticipation, a first mirroring of that marriage between the Church and Christ. Do not forget that here, too, there was a religious aspect, in that Isaac was imparting to Rebecca his faith, his worship of the one true God.

Responsory   *Hos 2:19-20; Rv 21:9*

I will betroth you to myself forever, betroth you with righteousness
and justice, with tenderness and love. † I will betroth you to myself
with faithfulness, and you will know the Lord.
V. Come, I will show you the Bride, the wife of the Lamb. † I will
betroth . . .

SATURDAY   Year II

First Reading   Genesis 25:7-11.19-34

Responsory   *Rom 9:10-12*

Rebecca's children had the same father, our ancestor Isaac, yet even
before they were born and had done nothing either good or bad,
she was told: † The elder shall serve the younger.
V. This was to show that God's choice is free and depends not on
human merit but on his call. † The elder shall . . .

Second Reading   From a homily by Philoxenus of Mabbug
                        (Hom. contre la gourmandise, 437-452: SC 44, 386-397)

Rise above all desire

To live a spiritual life means waging war against the desires of
the flesh. Would it not be ludicrous for spiritual people to be
overcome by their bodies? Would it not be shameful for those
invited to heaven to be mastered by the promptings of the flesh?

Not everyone is likely to accept what I am going to say because
the idea is new to them. Not many will understand it, few will put
it into practice. However, this is the rule that I lay down: it is better
for you to eat meat without greed than greedily to gulp down
lentils. Do you wonder why? Because if you eat meat without being
greedy you are not impelled by passion; if, on the other hand, you
eat a paltry plate of lentils greedily it is because you have a passion
for it. You are blamed for eating, then, not because of what you eat
but because of your greed.

If you know by experience that you have reached the height of
Christian freedom, if by the power of abstinence you have overcome your former bondage, if you eat without being aware that
you are eating, if you drink without being aware that you are

drinking, if you eat as though you were dead, then eat. But if you eat like one who is living take care, for the pleasure you experience from eating shows that passion is still alive in you, and that you eat for the sake of eating and not for the sake of living. Saint Paul has warned you to be careful not to be moved by greed, thinking you have achieved freedom when you are actually still a slave: *You, my friends, were called to freedom; only beware of making your freedom a pretext for your lower nature.*

It is, then, the desire with which one eats that is blameworthy, even if it is a matter of very ordinary food. To understand this, think of Esau's lentils and the meat brought to Elijah by the ravens. Esau was blamed for eating lentils: Saint Paul calls him immoral and irreligious because *he sold his birthright for a single meal.* Elijah, on the other hand, was spiritual even though he ate meat. Understand then by the example of Elijah and Esau that it is desire that is condemned. Rise above all desire: then you may eat anything.

Responsory   *Sir 37:29; 1 Cor 10:31*

Do not be greedy for any delicacy or eat without restraint. † Gluttony has been the death of many.

V. You may eat or drink, or do anything else, provided it is all done for the glory of God. † Gluttony has been . . .

Alternative Reading

From a commentary by Rupert of Deutz (De Trinitate et operibus eius, in Gen. VII, 2-3: CCCM 21, 430-432)

Faith might be helped by prayer

And Isaac prayed to the Lord on behalf of his wife, because she was barren; and the Lord granted his prayer, so that Rebecca conceived. Because it was God's gift and not by human will that all the nations should be blessed in Abraham's offspring, it was right that God's hand should thus be extended to give, so that the gratitude of humanity might not slumber in ignorance. But in a matter of this kind what could be more instructive for faith, or close the mouths of all, than the sterility of a woman. So the foresight of God prepared Rebecca well indeed, and Abraham's servant spoke only the truth in saying: *She is the one you prepared, Lord, for my master's son.* However he prepared her for such a destiny as not all humanity but only faith before God could glory in, namely, sterility. For in case you think this happened by chance, you must remember that not only Isaac, not only Abraham, but three leaders of the people and pillars of the patriarchs in succession, Abraham, Isaac and Jacob, were allotted barren wives: Abraham Sarah, Isaac Rebecca, and Jacob Rachel, for whom he served and could also even call his only wife. Therefore since their children, namely, Isaac, Jacob and Joseph, are not the sons of human desire but sons of the promise, it is rightly proved that in these the figure of the offspring of Abraham, which is Christ, in whom the whole promise is summed up, shines out with the utmost clarity. So it was clearly as a symbol of Christ that Isaac was sacrificed, that Jacob served, and Joseph was sold and after imprisonment called the savior of the world, and delivered Egypt from the threat of famine. Therefore the Lord granted Isaac's prayer on behalf of his wife, because he had clearly thus himself foreseen and prepared that faith might be helped by prayer, and the predestination of an offspring be fulfilled through a prayer to be released from sterility.

Responsory   *Is 55:8-9; Heb 11:2*
My thoughts are not your thoughts, nor are your ways my ways, says the Lord. † For as the heavens are high above the earth, so are my ways above your ways, and my thoughts above your thoughts. V. It was for their faith that the people of former times won God's approval. † For as the . . .

Alternative Reading

From a reading by Origen of Alexandria (In Gen. Hom. XI, 3: SC 7bis, 287-291)

The Lord blessed Isaac

And it happened, the text says, *after Abraham died, the Lord blessed Isaac his son and he dwelt at the well of vision.*

What more can we say about the death of Abraham than what the word of the Lord in the gospels contains, saying: *Concerning the resurrection of the dead, have you not read how he says in the bush: "the God of Abraham, and the God of Isaac, and the God of Jacob"? Now he is not God of the dead, but of the living. For all those are living. Let us also, therefore, choose this kind of death,* as also the Apostle says, that *we may die to sin, but live to God.* For indeed the death of Abraham should be understood to be such, which death has am-plified his bosom so much that all the saints who come from the four parts of the earth *may be borne by the angels into the bosom of Abraham.* But let us see now how, after his death, *the Lord blessed Isaac his son* and what that blessing is.

The Lord blessed Isaac, the text says, *and he dwelt at the well of vision.* This is the whole blessing with which the Lord blessed Isaac: that he might dwell *at the well of vision.* That is a great blessing for those who understand it. Would that the Lord might give this blessing to me too, that I might deserve to dwell *at the well of vision.*

What kind of man can know and understand what the vision is "which Isaiah the son of Amos saw"? What kind of man can know what Nahum's vision is? What kind of man can understand what that vision contains which Jacob saw in Bethel when he was departing into Mesopotamia, when he said: "This is the house of the Lord and the gate of heaven"? And if anyone can know and understand each individual vision or the things which are in the law or in the prophets, that man dwells "at the well of vision."

But also consider this more carefully, that Isaac deserved to receive such a great blessing from the Lord that he might dwell *at the well of vision.* But when shall we sufficiently deserve to pass by, perhaps, "the well of vision"? He deserved to remain and dwell in the vision; we, what little we have been illuminated by the mercy of God, can scarcely perceive or surmise a single vision.

If, however, I shall have been able to perceive some one meaning of the visions of God, I shall appear to have spent one day *at the well of vision.* But if I shall have been able to touch not only something according to the letter, but also according to the spirit, I shall appear to have spent two days *at the well of vision.* But if also I shall have touched the moral point, I shall have spent three days. Or certainly even if I shall not have been able to understand everything, if I am, nevertheless, busily engaged in the divine scriptures and *I meditate on the law of God day and night* and at no time at all do I desist inquiring, discussing, investigating, and certainly what is greatest, praying God and asking for understanding from him who "teaches man knowledge," I shall appear to dwell *at the well of vision.*

But if I should be negligent and be neither occupied at home in the word of God nor frequently enter the church to hear the word, as I see some among you, who only come to the church on festive days, those who are of this sort do not dwell *at the well of vision*. But I fear that perhaps those who are negligent, even when they come to the church, may neither drink from the well of water nor be refreshed, but they may devote themselves to the occupations and thoughts of their heart which they bring with them and may depart thirsty no less from the wells of the Scriptures.

You, therefore, hasten and act sufficiently that that blessing of the Lord may come to you, that you may be able to dwell *at the well of vision*, that the Lord may open your eyes and you may see *the well of vision*, and may receive from it *living water*, which may become in you *a fountain of water springing up into eternal life*. But if anyone rarely comes to church, rarely draws from the fountains of the scriptures, and dismisses what he hears at once when he departs and is occupied with other affairs, this man does not dwell *at the well of vision*.

Do you want me to show you who it is who never withdraws from the well of vision? It is the apostle Paul who said: *But we all with open face behold the glory of the Lord*.

You too, therefore, if you shall always search the prophetic visions, if you always inquire, always desire to learn, if you meditate on these things, if you remain in them, you too receive a blessing from the Lord and dwell *at the well of vision*. For the Lord Jesus will appear to you also "in the way" and will open the scriptures to you so that you may say: "Was not our heart burning within us when he opened to us the Scriptures?" But he appears to those who think about him and meditate on him and live *in his law day and night*. "To him be glory and sovereignty forever and ever. Amen."

Responsory   *Is 55:8-9; Heb 11:2*

My thoughts are not your thoughts, nor are your ways my ways, says the Lord. † For as the heavens are high above the earth, so are my ways above your ways, and my thoughts above your thoughts. V. It was for their faith that the people of former times won God's approval. † For as the . . .

FOURTH WEEK IN ORDINARY TIME

SUNDAY   Year II

First Reading   Genesis 27:1-29

Responsory   *Gn 25:22; Rm 9:11*
The Lord said to Rebekah: Two nations are in your womb. One will
be stronger than the other; † the elder will serve the younger.
V. This was to show that God's choice is free and depends not on
human merit but on his call. † The elder . . .

Second Reading   From a sermon by Saint Bernard of Clairvaux
(Sermo 28 in Cantica 2-3: PL 183, 921-922)

One thing is seen, another believed

It is better, it was said, *for one man to die for the people than for
the whole nation to be destroyed.* It is better that for the sake of all
one should be blackened by the likeness of sinful flesh, than that
the whole human race should be condemned for the blackness of
sin. Let the splendor and image of the divine nature be obscured
by the nature of a slave for the life of a slave; let the radiance of
eternal life be dimmed in the flesh to purify the flesh; let the fairest
of the children of humankind be darkened by the passion to
enlighten the children of humankind; let him be defiled on the
cross, let him grow pale in death, let him have no beauty or
comeliness, so that he may gain the Church as a beautiful and
comely bride, without spot or wrinkle.

I recognize the image and likeness of our sin-darkened nature;
I recognize those tunics of skin that clothed our first parents when
they had sinned. I know, Lord, that you are gentle by nature, meek
and humble of heart, pleasing in appearance, kindly, and anointed
with the oil of gladness above other kings. How is it then that you are
rough and shaggy like Esau? Whose is this wrinkled and blackened
face, whose this shaggy hair? They are mine, for these hands are
made hairy by their likeness to me, a sinner. I acknowledge this
shaggy growth as my own, and in my flesh I see God my Savior.

It was not Rebekah who clothed him in this fashion, but Mary.
As she who bore him was holier, so was he who received the

blessing more worthy. He has taken on my likeness because it is for me that the blessing is being claimed, the inheritance requested. He had heard the words: *Ask of me and I will give you the nations that are your heritage, and the ends of the earth that are your possession.* Your heritage? Your possession? How will you give it to him if it is his already? And why urge him to ask for what is his own? How can it be his own if he has to ask for it? But it is for me that he asks, he who clothed himself in my nature in order to plead my cause. *He bore the chastisement that brings us peace,* says the Prophet. *The Lord has laid on him the guilt of us all. He had to be made like his brothers in every way,* as the Apostle says, *so that he might be merciful.* That is why *the voice is Jacob's voice, but the hands are the hands of Esau.* What we hear from his lips is his, what we see in him is ours. The words he speaks *are spirit and life,* but what we see is mortal, subject to death. One thing is seen, another believed. Our senses tell us that he is black; our faith assures us that he is bright and beautiful.

Responsory   *Heb 2:9.11.18*
We see Jesus, who for a short time was made lower than the angels, crowned now with glory and honor because he suffered death, so that by the grace of God he might taste death for all. † For he who sanctifies and those who are sanctified are all of one stock.
V. Since he himself has suffered and been tempted, he is able to help those who are tempted. † For he who . . .

MONDAY   Year II

First Reading   Genesis 27:30-45

Responsory   *Gn 27:40; Rm 10:19*
Jacob said to Esau: You shall serve your brother, but the time will come when you grow restive and † then you will shake off his yoke.
V. I will make you jealous of a nation that is no nation, and use a foolish nation to rouse your anger. † Then you will . . .

Second Reading   From the writings of Saint Hilary of Poitiers
(Tract. Mysteriorum 25-26: SC 19bis, 116-120)

The door of salvation is open to all

In the Bible everything is carefully recounted and written down to enable us to perceive the superabundant mercy of God in the present prefiguration of what will take place in the future, for the same narrative of events applies both to the here and now and to what is hoped for in time to come.

When about to bless Jacob in place of Esau, Isaac was anxious not to be deceived in any way. This shows his love for Esau. Nevertheless, when a little later Esau returned from his hunting and presented himself to his father as his first-born to receive his blessing, Isaac showed no emotion on discovering that Jacob had stolen his blessing but rather confirmed the blessing he had given him.

Why did he change his mind? Why were his feelings inconsistent? Surely it must be because the words of scripture refer both to historical events and to those to which we look forward in hope. The concern Isaac showed by the questions he put to Jacob was prompted by his paternal affection; his refusal to revoke the blessing stemmed from spiritual insight. In the former he followed natural impulse, in the latter he held to providentially ordained symbolism. In the former the father was concerned to sanctify his first-born, in the latter, moved by the spirit of prophecy, he confirmed the blessing of the new people. The narrative recounts historical events, but at the same time points to the hope they prefigure.

Yet this is not the end of the prophecy, for the people of old could still aspire to a share in the blessing bestowed on the new people if only they would believe. The door of salvation is open to all, and the way of life is hard not because it is difficult in itself, which it is not, but because of our own will. That it is the human will which delays the reception of divine mercy is shown by the words addressed to Esau. He had asked for a blessing, but his father, moved by the Spirit, delayed the effects of the blessing he asked for until he had thrown off the yoke of his brother, who was to be his master. He was at liberty, then, to throw off the yoke, since it is the power of each of us, by an act of the will, to accept the faith.

When we have passed from the servitude of disbelief to the freedom of faith we shall deserve the blessing.

Responsory   *1 Pt 2:10; Rm 11:1.12*
Once you were not a people at all, but now you are God's people;
once you were outside God's mercy, but † now you are outside no
longer.
V. I ask then, has God rejected his people? By no means! If their
rejection meant the enrichment of the Gentiles, how much more
will their admission mean? † Now you are . . .

TUESDAY   Year II

First Reading   Genesis 28:10—29:14

Responsory   *Gn 28:11-12.16*
While Jacob slept, he saw a stairway rested on the ground, with its
top reaching to the heavens, and God's messengers were going up
and down on it; † and Jacob awaking from his sleep said: Truly the
Lord is here.
V. This is an abode of God and the gateway to heaven. † And
Jacob . . .

Second Reading   From a homily by Saint Augustine of Hippo
                      (Enarr. in Ps 44, 20: CCL 38, 508-509)

Jacob and the anointed stone, which is Christ

Jacob the patriarch set a stone under his head and while he
slept, with that stone under his head, he saw the heavens open and
a ladder stretching from heaven to earth, and angels ascending and
descending. After seeing this, he woke up, he anointed the stone,
and departed. In this stone he understood Christ, that is why he
anointed it. Just take a look at what forms the basis of this preaching Christ. What is meant by that act of anointing the stone,
especially in the time of the patriarchs, who worshiped the one
God? And this was done symbolically, and then he left. For he did
not anoint the stone, and keep going back there to worship, and to
offer sacrifices there. What happened was this: expression was
given to a mystery, it was not the grand opening of a sacrilege. And
take a look at the stone: *The stone which the builders rejected has
become the chief cornerstone.* And it is because Christ is the head of

man that the stone is placed at the head. Take note of this great symbol: the stone is Christ. *A living stone,* says Peter, *rejected by humankind, but specially chosen by God.* And the stone is at the head, because Christ is the head of the man. And the stone is anointed because the name Christ derives from anointing.

And as Christ unfolds this picture, a ladder is seen, from earth to heaven, or from heaven to earth, and angels ascending and descending. What this is all about we shall see better when we have rehearsed the testimony of the Gospel as spoken by the Lord himself. You know that Jacob himself is Israel. He wrestled with an angel and won; he was blessed by the one over whom he prevailed. His name was changed and he was called Israel. This is just like the situation with Jesus and the Jews. The people of Israel prevailed over Christ in such a way as to crucify him, and yet in the case of those who believed in Christ, Israel was blessed by the one over whom it prevailed. But many did not believe, and that is why Jacob has a limp — blessing and limping both. Blessing refers to those who have believed. For we know that afterward many from that nation did believe. But limping refers to those who have not believed. And because many have not believed, and few have believed, the angel touched the broad part of his thigh to bring about this limping. What is meant by the broad part of his thigh? The great number of his descendants.

You can therefore see that ladder. When the Lord saw Nathaniel in the gospel, he said: *Look, someone who really is an Israelite, in whom there is no guile.* For this is the sort of language that was used about Jacob himself: *And Jacob was free from guile and he lived at home.* The Lord remembered this when he saw Nathaniel free from guile, a member of that race and that people. *Look,* he said, *someone who is really an Israelite, in whom there is no guile.* He called him an Israelite, in whom there was no guile because of Jacob. And Nathaniel said: *How do you know me?* And the Lord said: *When you were beneath the fig tree I saw you.* This means, when you were within the Jewish people and under the law, which covered over that people with a bodily shadow, that is where I saw you. What is meant: that is where I saw you? That is where I took pity on you. And Nathaniel thought back to when he was under the fig tree in truth, and he was amazed because he thought that he had been seen by nobody when he was there. He made his confession and said: *You are the Son of God, you are the king of Israel.* Who said this? The person who had heard that he was a true Israelite, and that in him there was no guile. And the Lord said: *It is because I saw you under the fig tree that you have believed. You shall see things greater than these.* He is speaking with Israel, with Jacob, with the one who placed a stone under his head. *You will see things greater than these.*

What greater things? The fact that already that stone is by the head. *Truly I tell you, you shall see the heavens opened up, and God's angels ascending and descending on the Son of Man.* Let God's angels ascend and descend on that ladder. Let this happen in the Church. God's angels are heralds of the truth: let them ascend and see: *In the beginning was the Word, and the Word was with God, and God was the Word.* Let the angels descend and see that *The Word became flesh and dwelt among us.* Let them ascend so as to lift up those who are grown-ups. Let them descend so as to nourish the little ones. Watch Paul ascending: *If I have taken leave of my senses, it is to God that I am talking.* Watch him descending: *If I am making sense, then I am talking to you.* Watch him ascending: *I am speaking of wisdom among the perfect.* Watch him descending: *I have given you milk to drink, not solid food.*

This is happening in the Church: God's angels ascend and descend on the Son of Man. This is because the Son of Man is above. They ascend to him in their heart, that is, his head. And the Son of Man is below, that is, his body. His limbs are here, his head is up above. One rises up to the head, comes down to the limbs. It is the same Christ here and there. For were he there only, and not here, what would be the point of saying: *Saul, Saul, why do you persecute me?*

Responsory   *Ps 145:4-5.14*

One age shall proclaim your works to another, shall declare your mighty deeds. † People will speak of your splendor and glory, and tell of your wonderful works.

V. The Lord supports all who stumble and raises all who are bowed down. † People will speak . . .

Alternative Reading

From a sermon by Meister Eckhart (Sermon 69: *Die Deutschen Werke*, 159-180)

God is near to us

Our Lord says: *Know that the kingdom of God is close to you.* Indeed, the kingdom of God is within us; God is closer to me than I am to myself: my being depends on God's being near me and present to me. So he is also in a stone or a log of wood, only they do not know it. If the wood knew God and realized how close he is to it as the highest angel does, it would be as blessed as the highest angel. And so man is more blessed than a stone or a piece of wood because he is aware of God and knows how close God is to him. And I am the more blessed, the more I realize this, and I am the less blessed, the less I know this. I am not blessed because God is in me and is near me and because I possess him, but because I am aware of how close he is to me, and that I know God. The prophet says in the Psalter: *Do not be without understanding like a mule or a horse.* Again, the patriarch Jacob says: *God is in this place, and I knew it not.* We should know God and be aware that God's kingdom is near to hand.

Sometimes I declare that in whatever soul God's kingdom dawns, which knows God's kingdom to be near here, is in no need of sermons or teaching: she is instructed by it and assured of eternal life, for she knows and is aware how near God's kingdom is, and she can say with Jacob: *God is in this place, and I knew it not — but now I know it.*

If the soul is to know God, she must forget herself and lose herself: for if she were aware of herself, she would not be aware of God: but she finds herself again in God. By the act of knowing God, she knows herself and in him all things from which she has severed herself. To the extent that she has abandoned them, she knows herself totally. If I am truly to know goodness, I must know it there where it is goodness in itself, not where goodness is divided. If I am truly to know being I must know it where being subsists in itself, undivided: that is, in God.

No one should think it is hard to come to this, even though it sounds hard and a great matter. It is true that it is a little difficult in the beginning in becoming detached. But when one has got into it, no life is easier, more delightful or lovelier: and God is at great pains to be always with a man and to lead him inward, if only he is ready to follow. No man ever wanted anything so much as God wants to bring a man to knowledge of himself. God is always ready, but we are unready. God is near to us, but we are far from him. God is in, we are out. God is at home in us, we are abroad. The prophet says: *God leads the just through narrow paths to the highway, that they may come out into the open.*

May we all follow his lead and let him bring us to himself where we shall truly know him, so help us God. Amen.

Responsory   *Phil 2:12-13; Eph 3:20*
Work out your salvation with fear and trembling, for † God is at work in you, inspiring both the will and the deed for his own chosen purpose.
V. Glory be to him whose power, working in us, can do immeasurably more than we can ask or imagine. † God is at . . .

Alternative Reading

From the writings of Aphraates of Persia (Demonstration on Prayer IV, 5-6)

Symbols in the vision which Jacob saw

Our father Jacob prayed at Bethel and saw the gate of heaven opened, with a ladder going up on high. This is a symbol of our Savior that Jacob saw: the gate of heaven is Christ, in accordance with what he said: *I am the gate of life; everyone who enters by me shall live for ever.* David too said: *This is the gate of the Lord, by which the righteous enter.* Again, the ladder which Jacob saw is a symbol of our Savior, in that by means of him the just ascend from the lower to the upper realm. The ladder is also a symbol of our Savior's cross, which was raised up like a ladder, with the Lord standing above it; for above Christ is the Lord of all, just as the blessed apostle said: *The head of Christ is God.* Now Jacob called that place Bethel; and Jacob raised up there a pillar of stone as a testimony, and he poured oil over it. Our father Jacob did this too in symbol, anticipating that stones would receive anointing — for the nations who have believed in Christ are the stones that are anointed, just as John says of them: *From these stones God is able to raise up children for Abraham.* For in Jacob's prayer the calling of the nations was symbolized.

See, my beloved, how many symbols are hidden in that vision which Jacob saw. He saw the gate of heaven, which is the Messiah; he saw the ladder, symbol of the cross; he anointed the stones, a type for the nations. He also vowed to give tithes to Levi, and in him are hidden those who give tithes and receive first fruits. In his loins is Judah, the lion's whelp, in whom is hidden the king Messiah; and by him he points to baptismal anointing. And the tribes who were still within him vowed tithes to the Levites, and the kings still in his loins swelled his heart, and in him the spirit of the prophets discerned those of his seed who would come into being. *With only his staff he crossed the Jordan*: it was a wondrous symbol he held in his hand in anticipation — the sign of the cross of the great prophet. And he lifted up his feet onto the land of the people of the East, because it was from there that *a light shone out to the nations*. He reclined by the well that had a stone on its mouth which many people had not been able to lift — for many shepherds had been unable to lift it and open up the well, until Jacob came and, through the power of the shepherd who was hidden in his limbs, lifted up the stone and watered his sheep. Many prophets too had come without being able to unveil baptism before the great prophet came and opened it up by himself, and was baptized in it, calling out and proclaiming in a gentle voice: *Let everyone who thirsts come to me and drink.*

Responsory   *Phil 2:12-13; Eph 3:20*

Work out your salvation with fear and trembling, for † God is at work in you, inspiring both the will and the deed for his own chosen purpose.
V. Glory be to him whose power, working in us, can do immeasurably more than we can ask or imagine. † God is at . . .

WEDNESDAY   Year II

First Reading   Genesis 31:1-18

Responsory   *Gn 31:11-13.17*

The Lord said to Jacob; return to the land of your fathers, † and I will be with you.
V. Jacob proceeded to his children and wives on camels and left.
† And I will . . .

Second Reading   From a commentary by Rupert of Deutz
                     (De Trinitate et operibus eius, in Gen. VII, 41: CCCM 21, 477)

Receive the things promised of your forbears

How fortunate he was to hear the Lord God's voice saying: *Turn back to the land of your fathers*, and to your birthplace, and I will be with you.

It was good also that he should be a model of perpetual obedience and of perpetual pilgrimage, that he might inherit in perpetuity the blessing of Abraham his grandfather and Isaac his father, for whom it was not a light matter never to return thither whence God had decreed that they go forth. And therefore they were told: *But you shall not bring back my son thither*. And again: *But you shall not bring back my son thither*. This is the reason for those words already uttered along with what was later said to Rachel and to Lia: *But my father's love surrounded me and multiplied my reward tenfold*. These sayings combined to prosper the holy man, so that, impelled by adversity itself, he might the more speedily follow, whither God was calling him. Nevertheless there was also the hard-heartedness of an unlovable father working toward the same good end, through the spouses themselves. And of this they complain forthwith, saying: *Is there then no share remaining to us in the warmth and the security of our father's house? Has he not treated us as strangers, selling off and using up our rightful portion?* With this contrary wind happily forcing the bark onward, they look beyond the port and say: *But God has carried off our father's wealth and bestowed it on us and our children. So you must do all that he commands you.*

These events, I say, also prepared the way for their further well-being, that they might the more quickly follow this man and so, having forbears of such merit, receive the things promised of those forbears. In this way they set an instructive example in spiritual matters to those souls whom we have heard the Holy Spirit, or (shall we say?) God the Father of Christ, addressing in the psalm: *Hear, my daughter, and see, and incline your ear; forget your people and your father's house; and the king will find you desirable for your beauty.* For just as these adversities impelled Jacob's spouses to leave the father who had used up his daughters' portion and follow this man, so also are the adversities of the world apt to prosper the soul beloved of God to strive the more ardently for him.

Responsory   Lv 20:7.26
Consecrate yourselves and be holy, for I am the Lord your God. Keep my laws and obey them, for † it is I, the Lord, who make you holy.
V. You must be holy to me, because I, the Lord, am holy. † It is I . . .

Alternative Reading

From the writings of John Climacus (The Ladder of Divine Ascent, 85-87)

On Exile

There is such a thing as exile, an irrevocable renunciation of everything in one's familiar surroundings that hinders one from attaining the ideal of holiness. Exile is a disciplined heart, unheralded wisdom, an unpublicized understanding, a hidden life, masked ideals. It is unseen meditation, the striving to be humble, a wish for poverty, the longing for what is divine. It is an outpouring of love, a denial of vainglory, a depth of silence.

For followers of the Lord, this manner of thinking operates abundantly at the beginning and they are greatly disturbed by it, as though by some holy fire. I mean separation from their relations for the sake of hardship and simplicity which drives on the lovers of this good. Yet for all that it is praiseworthy, it requires discretion, since not every kind of exile is good if taken to extremes.

The Lord says that every prophet is without honor in his own country. If he is right, then we had better be careful that our act of renunciation is not for empty honor. Exile is a separation from everything, in order that one may hold on totally to God. It is a chosen route of great grief. An exile is a fugitive, running from all relationships with his own relatives and with strangers.

Detachment is good and its mother is exile. Someone withdrawing from the world for the sake of the Lord is no longer attached to possessions, that he should not appear to be deceived by the passions. If you have left the world, then do not begin to reach out for it. Otherwise your passions will come back to you. Eve had no wish to be driven from paradise, whereas a monk will abandon his homeland willingly.

Then again we manage for some time to live away from our relatives. We practice a little piety, compunction, self-control. And then the empty thoughts come tramping toward us, seeking to turn us back to the places we knew. They tell us what a lesson we are, what an example, what a help to those who witnessed our former wicked deeds. If we happen to be articulate and well informed, they assure us that we could be rescuers of souls and teachers to the world. They tell us all this so that we might scatter at sea the treasures we have assembled while in port. So we had better imitate Lot, and certainly not his wife. The soul turning back to the regions from which it came will be like the salt that has lost savor, indeed like that famous pillar. Run from Egypt, run and do not turn back. The heart yearning for the land there will never see Jerusalem, the land of dispassion.

Leaving home, some at the beginning are full of innocence. Their souls are clean. And then they want very much to go back, thinking, perhaps, that they might bring salvation to others, having attained it themselves. Moses, that man who saw God, returned. In his case it was to save the members of his tribe. Still, he ran into many dangers in Egypt and was caught up in the darkness of the world.

There is no greater example of renunciation than that great man who heard the command, *Leave your country and your family and the house of your father.* Obediently he went to a foreign country where the language was different. And so it is that anyone following this model of renunciation is glorified all the more by the Lord.

But even though this glory is given by God, it is still good to deflect it with the protective shield of humility. When demons or men lavish praise on us for our exile as if it were a great achievement, let us remind ourselves at once of him who came down from heaven for our benefit and exiled himself to earth. Nothing we could ever do would match that.

Responsory   *Lv 20:7.26*

Consecrate yourselves and be holy, for I am the Lord your God. Keep my laws and obey them, for † it is I, the Lord, who make you holy.

V. You must be holy to me, because I, the Lord, am holy. † It is I . . .

THURSDAY   Year II

First Reading   Genesis 32:4-31

Responsory   *Gn 32, 26.27.29*
The angel said to Jacob: Let me go for it is daybreak. Jacob responded: I will not let you go until you bless me, † and the angel
blessed him.
V. I bless you, and will increase you. † And the angel . . .

Second Reading   From a homily by Saint Gregory the Great
(Hom. in Ez. 1, 12: PL 76, 955)

The stronger we grow in our love for God alone,
the weaker becomes our love for the world

The pursuit of the contemplative life is something for which a
great and sustained effort on the part of the powers of the soul is
required, an effort to rise from earthly to heavenly things, an effort
to keep one's attention fixed on spiritual things, an effort to pass
beyond and above the sphere of things visible to the eyes of flesh,
an effort finally to hem oneself in, so to speak, in order to gain
access to spaces that are broad and open.

There are times indeed when one succeeds, overcoming the
opposing obscurity of one's blindness and catching at least a
glimpse, be it ever so fleeting and superficial, of boundless light.
But the experience is momentary only, so that all too quickly the
soul must again return to itself. From that light which is approached with bated breath, it must now, sighing and mournful,
go back once more to the obscurity of its blindness.

We have a beautiful illustration of all this in the sacred history
of the scriptures where the story is told of Jacob's encounter with
the angel, while on his return journey to the home of his parents.
On the way he met an angel with whom he engaged in a great
struggle and, like anyone involved in such a contest, Jacob found
his opponent, now stronger, now weaker than himself.

Let us understand the angel of this story as representing the
Lord, and Jacob who contended with the angel as representing the
soul of the perfect individual who in contemplation has come face
to face with God. This soul, as it exerts every effort to behold God
as he is in himself, is like one engaged with another in a contest of

strength. At one moment it prevails so to speak, as it gains access to that boundless light and briefly experiences in mind and heart the sweet savor of the divine presence. The next moment, however, it succumbs, overcome and drained of its strength by the very sweetness of the taste it has experienced. The angel, therefore, is, as it were, overcome when in the innermost recesses of the intellect the divine presence is directly experienced and seen.

Here, however, it is to be noted that the angel, when he could not prevail over Jacob, touched the sciatic muscle of Jacob's hip, so that it forthwith withered and shrank. From that time on Jacob became lame in one leg and walked with a limp. Thus also does the all-powerful God cause all carnal affections to dry up and wither away in us, once we have come to experience in our mind and hear the knowledge of him as he is in himself.

Previously we walked about on two feet, as it were, when we thought, so it seemed, that we could seek after God, while remaining at the same time attached to the world. But having once come to the knowledge and experience of the sweetness of God, only one of these two feet retains its life and vigor, the other becoming lame and useless. For it necessarily follows that the stronger we grow in our love for God alone, the weaker becomes our love for the world.

If therefore like Jacob we hold fast to the angel and do not let him go, we will then like him be stricken with lameness in one foot. For, as our love for God grows in strength, our carnal appetites decrease in strength. Everyone who is lame in one foot leans for support on the foot that is healthy and strong. In the same way he, in whom the desire and love of earthly allurements have dried up as it were and withered away, will lean for support and with all his strength on the one foot of the love of God.

Responsory   *Jn 8:12; Rm 13:12*

I am the light of the world. † Anyone who follows me will not walk in darkness, but will have the light of life.

V. Let us cast off the deeds of darkness and put on the armor of light. † Anyone who follows . . .

Alternative Reading

From a sermon by Guerric of Igny (In nat. Joannis Baptistae, sermo II: PL 185, 167-169)

No longer is love as strong as death, but stronger than death

Since the days of John the Baptist the kingdom of heaven suffers violence and the violent are even now seizing it.

Did not the untiring wrestler, the patriarch Jacob, do violence to God? As it is written, he was strong against God and prevailed, wrestled with him until morning perseveringly and with all his might held fast to him when he asked to be let go. *I will not let you go,* he said, *unless you bless me.* I say that he wrestled with God, for God was in the angel with whom he wrestled. Otherwise the angel would not say: *Why do you ask for my name? It is wonderful,* and Jacob would not say: *I have seen the Lord face to face.*

It was a good sort of violence then that extorted a blessing; happy the wrestling in which God yielded to man and the vanquished rewarded the victor with the grace of a blessing and the honor of a holier name. What if he touched the sinew of his thigh and it withered, and so he went limping? A man will readily sacrifice his body and soon be comforted for the harm done when it is compensated for by such a gift, especially the man who could say: *I have loved wisdom more than health and all beauty.* Would that not only the sinew of my thigh but the strength of my whole body would wither, provided I might win but one blessing from an angel. Would that I might not only limp with Jacob but also die with Paul so as to obtain the grace and name of Israel as an everlasting gift. Jacob bears a withered hip, but Paul a dead body, because the mortification of the body's members begun by the first practices of the prophets was brought to completion by the gospel. Jacob goes limping, because in part his thoughts dwell on the things of the world while his other foot he bears raised up from the earth. Paul's thoughts dwell only on the things of God whether in the body or out of the body I know not, God knows; he is wholly free in spirit and flies up to heaven.

So to you, brethren, we say, you whose set purpose it is to win heaven by force, you who have come together to wrestle with the angel who guards the way to the tree of life, to you we say: it is wholly necessary that you should wrestle perseveringly and without remission.

But God forbid, brethren, God forbid that he who willed to become weak, and even to die for you, will be strong against you who ask for what is pleasing to him. He has been pierced with so many wounds, his whole body has suffered crucifixion; from where can he draw strength to resist that charity which led him, as if conquered and a prisoner, through every kind of weakness even to death, death on a cross? No longer is love as strong as death, but stronger than death, since God's strength through the power of his love has been made weak unto death. Yet his weakness has been found stronger than all the strongest, his death has been proved to be your death, O death.

Be armed then with the power of love, whoever you are who in your devotion would force an entry into the kingdom of heaven and make it your prize; and be assured that you will easily conquer the king of heaven himself. If he seems to oppose you with difficulties or hardness, do not be fainthearted but understand what his purpose is in so acting. By the very contradiction he seeks to give a finer edge to your spirit, as the nature of the magnanimous and the strong is wont to be; he seeks to exercise your forces, to prove your constancy, to multiply your victories and increase your crowns.

Responsory   *1 Jn 4:9.16b; Jn 3:16*
God's love for us was revealed when he sent his only Son into the world so that we might have life through him. † God is love, and whoever lives in love lives in God and God lives in him.
V. God loved the world so much that he gave his only Son, so that whoever believes in him should not perish but have eternal life. † God is love . . .

FRIDAY   Year II

First Reading   Genesis 35:1-29

Responsory   *Gn 35:1-3*
God said to Jacob: Go to Bethel. Settle there and build an altar there † to the God who appeared to you while fleeing from Esau.
V. Jacob told his family: We are now to go up to Bethel. † To the God . . .

Second Reading   From a commentary by Saint Bede of England
(Gen. III, 13, 18; CCL 118A, 181-182)

Through faith and through the sacraments we are saved and rendered just

Moving his tent, Abraham came and dwelt near the vale of Mambre, which is in Hebron.

And there he built an altar to the Lord. This was the third altar built by Abraham; the first was close to Sichem, the second between Bethel and Ai. In all this it is to be noted that nowhere does he offer sacrifices; scripture records only his calling on the name of the Lord. But neither in the later writings is there mention of any victim or sacrifice being offered to God, apart from a ram which Abraham offered as a holocaust to the Lord for his son, thereby most plainly symbolizing the passion of the mediator between God and man. But neither is Isaac his son said to have offered any sacrifice to the Lord: only to have built an altar to God. Likewise Jacob, having made an altar at God's bidding, is not found to have slaughtered victims on it either, except when, leaving the land of promise, he was about to enter Egypt because of Joseph. For then, on arriving at Beersheba and slaughtering victims, he is said to have received an oracle from God. What kind of victims, and how many of them, we are not told. Nor are we told of any from then on until the time of the Passover, which was sacrificed in Egypt by the blood of a lamb. For many years afterwards, however, the ancient Hebrews offered sacrifices.

It is found that offerings were made to God by the forefathers throughout all these years. Why is it, then, that from the time of the promise made to Abraham to the time when the law was given no victims were offered, apart from the one which the father immolated, prefiguring God the Father, who spared not his own Son, but gave him up for all of us? And in fact what an abundance of victims were ceaselessly offered thereafter every day! Surely it was all to give a clear sign that the grace and truth promised to Abraham and his seed were to be bestowed on the world, not in sacrificial offerings, but in Christ's passion.

Through faith and through the sacraments stemming from that passion, not only we ourselves but those who lived before the time of his passion also are saved and rendered just. This idea is consistent with the fact that the priest of God Melchizedek, living in the time of the patriarchs, is said to have offered to the Lord on high, not the blood of victims, but both bread and wine, thereby anticipating the nature, not of the priesthood of the old law, but of that of the gospel. For he it was also who blessed Abraham himself, to whom and in whom had been promised the blessing on all the nations, so that all this might make it evident that the promise made to the fathers would be fulfilled, not through the ceremonies of the Mosaic law, but through the grace coming from our Lord's passion.

Responsory   *Mi 6:8; Acts 17:28*
The Lord has shown us what is good; † what he requires of us is only this: to act justly, to love tenderly and to walk humbly with our God.
V. He is not far from any one of us, for in him we live and move and have our being. † What he requires . . .

SATURDAY   Year II

First Reading   Genesis 37:2-4.12-36

Responsory   *Gn 37:18-20.4*
They noticed Joseph from a distance and said: Here comes the dreamer; † let us kill him and see what comes of his dreams.
V. When his brothers saw that their father loved Joseph best they said: † Let us kill . . .

Second Reading   From a commentary by Saint Cyril of Alexandria (Glaphyrorum in Genesim VI: PG 69, 304-305)

The story of Joseph

The devout Joseph obeyed his father's command to go to Shechem to see if his brothers were well, and where and how they were feeding their flocks. But when they saw him coming they smiled a cruel and hateful smile, saying: *Here comes that dreamer!* And they cast him into a pit. But a little later they drew the boy out of the pit, and sold him to the Ishmaelites who were going to Egypt. And so Joseph was led away to Egypt.

In the same way our Lord Jesus Christ was sent by God the Father to see if the Israelites continued to be well, obviously in a spiritual sense, and if the sheep in their care were still in a good state, and the shepherds not lacking in gentleness towards them. But people were aware that the beloved Son, the spiritual Joseph, was among them in person. For the blessed evangelist John said: *Yet many even of the people in authority believed in him, but they kept it to themselves because of the Pharisees.* So the fact that they recognized him did not prevent them from insulting him. Indeed they killed him and the cowards threw him into a kind of pit, the deep and dark pit of death, that is, Hades. For that is just how the inspired David showed him to us, speaking as if addressing his words to God the Father in heaven, as if in the person of Christ: *Lord, you brought my soul out of Hades, you saved me from the fate of those who go down to the pit.*

We are told: *The pit was empty, there was no water in it,* to show us distinctly and clearly that this was meant to represent Hades. And I shall tell you why: water is a symbol of life, as something life-giving. It is said there was no water in the pit, naturally, for Hades was thought of as the home and dwelling-place of those deprived of life. However, the boy was raised from the pit. Christ too came back to life from the dead. For just as Joseph was not kept down in the pit, so neither did Christ remain in Hades, and what is more he left it empty. "For he said to the prisoners: Come out!"

It was not long after he had been raised from the pit that the devout Joseph went away to Egypt, when the Ishmaelites bought him. Christ too came back to life and rose from the pit. Then leaving Judea he went to the land of the Gentiles, taken there by the spiritual Ishmaelites, those in obedience to God, for that is the literal meaning of their name. Who would such people be? Again they were the blessed disciples, who had listened to Christ's teaching and were the first-fruits of those distinguished in their obedience, their faith and glorious achievements above the law. It was these who in a way bought Jesus, giving up all the treasure they possessed in the law to buy that *single pearl of great value,* in the words of our Savior's own parable. It was they who conveyed Christ to the gentiles as ministers of the gospel. Throughout every land under the sun they proclaimed him as God and Lord, and as the chosen stone, rejected by those who clung to the law, the spiritual builders, but chosen and precious in God's sight, and laid as the cornerstone of the building.

Responsory   *1 Jn 4:16.7*
God is love, and those who live in love live in God, † and God lives in them.
V. Let us love one another, for love comes from God and knows God. † And God lives . . .

Alternative Reading

From a sermon by Saint Caesarius of Arles (Sermo 90, 4.6: CCL 103, 372-374)

Combating envy

Having experienced the poisonous effect of envy upon his brothers the blessed patriarch Joseph strove, with God's help, to banish this vice from his own heart by constantly pondering on the beauty of true love.

There is no place for jealousy or for envy among Christians: they are to grow to the heights by humility. Listen to Saint John the Apostle in his letter: *Everyone who hates his brother is a murderer;* and again: *A man may say "I am in the light" but he who hates his brother is in darkness; he walks in the dark and has no idea where he is going, because the darkness has made him blind.* Saint John says that the one who hates his brother walks in the dark and has no idea where he is going. He is slipping down to hell without knowing it, plunging headlong into torment because he cannot see. He has turned his back on Christ, the light, despite his words of warning: *I am the light of the world* and, *He who believes in me shall not wander in darkness; he shall have the light of life.*

The person who is subject to the vice of envy is neither at peace nor free from care; how then can the love of the Lord abide within him? With the help of God, then, my brothers, let us avoid this poison of envy and jealousy. Let us show gentleness and love to good and bad alike. In this way, Christ will not reject us for the sin of jealousy but will, instead, praise us and invite us to our reward, saying: *Come, you who have blessing; enter and possess the kingdom.*

Always have a spiritual book in your hands and the Lord's sentiments in your hearts. Pray continually, without ceasing, and persevere in deeds which promote salvation.

Thus whenever the enemy comes to tempt us, he will always find us engaged in good works. Each and every one of us should examine his conscience. If anyone perceives that he is envious of his neighbor's good fortune, he should uproot the thorns and weeds from his heart. In this way the seed of the Lord will be multiplied within him as in a fertile field of rich corn; God's spiritual produce will be as abundant as the richness of a plentiful harvest.

Let each of us contemplate the joys of paradise and yearn for the kingdom of heaven, for Christ will not receive us unless we are one in mind and heart. Let us be mindful, my brothers, that only the peacemakers are called the sons of God. It is written, *By this shall all know that you are my disciples, if you love one another*. May our good Lord grant you his protection and lead you to this mutual love through the practice of good works. To him be honor and glory, with the Father and Holy Spirit for all eternity. Amen.

Responsory   *Ps 11:4-5.7*

The eyes of the Lord look down upon the world; his gaze tests humankind. † The Lord tests the just and the unjust; he hates all who love violence.

V. The Lord is just and loves justice; the upright shall see his face. † The Lord tests . . .

FIFTH WEEK IN ORDINARY TIME

SUNDAY

Year II

First Reading Genesis 39:1-23

Responsory Ps 81:6; 105:18

Joseph, when he entered Egypt, heard an unfamiliar speech. † The Lord was with him and brought success to all he did.

V. They had weighed him down with fetters, and he was bound with chains until his prediction came to pass. † The Lord was . . .

Second Reading From a sermon by Saint Chromatius of Aquileia (Sermo 24, 2: SC 64, 70-72)

The saintly Joseph

As you have just heard in the reading, the saintly Joseph was of good appearance but even better in mind, because he was both physically and mentally chaste. He shone in outward appearance but even more so in the excellence of his mind. And though for many people good looks are usually a hindrance to a good life, they could not harm this saintly man because his handsome appearance was governed by the excellence of his mind. So the soul must rule the body, not the body the soul, because the soul is mistress of the body; the body is really a servant to the soul. Hence the unhappiness of the soul which is ruled by the body, and after being mistress becomes servant, because it breaks faith with the Lord and submits to the slavery of sin.

But the soul of the patriarch Joseph was faithful to its dominion, and there was no question of the body usurping its power. In fact when his master's wife, an unchaste woman, asked him to live with her he refused to do so, because even in his state of slavery he had not lost command of his soul. As a result he was falsely accused and put into prison. But the saintly man regarded that prison as a palace, or rather was himself a palace in the prison, because where there is faith, chastity and modesty, there is the palace of Christ, the temple of God, the abode of the Holy Spirit. So if any man prides himself on his good looks, or any woman boasts of the beauty of her body, let the man follow Joseph's example and the woman Susanna's: let them be chaste in body and mind; then they will also be beautiful not only to their fellow human beings but to God. For there are three examples of chastity in the Church, so that all have someone to copy: Joseph, Susanna, and Mary; Joseph for men to copy, Susanna for women, and Mary for virgins.

Responsory   *Ps 16:7-8; Mt 19:17*

I will bless the Lord who gives me counsel, who even at night directs my heart. I keep the Lord always before me: † since he is at my right hand, I shall stand firm.

V. If you wish to enter into life, keep the commandments. † Since he is . . .

Alternative Reading

From the writings of Novatian (De bono pudicitiae VIII, 1: CCL 4, 119-121)

God was with Joseph

Joseph is an example of purity. He was an illustrious Hebrew youth by birth. His spotless life, however, was his real title to nobility. Hated because of his dreams and sold by his brothers to the Ishmaelites, he had come into the household of an Egyptian. By obedience, irreproachable conduct, and utterly faithful service, Joseph had earned the favor and good will of his master. His appearance, that of a free man though he was a slave, which his youth and noble qualities had commended to all, was observed, though not fittingly, by his master's wife.

Unobserved, in a secluded area of the house, a hiding place suitable for wicked acts, the incontinent, brazen woman thought she could overcome by means of blandishments and threats the young man's purity. Since he was endeavoring to get away from her, she seized him by his clothes. Bewildered at the daring boldness of such a heinous action, he left behind his very clothes. The purity of his naked body furnished sufficient evidence of his integrity. The impudent woman did not hesitate to add the foolhardiness of calumny to the crime of immorality. Rejection infuriated and crushed her. Feigning grief, she charged the Hebrew youth with endeavoring to inflict on her the very violence that she herself had tried to bring to bear on him.

The passionate husband, in ignorance of the facts, was greatly aroused by his wife's accusation. The chaste young man was thrown into the lowest cell of the prison because he had refused to stain his conscience with sin. But purity was not alone in the prison. God was with Joseph, and the evildoers were in his control because his spirit had been vigilant in time of trial. The Lord finally set him free. He who in a house of lower status had done a servant's work, and this amidst dangers, was now master of the royal household free of any peril. His noble status was restored to him, and he received by the judgment of God, from whom he had merited it: the fruit of his purity and integrity.

Responsory   *Ps 16:7-8; Mt 19:17*
I will bless the Lord who gives me counsel, who even at night directs my heart. I keep the Lord always before me: † since he is at my right hand, I shall stand firm.
V. If you wish to enter into life, keep the commandments. † Since he is . . .

MONDAY   Year II

First Reading   Genesis 41:1-7.25-43

Responsory   *Wis 10:13-14*
Wisdom did not abandon the just man when he was sold, but delivered him from sin until she brought him the scepter of royalty † and authority over his oppressors.
V. Wisdom showed those who had defamed him false, and gave him eternal glory. † And authority over . . .

Second Reading   From the writings of Quodvultdeus of Carthage (Liber Promissionum I, 24, 41: SC 101, 240-242)

Joseph and Christ

After two days which seem like two years, Joseph is let out of prison on the third. Likewise our Joseph, who is Christ our Lord, rose from the dead on the third day. He is presented to Pharaoh. The resurrection is manifested to the world. Joseph interprets Pharaoh's dreams to him and gives him sound advice about what must be done, the store for seven years of plenty to be laid up under the supervision of a prudent man, for them to withstand the famine threatening thereafter. Likewise our Joseph, Christ our Lord, gave this counsel to a world running toward its end, in fulfillment of a sevenfold symbolism: For he said that *unless a grain of wheat falling into the earth should die, it remains but what it is; but if it dies, it yields much fruit.* For, again: *they who sow in tears shall reap in joy.*

Joseph was given authority by Pharaoh over the whole of Egypt. So also our Joseph, Christ our Lord, said after his resurrection: *All authority in heaven and on earth has been given to me.* Joseph sent his men all over Egypt and *collected corn in abundance like the sand on the seashore.* So also our Joseph, Christ our Lord, sent his men out into the world, saying: *Go forth and baptize the nations in the name of the Father, the Son, and the Holy Spirit.* And the tally of the believers was beyond counting, like the sand on the seashore. Joseph set up barns all over Egypt. And Christ our Lord has consecrated churches throughout the world. About that, Saint John said: *He will store the corn in his barn.* Joseph opened up the barns in the time of famine and served out to the people. Of our Joseph, this is said: *The Lord's eyes are on the just.* And then: *May he in his power and might draw out their souls from death and feed them in their hunger.* Amos the prophet mentions this hunger of the soul: *I will give them, says the Lord, a hunger not for bread and water, but to hear the word of God.* And in the gospel the Lord himself says: *Because iniquity has been there in abundance the charity of many has grown cold.* To those affected by this famine, our Joseph, the one who is Christ our Lord, supplies from his granaries the daily allowance of the bread of his body; and on tasting it we see *that the Lord is sweet.* It was said that Joseph gained from Pharaoh the whole of Egypt. Of our Joseph it is said that *God was in Christ, reconciling the world to himself.*

Responsory   *Ps 20:7-8; 121:2*

Some put their trust in chariots or horses, but our trust is in the name of the Lord. † They will collapse and fall, but we shall rise and stand firm.

V. My help shall come from the Lord, the creator of heaven and earth. † They will collapse . . .

Alternative Reading

From a commentary by Saint Procopius of Gaza (In Gen.: PG 87/1, 468-469.475-478)

The father wept for the son he loved

Not only does God pour out his gifts upon us, he also draws good out of evil. Had Joseph remained in his father's house, Egypt would have had no one to act in advance to prevent the full effects of the impending famine. In the same way, had the only Son of God remained hidden from us in the glory of the Father, the whole world would still be unredeemed.

Joseph was born in his father's old age, and for this reason Jacob loved him all the more. There is a foreshadowing here of the events of these last days. With immeasurable love God looked upon his Son as he came into the world in the fullness of time, at the end of a long line of prophets and saintly men and women. This Son of his encountered the hate of the Pharisees because the Father had clothed him with a garment of many glorious attributes — rather as Jacob had clothed Joseph with a tunic of many colors. Christ was the light, and he was the life. He cleansed those dead in sin, commanded the sea and walked on the water. The fire of envy, however, smoldered in the hearts of the Pharisees when they considered that the time would come when the whole world, and not merely the Jews, would worship this man. Here is the heir. Let us kill him and take his inheritance.

Joseph was handed over to the Ishmaelites and went down into Egypt. Christ, too, was delivered to the Gentiles: *Behold we go to Jerusalem, and the Son of Man will be handed over to the Gentiles.* When Joseph first arrived in Egypt, he was deeply afflicted. Christ, too, suffered persecution at the hands of both Jews and Gentiles. Both men were falsely accused. Joseph was thrown into prison, Christ was consigned to the grave. Joseph rose to a position of eminence and ruled over his captors. Christ's rule extends to the living and the dead.

Think, however, with what constancy of mind Joseph was endowed. Though oppressed by servitude and imprisonment, he possessed true freedom of mind. He languished in prison, but one day he would be clothed with royal dignity. Doubts never violated his faith. What was the source of his watchfulness and self-control?

If he had no faith in the divinely inspired gift of interpretation, why did he interpret the dreams of Pharaoh's servants in prison with him? Why did he not rather persuade them that nothing was to be gained by self-discipline?

When the time came, not one of his brothers was able to recognize Joseph. Envy obscures the truth, and too much cunning can lead to a form of slavery. It was Joseph's father who paid him the highest tribute of all when he wept for the son whom he loved. The envy of the Jews obscured the truth concerning the Christ, and so does the hate of the Greeks. Christ is not truly recognized either by those bogged down in heresy. But if you desire to attain true knowledge of Christ, you must hear God saying to you: *This is my beloved Son; listen to him.*

Responsory   *Ps 20:7-8; 121:2*

Some put their trust in chariots or horses, but our trust is in the name of the Lord. † They will collapse and fall, but we shall rise and stand firm.

V. My help shall come from the Lord, the creator of heaven and earth. † They will collapse . . .

TUESDAY   Year II

First Reading   Genesis 41:56—42:26

Responsory   *Gn 42:25-26*

Joseph gave orders to have † their containers filled with grain, their money replaced, and provisions given for their journey.

V. After this had been done, they departed, † their containers filled . . .

Second Reading   From the writings of Quodvultdeus of
                         Carthage (Liber Promissionum I, 30, 42: SC 101, 242-246)

Benjamin and Saul

Impelled by the famine, Joseph's brethren came to Egypt to buy corn from their brother, whom they had sold. Those who had crucified our Joseph, that is to say Christ our Lord, came to him to be revived by his bread, and so take away the hunger which was distressing their souls. The former, Joseph's brethren, do him reverence; the latter,

Christ's brethren, likewise do him reverence. On seeing his brothers, Joseph recognized them; but they did not know who he was. This applies to us also: for his brethren knew him not. *For if they had known who he was, they would never have crucified the Lord of glory.* Joseph was estranged from his brethren and said to them, through an interpreter: *You are spies, you have come to spy out the roads and the tracks and the pathways of this country.* So also our Joseph, Christ our Lord, said to his persecutors through his interpreter Peter: *You have denied what is holy and just and you have killed the prince of eternal life.* Joseph's brethren are sorry for what they did. To those others also, Christ's persecutors, the word is: *Repent.* They, of the olden times, say: *We are at fault over our brother.* So also the Jews who had told Pilate: *His blood be upon us and our children,* now say to the apostles: *What are we to do, brethren?* Show us. So as not to be thought spies, Joseph's brethren state that they are the sons, twelve in all, of one father; and they say that one of them is no more (since it was he to whom they were telling this), while the youngest is at home with their father.

On hearing mention of his younger brother, Joseph, ardently longing for him, says: *I will test your claim not to be spies by seeing whether your younger brother will come with you.* And he took Simeon apart from them, had him fettered in their presence, and put him under guard. Surely our latter day Benjamin and youngest brother, sought after by the Joseph who is Christ our Lord, is none other than Paul, formerly Saul, of the tribe of Benjamin, as he himself says, calling himself the least of the apostles. Simeon, bound by the three bonds of his denial, he whom fear held bound and love released, this Simeon we may take as Peter. That said, we had better acknowledge that it is by him that sins are bound and loosed: him indeed to whom it was said that *What you hold bound on earth will be bound in heaven; and what you loose on earth will be loosed in heaven.*

Responsory   *Ps 141:1-2; 143:1*

I call to you, Lord, hasten to help me; hear my voice when I cry to you. † Let my prayer rise before you like incense, the raising of my hands like an evening sacrifice.

V. Lord, hear my prayer; listen to my plea. † Let my prayer . . .

WEDNESDAY   Year II

First Reading   Genesis 43:1-11.13-17.26-34

Responsory   *Gn 43:13.14.11*
Take gifts with you and go to the Lord of the earth and adore him.
† May God Almighty dispose the man to be merciful toward you.
V. Put some of the land's best products in your baggage and take
them down to the man as gifts. † May God Almighty . . .

Second Reading   From a commentary from Saint Cyril of
                     Alexandria (Claphyrorum in Genesim IV: PG 69, 324-325)

The inheritance

When the sons of Jacob arrived with Benjamin, Joseph called
them to the feast, and after they had washed with water he fed
them to the full with food and wine. For at the right moment the
Jews, distressed and as if overwhelmed by unbearable hunger,
obviously in a spiritual sense, will abandon their haughty and
arrogant pride and come to Christ, longing to be fed by him, I mean
with holy, spiritual and life-giving food. But he will not receive
them without the new people, of whom Benjamin is the symbol.
And when they come as it were in concord and unanimity he will
receive them cheerfully, and welcome them as if to his own house,
that is, the Church. Then after he has washed them with pure
water, the baptismal water of spiritual rebirth, he will feed them
with bread and wine.

This is the spiritual interpretation. But we may take it further.
For Joseph made himself known to his brothers when they arrived
with Benjamin, and even thought them worthy to eat at his table,
as I said just now. But he gave them no inheritance, and actually
ordered them to return home and fetch their father, Jacob. But
when Jacob went down and Joseph now saw him there with his
children, then and only then he assigned them the best of all his
land. This too is a clear indication that Christ will receive the
Israelites converted in the last days of this age, since the new people
are obviously united with them in unity of soul. The new people,
as I said, are foreshadowed in Benjamin. But the inheritance we
hope for will not be given to us without the holy Fathers. For just
as they, although they died in faith, in the words of the wise Paul:

did not obtain what was promised, since God had foreseen something better for ourselves, that they should not attain perfection without us, so we too shall wait for the Fathers, so as not to attain perfection without them. Therefore with the holy Fathers, the first, middle, and last people, we shall receive the best and inalienable inheritance of the kingdom of heaven in Christ, through whom and with whom glory be to God the Father with the Holy Spirit for ever. Amen.

Responsory   *Zep 2:3; Ps 22:26*
   Seek the Lord, all you in the land who live humbly, obeying his commands. † Seek integrity, seek humility.
   V. The poor shall eat and be satisfied; those who seek the Lord shall praise him. † Seek integrity . . .

THURSDAY   Year II

First Reading   Genesis 44:1-20.30-34

Responsory   *Gn 43:29.30*
   Is this your younger brother, of whom you told me? May God be gracious to you, my boy. † He went into a private room and wept there.
   V. When Joseph's eye fell on his brother Benjamin he was moved. † He went into . . .

Second Reading   From the writings of Quodvultdeus of
                       Carthage (Liber Promissionum I, 31, 43: SC 101, 246-250)

The cup of Christ's suffering, given in secret,
is recognized for what it is by grace

   Joseph ordered his brothers' sacks to be filled with corn and the money they had brought to be returned to each one. This was to show that the grace of Christ, who is our Joseph, does not come from works; for otherwise grace would not be grace. Joseph's brethren come the second time, with Benjamin as they had promised; and for the second time five thousand Jews come to Christ, followed by Paul, the least — or last — of the Apostles. Joseph saw Benjamin, his brother and his mother's son, and he wept at the sight. Jesus saw Paul savaging our mother the Church and he took pity on him. The same Paul says that Jesus appeared to him, as it were, born after his time. Benjamin's delivery and birth, on the other hand, hastened his mother's death: and so he was called the child of grief. Thus Paul, our Benjamin, says: *I am not worthy to be called an apostle, for I persecuted the Church of God.* Joseph said of his brothers, to the head of his household: *Take them into the house; for they are to eat bread with me.* So our Joseph says, through the prophets, to his brethren: *Come, eat of my bread and drink of the wine I have made ready for you.* Joseph gave his brethren gifts; and Christ our Joseph made gifts to men when he gave, when he sent, the Holy Spirit to his disciples. Joseph's gifts to his younger brother were more lavish than those to the others. This is what Paul, our Benjamin, said of himself in his preaching: *I have labored more than all those* (he says): *but not I, but God's grace working in me.* Again, Joseph ordered his brothers' sacks to be filled with corn and the money to be given back. Our brethren remonstrate to Joseph at receiving grace upon grace. Joseph orders his own goblet to be placed secretly in Benjamin's sack: and it troubled his brethren when it was sought and found in Benjamin's sack. The cup of Christ's suffering, given in secret, is recognized for what it is by grace, when afflicting Paul's body. For this is what he meant when he berated the entire synagogue, as if to say he had found the cup in his sack: *For I bear in my body* (he says) *the marks of our Lord Jesus Christ.*

Responsory   *Ps 119:161-162; see Jn 6:63*
Though princes persecute me without cause, I stand in awe of your word. † I delight in your word like one who finds a treasure.
V. Your words are spirit, Lord, and they are life. † I delight in . . .

FRIDAY   Year II

First Reading   Genesis 45:1-15.21-28; 46:1-7

Responsory   *See Gn 45.3.4.5.2*
Joseph speaking to his brothers said: † Do not be distressed and do not reproach yourselves.

V. His sobs were so loud that the Egyptians heard him and so the news reached Pharaoh's palace, and he said to his brothers: † Do not be . . .

Second Reading   From a sermon by Cardinal John Henry Newman *(Parochial and Plain Sermons* IV, 251-259.261-263)

The Lord was with Joseph

It is God's rule in scripture to dispose his blessings, silently and secretly, so that we do not discern them at the time, except by faith, afterwards only.

Consider how parallel this is to what takes place in the providences of daily life. Events happen to us pleasant or painful; we do not know at the time the meaning of them, we do not see God's hand in them. If indeed we have faith, we confess what we do not see, and take all that happens as you; but whether we will accept it in faith or not, certainly there is no other way of accepting it. We see nothing. We see not why things come, or whither they tend. Jacob cried out on one occasion, *All these things are against me*; certainly so they seemed to be. One son made away with by the rest, another in prison in a foreign land, a third demanded; "You have me bereaved of my children; Joseph is not, and Simeon is not, and you will take Benjamin away: all these things are against me." Yet all these things were working for good. Or pursue the fortunes of the favorite and holy youth who was the first taken from him: sold by his brethren to strangers, carried into Egypt, tempted by a very perilous temptation, overcoming it but not rewarded, thrown into prison, the iron entering into his soul, waiting there till the Lord should be gracious, and *look down from heaven*; but waiting — why? and how long? It is said again and again in the sacred narrative, *The Lord was with Joseph*; but do you think he saw at the time any tokens of God? Any tokens, except so far as by faith he realized them, in faith he saw them.

Yet afterwards he saw what was so mysterious at the time — *God did send me before you*, he said to his brethren, *to preserve life. It was not you that sent me hither, but God; and he hath made me a father to Pharaoh, and lord of all his house and a ruler throughout all the land of Egypt.* Wonderful providence indeed, which is so silent, yet so efficacious, so constant, so unerring.

Let a person who trusts he is on the whole serving God acceptably look back upon his past life, and he will find how critical were moments and acts, which at the time seemed the most indifferent: as for instance, the school he was sent to as a child, the occasion of his falling in with those persons who have most benefited him, the accidents which determined his calling or prospects whatever they were. God's hand is ever over his own, and he leads them forward by a way they know not of. The utmost they can do is to believe what they cannot see now, what they shall see hereafter; and as believing, to act together with God toward it.

Responsory   *Ps 119:137.138.142; 7:12*
Lord, you are just indeed, you have imposed your will with justice.
† Your justice is an eternal justice, and your law is truth.
V. God is a just judge, slow to anger, but he threatens the wicked every day, people who refuse to repent. † Your justice . . .

SATURDAY   Year II

First Reading   Genesis 49:1-28.33

Responsory   *Rv 5:5; Gn 49:10*
The lion of the tribe of Judah, the root of David, has won the right by his victory † to open the scroll with its seven seals.
V. The scepter shall never depart from Judah until tribute is brought to him † to open the . . .

Second Reading   From a commentary by Rupert of Deutz
                     (De Trinitate et operibus eius, in Gen IX, 29: PL 167, 554)

Through your offspring all the nations will be blessed

The scepter will not be taken away from Judah, nor a prince of his own blood. So the scepter was taken away from Judah, for the first time when Herod seized it, who was certainly not a Jew. But as everyone knows it was then that one came who was destined to be sent. For it was then that Jesus Christ, the Son of God, consented to be born of the Virgin at Bethlehem in Judea. So when Jacob said: *the scepter will not be taken away from Judah, nor a prince of his own blood, until he comes who is destined to be sent,* the holiest of prophets raised aloft his firm prophetic message like a lamp shining *in a dark place*. He wanted those who were searching for the kingdom of God to know the time or circumstance that would make them sure of the coming of one, whom all his brothers and sisters, all the children of his Father, must praise and worship.

Through the holy Spirit, Simeon, an old man, *righteous and devout,* turned his attention to this lamp, this prophetic message. When he knew and saw that an alien ruled, and the scepter and the prince of his own blood had been taken away from Judah, he understood that now was the appointed time for the one to come who was destined to be sent. And so with long-continued anxious prayer he knocked at the doors of heaven, from where he expected him to come, until he received *the answer from the holy Spirit: that he would not see death before he had seen Christ the Lord.* He indeed saw him; and as he had read in this passage of Scripture: *and he will be the expectation of the nations,* he believed and confessed that he was *a light for the revelation to the Gentiles.*

But from whom could the patriarch Israel himself have learned to say: *and he will be the expectation of the nations?* From God of course, not only as a prophet but because God had spoken these words to Abraham: *through your offspring all the nations will be blessed.*

Responsory   *Ps 119:97.105.135; 19:11*
Lord, how I love your law! Your word is a lamp for my feet, a light for my path. † Let your face shine on your servant and teach me your decrees.
V. By them your servant is instructed; in keeping them there is great reward. † Let your face . . .

SIXTH WEEK IN ORDINARY TIME

SUNDAY   Year II

First Reading   1 Thessalonians 1:10—2:12

Responsory   *1 Thes 1:9; 3:12.13*
You are turned toward God to serve the living and true God and to await from heaven the Son he raised from the dead, † who delivers us from the wrath to come.
V. May the Lord increase you and make you overflow with love for one another and may God strengthen your hearts in holiness for the coming of our Lord Jesus Christ † who delivers us . . .

Second Reading   From a homily by Saint John Chrysostom
(Première Epître aux Thessaloniens: Bareille XIX, 184-186)

The joy of the Spirit brings gladness
in place of what seemed like affliction

You have become imitators of the Lord, says the Apostle, *by receiving the word amidst much oppression, with the joy of the Holy Spirit.* Oppression in what pertains to the body, but joy in the spirit. You wonder, perhaps, how that can be. Well, what happened was distressing for you, but not so what came of it: the Holy Spirit does not allow it to be. On the one hand, you cannot be joyful while suffering for your sins; but on the other, you can find joy even in being scourged, when you suffer for Christ.

For that is how the joy of the Spirit shows itself: it brings gladness in place of what seemed like affliction. They have oppressed you, he says, and persecuted you, but the Spirit has not forsaken you all the while. Just as the three young men were refreshed in the fiery furnace, so it has been with you in your oppression. Whereas it is not in the nature of fire to refresh, but of the revivifying Spirit, it is likewise not in the nature of oppression to beget joy and gladness: that comes of suffering for Christ, and of the revivifying Spirit bringing relief even through the furnace of trials and temptations.

With joy, Saint Paul says, but, more than that, *with great joy*: for it comes from the Holy Spirit. *This has made you an example to all the faithful in Macedonia and Achaia.* Indeed, he tells them that they have shone so brightly that they have become teachers of those who preceded them. That is what it means to be apostolic. He did not say, "So as to set an example in believing," but "to set an example to those who already believe." That is to say, "You have taught them how to have faith in God, by enduring hardships from the very first days." And when he says Achaia, he means the whole of Greece.

Do you see what zeal can do? No need for time, no procrastination or delay; it only has to show itself and everything is accomplished. For thus it was that people who had only later heard the preaching of the gospel became teachers of the first to do so. Let no one despair, then. Even those who have spent a good deal of time unprofitably may nevertheless do as much in a short time as they previously failed to do. For if people who did not believe could become such shining lights once they did believe, how much more could those do so who already believed?

On the other hand, let no one pondering all this slacken off, on learning that everything can be put right in a short while: for the future is always unclear, and the day of the Lord is like a thief that comes upon us suddenly as we sleep. But if we are not asleep, it will not come upon us like a thief, or take us all unaware. For if we stay awake and keep watch, it will arrive not like a thief, but like a royal messenger calling us to the good things prepared for us.

Responsory   *Is 55:6; Eccl 12:1*
Seek the Lord while he may be found; † call on him while he is near.
V. Remember your Creator in the days of your youth. † Call on him . . .

MONDAY   Year II

First Reading   1 Thessalonians 2:13—3:13

Responsory   *See 1 Thes 3:12.13; 2 Thes. 2:16-17*
May the Lord be generous in making your hearts overflow with love for one another and for all peoples, † and may he confirm your hearts in holiness.
V. May our Lord himself inspire your hearts with courage. † And may he . . .

Second Reading   From a commentary by Saint John
Chrysostom (Première Epître aux Thessaloniens: Bareille
XIX, 226-227)

God's way of love

*May God our Father himself, and our Lord Jesus Christ, direct our
way to you. And may the Lord make your love for one another and for
all grow as strong as ours is for you.* True divine charity embraces
everyone. If you love one person but cease to love someone else,
yours is a merely human love. Our love is not like that.

*So may he confirm your hearts in holiness and make you blameless
in the sight of God our Father when our Lord Jesus Christ comes with
all his saints.* Daniel shows that they will profit from their charity
as much as those who receive it. He says he wants their love to
increase so that they may be blameless. He did not say, "May he
confirm you" but *may he confirm your hearts,* for *evil thoughts come
from the heart.* It is possible to be evil without doing anything, as
are those who are envious, disbelieving, deceitful, who delight in
wrong-doing, are unfriendly or hold perverted opinions.

All these sins come from the heart, and to be free from them is
holiness. Chastity in particular is rightly called holiness, since
fornication and adultery are called impurity. Speaking generally,
every sin is impurity and every virtue is purity. Our Lord said:
Blessed are the pure in heart, affirming that the pure are those who
are pure in every way.

I am well aware that other sins make the soul unclean just as
much as unchastity. Listen to the prophet saying that evil thoughts
or deeds defile the soul: *Jerusalem, wash your hearts clean of wickedness;* and again: *Wash, make yourselves clean, get rid of the wickedness in your souls.* He did not say unchastity, so it is not only
unchastity that defiles the soul but all the other sins as well.

Responsory   *Ps 76:4; Hb 3:2*

You are awesome, O Lord, more majestic than the everlasting
mountains. † Who can stand when your anger is roused?
V. Lord, I have heard of your fame; I stand in awe of your deeds.
† Who can stand . . .

TUESDAY   Year II

First Reading   1 Thessalonians 4:5-18

Responsory   *1 Thes 4:15; Mk 13:27; see Mt 24:31*
At the word of command, at the call of the archangel's voice and
the sound of God's trumpet, the Lord himself will come down from
heaven; † he will gather his elect from the four winds, and from the
depths of the earth to the heights of heaven.
V. When the Son of Man comes, he will send forth his angels with
a mighty trumpet blast. † He will gather . . .

Second Reading   From the writings of Saint Cyprian of
                     Carthage (De Mortalitate 20-22.24: CSEL 3/1, 309-312)

Let us be ready for every manifestation of God's will

   How often has it been revealed to us also, the least and the last,
how frequently and manifestly have I been commanded, through
God's vouchsafing, that I should bear witness constantly, that I
should preach publicly that our brethren who have been freed
from the world by the summons of the Lord should not be
mourned, since we know that they are not lost but sent before; that
in departing they lead the way; that as travelers, as voyagers are
wont to be, they should be longed for, not lamented; and that dark
clothing should not be worn here, inasmuch as they have already
assumed white garments there; and that no occasion should be
given to the pagans to censure us deservedly and justly, on the
ground that we grieve for those who we say are living with God,
as if entirely destroyed and lost, and that we do not show by the
testimony of the heart and breast the faith which we declare in
speech and word! We are prevaricators of our hope and faith, if
what we say seems pretended, feigned, falsified. It profits nothing
to show forth virtue in words and destroy truth in deeds.
   Finally, the apostle Paul censures rebukes, and blames any who
are sorrowful at the death of their dear ones. *We will not*, he says,
*have you ignorant, brethren, concerning them that are asleep, that you
be not sorrowful, even as others who have no hope. For if we believe
that Jesus died, and rose again; even so those who have slept through
Jesus will God bring with him.* He says that they are sorrowful at
the death of their dear ones who have no hope. But we who live in

hope and believe in God and have faith that Christ suffered for us and rose again, abiding in Christ and rising again through him and in him, why are we ourselves either unwilling to depart hence from this world, or why do we mourn and grieve for our departing ones as if they were lost, since Christ our Lord and our God himself admonishes us and says: *I am the resurrection: he who believes in me, although he be dead, shall live: and everyone that lives and believes in me shall not die forever!* If we believe in Christ let us have faith in his words and promises, that we who are not to die forever may come in joyful security to Christ with whom we are to conquer and reign for eternity.

He who is to come to the abode of Christ, to the glory of the heavenly kingdom, ought not to grieve and mourn. Rather, beloved brethren, with sound mind, with firm faith, with rugged virtue, let us be ready for every manifestation of God's will; freed from the terror of death, let us think of the immortality which follows. Let us show that this is what we believe, so that we may not mourn the death even of our dear ones and, when the day of our own summons comes, without hesitation but with gladness we may come to the Lord at his call.

Responsory   *Ps 41:1; Gal 6:2*
   Blessed are those who are concerned for the poor and the weak;
   † the Lord will save them in time of trouble.
   V. Bear one another's burdens, and so fulfill the law of Christ. † The
   Lord . . .

Alternative Reading

From a letter by Saint Fulgentius of Ruspe (Ep. ad Gallam viduam 3-5: CCL 91, 198-199)

Sent on ahead of you

So, if we hold on to the true faith, if we harbor no doubts about the words of God, if we, with most certain hope, progress toward the future life, if we love God and neighbor worthily, if we do not await a vainglory from human beings but the true glory of the Christian name from God, we must not like the unbelievers have any sadness concerning the faithful departed and, to speak more precisely, our people who have fallen asleep. There must remain in our heart a distinction between a salutary and a harmful sadness by which it comes about that a spirit, given over to eternal things, does not collapse because of the loss of temporal solace and assumes a salutary sadness concerning these things in which it considers that it did either something less or differently than it should have. So Paul teaches that each type of sadness is different no less in deed than in word. Finally, he shows that in one there is progress toward salvation but in the other an ending in death, saying, "For godly sorrow produces a salutary repentance without regret but worldly sorrow produces death."

Therefore, do not have an undifferentiated sadness over the death of your husband beyond the way of the Christian faith. You should not think of him as lost but as sent on ahead of you. You should not think of his youth as prematurely cut off but rather see him confirmed in an endless eternity. To the faithful souls it is said: "Your youth shall be renewed like the eagle's."

Far be it from us, agreeing with the errors of the unbelievers, to think or to say that "A black day has carried off and plunged in bitter death" that young Christian man. For black day carries off those who, according to the saying of the Apostle John, "are in darkness and walk in darkness and do not know where they are going because the darkness has blinded their eyes." Black day has carried off those whom the true light itself vehemently rebukes: "This is the verdict," he says, "that the light came into the world but people preferred darkness to light because their works were evil." Such are they who live in such a way that when they hear the voice of the Son of God, they are called forth, not to life, but to judgment, as the Lord says, "The hour is coming in which all who are in the tombs will hear his voice and will come out, those who have done good deeds to the resurrection of life, but those who have done wicked deeds to the resurrection of condemnation." And since neither a short nor a long life can avail these people, consequently in the book of Wisdom it is said of such people: "Even if they live long, they will be held of no account and, finally, their old age will be without honor. If they die young, they will have no hope and no consolation on the day of judgment."

Responsory   *Ps 41:1; Gal 6:2*
    Blessed are those who are concerned for the poor and the weak;
    † the Lord will save them in time of trouble.

V. Bear one another's burdens, and so fulfill the law of Christ. † The Lord . . .

WEDNESDAY   Year II

First Reading   1 Thessalonians 5:1-28

Responsory   *1 Thes 5:9; Col 1:13*
God has not destined us to endure his wrath but to win salvation through our Lord Jesus Christ, † who died for us, so that we might live in him.
V. God rescued us from the power of darkness and brought us into the kingdom of his own beloved Son, † who died for us, so that we might live in him.

Second Reading   From a homily by Saint Symeon the New Theologian (Traités Théologiques et Éthiques II, 10: SC 129, 266-270)

Children of the light

Grace reveals itself perceptibly to those who through faith, in fear and trembling, fulfill the commandments and show due repentance, and there can be no doubt that of itself it brings about in them the future judgment. Or rather, it becomes in them the day of divine judgment which continually enlightens those who have been purified, so that they can see what they really are in themselves, and the nature in every detail of their actions, both natural and spiritual. Nor is this all, for they are tried and examined by the fire, and bathed in the water of tears streaming all over the body, little by little they are thoroughly washed by the divine fire and the Spirit, and become wholly pure and unstained. They are children of the light and of the day, and no longer mortal.

This is why such people are not judged in the coming judgment and trial, for they have been judged beforehand. They are not put to shame by that light, for they have already been enlightened. Neither are they tested or burnt when they come into this fire, for they have already been tested. They do not regard the Day of the Lord as being then revealed, for association and companionship with God has completely transformed them into a radiant day and lamp. Nor are they then in the world or with the world, but wholly outside it. For the Lord says, *I have chosen you out of the world*, and the Apostle declares: *If we judged ourselves, we should not be judged. But when we are judged by the Lord, we are corrected in order that we may not be condemned with the world*; and elsewhere he says, *Walk as children of the light.*

Therefore, the Day of the Lord will never come upon those who are children of that light, and sons and daughters of the coming day, and who are able to live decently, as in the daytime; for they are in that light always and continually. The Day of the Lord will be revealed suddenly not to those upon whom the divine light is always shining, but to those who are in the darkness of the passions, who live in the world and desire the things of the world. For them that day will be fearful, like unbearable fire.

But you are not living in darkness for that day to surprise you like a thief. You are all children of light and children of the day. We do not belong to the night or to darkness. Let us not sleep, then, as others do, but let us stay awake and be sober. And further on the Apostle continues: *For God has not destined us for wrath but for salvation, so that whether we wake or whether we sleep we may live with him.*

Responsory   Ps 103:8-9.13-14
The Lord is merciful and loving, slow to anger and full of compassion. He will not always reprove us; his wrath will come to an end.
† As tenderly as a father treats his children, the Lord treats those who stand in awe of him.
V. He knows what we are made of; he remembers that we are dust.
† As tenderly . . .

Alternative Reading

From a sermon by Saint Augustine of Hippo (Enarr. in Ps. 37, 14: CCL 38, 391-392)

Inner prayer without ceasing

Your desire is your prayer. And if your desire is unending, so is your prayer unending. For it was not without good reason that the apostle spoke: *Pray without ceasing.* We are hardly expected to go down on our knees without a break, are we, or to prostrate ourselves, or raise our hands? Is this really what he means by saying: *Pray without ceasing?* If we are saying that this is how we are to pray, I think it is frankly impossible to do so without ceasing.

There is another, inner prayer without ceasing. It is the desire which consists in longing. Whatever else you do, if you long for that sabbath, you never cease praying. If you do not want to cease praying, do not cease longing. Your unending stream of longing is your unending stream of speech. If you cease loving, you will cease speaking. Who are those who have ceased speaking? Those of whom it is said: Because there is an abundance of iniquity, the love of many shall grow cold. The cooling-off of love is the silence of the heart. The leaping flames of love are the shouting of the heart. If love lasts for ever, then you are always shouting. If you are always shouting, you are always longing. If you are longing, then you are recollecting the future rest. And you ought to understand before whom the roaring of your heart takes place.

Consider now what sort of longing it ought to be which is before the eyes of God. Should it really be a longing for the death of our enemy? This is the sort of thing people think they are right to ask for. Indeed sometimes we do pray for the thing we ought not to. Let us have a look at what people think they are entitled to pray for. For they pray for the death of someone, and for an inheritance to come their way. But let even those who pray for their enemies to die listen to the Lord when he says: *Pray for your enemies.* Let them not, therefore, pray for the death of their enemies, but let them pray for their improvement. Indeed their enemies will in a very real sense be dead, for once they have been corrected, they will no longer be enemies.

And before you is all my longing. What if their longing is before God, and their groaning is not before God? How can this possibly be, when the voice of that longing is groaning? That is why the psalm says: *And my groaning is not hidden from you.* For you it is not hidden, but it is hidden from many people. Sometimes God's humble servant is seen to be saying: And my groaning is not hidden from you. Sometimes God's servant is seen also to laugh. You could hardly say that the longing for God was dead and buried in his heart, could you? And if there is longing within it, there is also groaning. It does not always filter through to the ears of people like you and me, but it never escapes the attention of God's ears.

Responsory   *Ps 103:8-9.13-14*
    The Lord is merciful and loving, slow to anger and full of compassion. He will not always reprove us; his wrath will come to an end.

† As tenderly as a father treats his children, the Lord treats those
who stand in awe of him.
V. He knows what we are made of; he remembers that we are dust.
† As tenderly . . .

THURSDAY   Year II

First Reading   2 Thessalonians 1:1-12

Responsory   *See 2 Thes 1:10; Ps 145:13*
The Lord will come to be glorified in his holy ones † and to be
adored by all who have believed in him.
V. The Lord is faithful in all his words and loving in all his deeds,
† and to be . . .

Second Reading   From the writings of Jean Pierre de Caussade
                      (*Abandonment to Divine Providence*, 48-49)

We rejoice our whole life in the fact that God is God

Offer a righteous sacrifice, the prophet says, *and trust in the Lord.*
This shows us that the great and solid foundation of the spiritual
life is to give ourselves to God, to be subject to his good will in all
things, inwardly and outwardly; and after that to forget ourselves
so thoroughly that we regard ourselves as something sold and
handed over, to which we no longer have any right: so that God's
good will becomes all our joy, and his happiness, his glory and his
being become our sole good.

Once we have laid this foundation, we have only to spend our
whole life rejoicing in the fact that God is God, abandoning ourselves so entirely to his good will that we are equally content to do
this or that or the opposite, as his good will disposes, without
complaining of the use that good will makes of us.

So, to abandon ourselves is the great duty that remains to be
fulfilled, after we have faithfully discharged all the obligations of
our position in life. The perfection with which that duty is carried
out will be the measure of our holiness.

Holiness only means our free submission to the divine will,
with the help of grace. All that follows such pure acquiescence is
the work of God, and not the work of any human being. To give
ourselves up blindly in total renunciation and indifference: that is

all God asks us to do; the rest he decides and chooses in accordance with his plans, as an architect marks off and specifies the stones for the building he wants to construct.

Therefore we must love God and his command completely; we must love this as it appears, without wanting anything more. The fact that such or such things are offered to us is not our affair but God's; and what he gives us is the best for our souls. The whole of spirituality is summed up in this maxim: to give ourselves up purely and entirely to God's command; and then, in constant self-negation to fill our time eternally with loving and obeying him, without one of those fears, complaints, changes of mind and worrying, which concern for our salvation and our own perfection sometimes gives us. Since God offers to manage our affairs for us, let us then hand them over once and for all to his infinite wisdom, so that from now on we can center our thoughts in him and what concerns him alone.

Responsory   *Ps 146:5-7; 118:8-9*
Happy are those who are helped by Jacob's God, whose hope is in the Lord their God. † It is he who keeps faith forever, and is just to those who are oppressed.
V. It is better to take refuge in the Lord than to trust in human help; better to take refuge in the Lord than to rely on princes. † It is he who . . .

FRIDAY   Year II

First Reading   2 Thessalonians 2:1-17

Responsory   *Mt 24:30; 2 Thes 2:8*
The sign of the Son of Man will appear in the sky † and all on earth will see the Son of Man coming with great power and majesty.
V. Then the evil one will be revealed, and the Lord Jesus will slay him with the breath of his mouth. † And all on . . .

Second Reading   From a sermon by Cardinal John Henry
                       Newman *(Parochial and Plain Sermons VI, 235-237.245-246)*

Signs

In one place Saint Paul cautions his brethren against expecting
the immediate coming of Christ; but he does not say more than that
Christ will send a sign immediately before his coming — a certain
dreadful enemy of the truth — which is to be followed by himself
at once, and therefore does not stand in our way, or prevent eager
eyes from looking out for him. And, in truth, Saint Paul seems
rather to be warning his brethren against being disappointed if
Christ did not come, than hindering them from expecting him.

Now it may be objected that this is a kind of paradox; how is it
possible, it may be asked, ever to be expecting what has so long
been delayed? What has been so long coming may be longer still.
It was possible, indeed, for the early Christians, who had no
experience of the long period which the Church was to remain on
earth, to look out for Christ; but we cannot help using our reason:
there are no more grounds to expect Christ now than at those many
former times, when, as the event showed, he did not come. Christians have ever been expecting the last day, and ever meeting with
disappointment. Now I shall attempt to say something in answer
to this objection.

If it be true that Christians have expected him when he did not
come, it is quite as true that when he does come, the world will not
expect him. If it be true that Christians have fancied signs of his
coming when there were none, it is equally true that the world will
not see the signs of his coming when they are present. His signs
are not so plain but you have to search for them; not so plain but
you may be mistaken in your search; and your choice lies between
the risk of thinking you see what is not, and of not seeing what is.
True it is that many times, many ages, have Christians been mistaken in thinking they discerned Christ's coming; but better a
thousand times think him coming when he is not, than once think
him not coming when he is.

Always since the first, Christians have been looking out for
Christ in the signs of the natural and moral world. If they have been
poor and uneducated, strange sights in the sky, or tremblings of
the ground, storms, failure of harvest, or disease, or anything

monstrous and unnatural, has made them think that he was at hand. If they were in a way to take a view of the social and political world, then the troubles of states — wars, revolutions, and the like — have been additional circumstances which served to impress them, and kept their hearts awake for Christ. Now all these are nothing else but those very things which he himself has told us to dwell upon, and has given us as signs of his coming. *There shall be signs*, he says, *in the sun, and in the moon, and in the stars; and upon the earth distress of nations with perplexity, the sea and the waves roaring; men's hearts failing them for fear, and for looking after those things which are coming on the earth; for the powers of heaven shall be shaken. And when these things begin to come to pass, then look up and lift up your heads, for your redemption draws near.* One day the lights of heaven *will* be signs; why, then, is it superstitious to *look* toward them? It is better to be wrong in our watching, than not to watch at all.

Responsory   *Ps 106:45; 89:34*

For their sake he remembered his covenant; † in his boundless love he relented.

V. I will never violate my covenant, nor go back on the promise I have made. † In his . . .

SATURDAY   Year II

First Reading   2 Thessalonians 3:1-18

Responsory   *See 1 Thes 2:13; see Eph 1:13*

When you opened your hearts to the message of God, † you received it, not as the word of men, but as what it truly is, the word of God.

V. You have heard the word of truth, the good news of your salvation. † You received it . . .

Second Reading   From the writings of Pierre Teilhard de Chardin *(The Divine Milieu, 37-39)*

Spiritual encumbrance

I do not think I am exaggerating when I say that nine out of ten practicing Christians feel that man's work is always at the level of

a "spiritual encumbrance." In spite of the practice of right inten-
tions, and the day offered every morning to God, the general run
of the faithful dimly feel that time spent at the office or the studio,
in the fields or in the factory, is time taken away from prayer and
adoration. It is impossible not to work — that is taken for granted.
Then it is impossible, too, to aim at the deep religious life reserved
for those who have the leisure to pray or preach all day long. A few
moments of the day can be salvaged for God, yes, but the best
hours are absorbed, or at any rate cheapened, by material cares.
Under the sway of this feeling, large numbers of Catholics lead a
double or crippled life in practice; they have to step out of their
human dress so as to have faith in themselves as Christians — and
inferior Christians at that.

There are, of course, certain noble and cherished moments of
the day — those when we pray or receive the sacraments. Were it
not for these moments of more efficient or explicit commerce with
God, the tide of the divine omnipresence, and our perception of it,
would weaken until all that was best in our human endeavor,
without being entirely lost to the world, would be for us emptied
of God. But once we have jealously safeguarded our relation to
God encountered, if I may dare use the expression, "in his pure
state" (that is to say, in a state of being distinct from all the
constituents of the world), there is no need to fear that the most
trivial or the most absorbing of occupations should force us to
depart from him. By virtue of the creation and, still more, of the
incarnation, *nothing* here below *is profound* for those who know
how to see. Try, with God's help, to perceive the connection —
even physical and natural — which binds your labor with the
building of the kingdom of heaven; try to realize that heaven itself
smiles upon you and, through your works, draws you to itself;
then, as you leave church for the noisy streets, you will remain with
only one feeling, that of continuing to immerse yourself in God. If
your work is dull or exhausting, take refuge in the inexhaustible
and becalming interest of progressing in the divine life. If your
work enthralls you, then allow the spiritual impulse which matter
communicates to you to enter into your taste for God whom you
know better and desire more under the veil of his works. Never, at
any time, "whether eating or drinking," consent to do anything
without first of all realizing its significance and constructive value

in Christo Jesu, and pursuing it with all your might. This is not simply a commonplace precept for salvation: it is the very path to sanctity for each person according to his or her state and calling. For what is sanctity in a creature if not to adhere to God with the maximum of strength? And what does that maximum adherence to God mean if not the fulfillment — in the world organized around Christ — of the exact function, be it lowly or eminent, to which that creature is destined both by natural endowment and by supernatural gift?

Responsory   *Ps 113:4.6-7*
High above all nations is the Lord, yet he stoops from the heights to look down upon heaven and earth. † He lifts up the lowly from the dust, the needy from the dung-heap.
V. He has pulled down princes from their thrones and exalted the lowly. † He lifts up . . .

SEVENTH WEEK IN ORDINARY TIME

SUNDAY Year II

First Reading   2 Corinthians 1:1-14

Responsory   *Ps 94:18-19*
Your love, O Lord, sustains me. † In the midst of all my troubles,
your consolation gladdens my soul.
V. As we share abundantly in Christ's suffering, so through Christ
we share abundantly in his consolation. † In the midst . . .

Second Reading   From the writings of Leander of Seville (PL 72,
894-895)

How sweet is love and how delightful is unity

Rejoice and be glad, O Church of God, exult and arise as one
body of Christ, put on your strength, and sing for joy, for your
sorrows have changed to gladness and your mourning clothes to
robes of gaiety. Lo, suddenly forgetful of your sterility and your
poverty, you have at one birth borne innumerable peoples for your
Christ, in that you make gain from your losses and profit from your
persecution. So strong is your bridegroom by whose command
you are ruled, that, although he allows you to be dispossessed of
a few things, yet he lets you recover the spoils and even subjects
your enemies to you. So a farmer or a fisherman, looking toward
future gains, does not count as loss the seed he sows or the bait on
his hook.

Weep no longer, then; grieve not that for a while you had lost
those whom you now see returned to you with great pain. Exult in
the strength of your faith, and in the service of your head be of
robust belief, as you behold how you have recovered what it was
once promised that you would regain; for truth itself says in the
gospel: *Christ had to die for the nation; and not only for the nation,
but that he might gather together into one the children of God who
were scattered abroad.* Proclaim as in the psalms, saying to those
who hate peace: *Glorify the Lord with me, let us together extol his
name.* And again: *When the peoples and kingdoms gather together to
serve the Lord.*

How sweet is love and how delightful is unity you know well through the foretelling of the prophets, through the divine word in the gospels, through the teachings of the apostles. Therefore, preach only the unity of nations, dream only of the oneness of all peoples, spread abroad only the good seeds of peace and love. Rejoice, therefore, in the Lord that you were not cheated of your desire, for now, after the winter's ice, after the harsh cold, after the austerity of the snow, like the fruit which is the delight of the fields and the joyous flowers of springtime and the branches smiling with the offshoots of leaves, you have suddenly and joyously recovered those whom you embraced for so long with constant mourning and continual prayers.

Responsory   *Sir 42:15-16; 43:28*

By the words of the Lord his works come into being, and all creation obeys his will. † As the sun as it shine looks upon all things, so the work of the Lord is full of his glory.

V. Where can we find the power to praise him, since he is greater than all his works? † As the sun . . .

Alternative Reading

From a sermon by Cardinal John Henry Newman (*Parochial and Plain Sermons* V, 300.307-311)

Paul knew how to console, for he knew the sorrow

If there is one point of character more than another which belonged to Saint Paul, and discovers itself in all he said and did, it was his power of sympathizing with his brethren, nay, with all classes of people. He went through trials of every kind, and this was their issue, to let him into the feelings and thereby to introduce him to the hearts of high and low, Jew and Gentile. He knew how to persuade, for he knew where lay the perplexity; he knew how to console, for he knew the sorrow.

When a man, in whom dwells God's grace, is lying on the bed of suffering, or when he has been stripped of his friends and is solitary, he has, in a peculiar way, tasted of the powers of the world to come and exhorts and consoles with authority.

Some such thoughts as these may be humbly entertained by every one of us, when brought even into any ordinary pain or trouble. Doubtless if we are properly minded, we shall be very loath to take to ourselves titles of honor. We shall be slow to believe that we are specially beloved by Christ. But at least we may have the blessed certainty that we are made instruments for the consolation of others.

Taught by our own pain, our own sorrow, nay, by our own sin, we shall have hearts and minds exercised for every service of love toward those who need it. We shall in our measure be comforters after the image of the Almighty Paraclete, and that in all senses of the word — advocates, assistants, soothing aids. Our words and advice, our very manner, voice, and look, will be gentle and tranquilizing, as of those who have borne their cross after Christ. We shall not pass by his little ones rudely, as the world does. The voice of the widow and the orphan, the poor and destitute, will at once reach our ears, however low they speak. Our hearts will open toward them, our word and deed befriend them. The ruder passions of man's nature, pride and anger, envy and strife, which so disorder the Church, these will be quelled and brought under in others by the earnestness and kindness of our admonitions.

Thus, instead of being the selfish creatures which we were by nature, grace, acting through suffering, tends to make us ready teachers and witnesses of truth to all. Time was when, even at the most necessary times, we found it difficult to speak of heaven to another; our mouth seemed closed, even when our heart was full; but now our affection is eloquent, and *out of the abundance of the heart our mouth speaks.*

Such was the high temper of mind instanced in our Lord and his apostles, and thereby impressed upon the Church of Christ. And this great truth she never has forgotten, that we must all *take up our cross daily,* and *through much tribulation enter into the kingdom of God.* She has never forgotten that she was set apart for a comforter of the afflicted, and that to comfort well we must first be afflicted ourselves.

Responsory   *Sir 42:15-16; 43:28*

By the words of the Lord his works come into being, and all creation obeys his will. † As the sun as it shines looks upon all things, so the work of the Lord is full of his glory.

V. Where can we find the power to praise him, since he is greater than all his works? † As the sun . . .

MONDAY   Year II

First Reading   2 Corinthians 1:15—2:11

Responsory   *2 Cor 1:21-22; Dt 5:2.4*
God firmly establishes us in Christ. He anointed and sealed us,
† and as his pledge to us he sent his Spirit to dwell in our hearts.
V. The Lord our God made a covenant with us and spoke to us face
to face. † And as his . . .

Second Reading   From a commentary by Saint Cyril of
                     Alexandria (In Ep. II ad Corinthios: PG 74, 921-923)

Christ is God by nature and in truth

God the Father makes us firm in Christ and establishes in all
souls a faith that is correct and unshakable in holding that Christ
is God by nature and in truth. That is so even if he was visibly in a
form like ours, being born from a woman according to human
nature and yet being above every created thing. At any rate, when
Peter confessed his faith, saying clearly that *You are the Christ, the
Son of the living God,* Jesus Christ our Lord replied himself, saying,
*Blessed are you, Simon Bar-Jona, for flesh and blood did not reveal this
to you, but my Father who is in heaven.* For since the mystery is an
enormous one, it has reasonable need of the revelation which is
from above, from the Father.

It is God, therefore, who makes us firm in Christ, God who seals
and anoints us and gives the Spirit as the guarantee, so that it might
not be obscure for us, and derived from these things around us,
that the Son is not "yes" and "no" but, rather, is truly God and that
the "yes" to all good things is in him. God is said to seal and to
anoint us, giving the guarantee of the Spirit, so that Christ might
be the one who fulfills these things in us, not in a servile way nor
as one anointing and sealing us with an alien spirit, but with the
Spirit which is his own and the Father's. For the Holy Spirit is in
both Father and Son by means of the identity of nature, not as
something shared between them but rather as coming forth from
the Father through the Son to the created universe. Christ breathed
on the holy apostles and said *Receive the Holy Spirit,* and it is
through him and in him that we have received the impress of the
divine and intelligible image. For the divine apostle himself said

in the letter to the Galatians *My children, with whom I am again suffering labor pains until such time as Christ is formed in you.* Now if we are conformed to Christ, and if we are enriched by the divine image within us, then Christ himself is the image of God the Father, and his exact resemblance, and we are called to his likeness, not by means of a participation in holiness but rather in nature and essence.

For it is not unreasonable that the one who, by nature, is related to the true God by nature and who is generated from his substance should himself be God. He has been sealed by God the Father, as John the wise says, *He who receives his witness has put his seal to the fact that God is true.* But he has not been sealed in the same way as we have been, for the Father writes to the effect that he himself is wholly in the nature of the Son, and substantially intimates such. Thus Christ says, *He who has seen me has seen the Father.*

Responsory   *Ps 118:33.34; Ps 18:8*
Teach me the demands of your statutes and I will keep them to the end. † Train me to observe your law, to keep it with my whole heart.
V. The precepts of the Lord are right, they gladden the heart. † Train me to . . .

TUESDAY   Year II

First Reading   2 Corinthians 2:12—3:6

Responsory   *2 Cor 3:4.6.5*
Through Christ we have full confidence in God, † who has made us suitable ministers of his new covenant, not of a written code but in the Spirit.
V. We know that we cannot of ourselves take credit for anything, for all of our sufficiency comes from God, † who has made . . .

Second Reading   From a homily by Ralph the Fervent
(Hom. In Epist. et Evang. Domini XXVI: PL 155, 2033-2035)

Confidence in God

Such is the confidence we have in God through Christ; not that we are capable of thinking anything by ourselves as if it came from ourselves, but our capacity comes from God. The apostle tells us three things about confidence: whom we are to have confidence in, through whom, and what kind of confidence. He shows us whom we are to have confidence in, saying: *in God*. He himself, he says, has confidence in God, and he teaches us to have the same by his own example. For God alone is able to save us, and truly loves us and is truthful, whereas worldly kings, princes, relations and friends can save neither themselves nor us. Hence the psalmist's words: *Put no trust in princes or in any human being, in whom there is no security. Their breath will leave them, and they will return to their own earth*. But neither do they truly love, since none of our worldly friends love us for our own good but rather for theirs. It is only God who loves us not for his own advantage but ours. Again they are not even truthful, since it is written: *Every man and woman is a liar*. But God is truthful. Therefore, my friends, we must put the whole of our trust in God alone, not in anything transient; for relations, friends and all transient things deceive us. God alone never abandons those who hope in him. Hence it is written: *Has anyone ever hoped in the Lord, and been put to shame?* And David says: *For me it is good to cling to God, to put my hope in the Lord my God*.

He shows us through whom we are to have confidence, saying: *through Christ*. For it is only through Christ that we have access to the Father. It is he who reconciles and mediates between God and humanity, and is always interceding for us, insofar as he is man, and like the Father saves us, insofar as he is God. Therefore, my friends, we must love him with all our heart, for, as the apostle says, there is no other name in heaven or on earth by which we are destined to be saved.

As to what kind of confidence we should have in God, this he shows us in saying: *not that we are capable of thinking anything by ourselves*. He means: we have no confidence in ourselves, neither complete nor partial, as some people usually have, but total confidence, and about everything, in God. For such is our trust in God that we have no confidence that comes from ourselves even in thinking, speaking or doing anything at all, but it comes from God. And so he confounds those who rely on their own free will, or their own talents, strength or wealth, since it is written: *A king is not saved by his own great power; nor can a giant be saved by his own immense strength*. And elsewhere: *Those who trust in their own wealth are certain to be ruined. But our capacity comes from God,* as regards everything good, of course. For we cannot enjoy anything good, either material, spiritual or heavenly, except through him. And unless he works through us, our own labor for material things, our devotion to spiritual things and our effort to obtain the rewards of heaven are useless. Hence Christ's words to his disciples: *Without me you can do nothing.*

Responsory   *Ps 68:3; 1 Cor 2:9*
The righteous shall rejoice before God, † they shall exult and dance for joy.
V. Eye has not seen, nor ear heard, nor human heart conceived what God has prepared for those who love him. † They shall exult . . .

WEDNESDAY   Year II

First Reading   2 Corinthians 3:7—4:4

Responsory   *2 Cor 3:18; Phil 3:3*
With our faces unveiled, † all of us, reflecting as in a mirror the glory of God, are being transformed from splendor to splendor.
V. We worship in the Spirit of God and we glory in Christ Jesus. † All of us . . .

Second Reading   From a homily by Saint John Chrysostom
(Second Epître aux Corinthiennes 7, 5: Bareille XVII, 421-422)

Reflecting the Lord's glory

What does it mean, to say (as Saint Paul does) that: *Reflecting the Lord's glory, we are refashioned — transformed — to his likeness?* This was clearer in evidence when the grace of miracles was actively at work; but it is not hard to see even now, for anyone with the eyes of faith. For on receiving baptism the soul shines brighter than the sun, being purified by the Holy Spirit; and not only do we behold God's glory, but from it we receive a certain gleam ourselves. Just as bright silver, when struck by beams of light, can send out beams in its turn, not simply of its own nature but from the sun's brilliance, so also the soul, once purified and become brighter than silver, receives a beam from the glory of the Holy Spirit — and sends that on. That is why he says, *Reflecting, we are refashioned to the same pattern from — or of, or by — his glory,* that of the Holy Spirit, into a glory, our own, which is contingent, modeled on the Spirit of the Lord. See how he calls the Spirit "Lord," or "Master." He it is who transforms us, who does not permit us to conform to this world, the maker and first cause of creation as he is. As he says: *You have been established in Christ Jesus.*

This can be explained in more concrete terms from the apostles. We think of St. Paul, whose very clothes were activated; of St. Peter, whose very shadow had power. That could never have been, if they had not borne the king's likeness; if they had not had something of his unapproachable brightness — so much, it appears, that their clothes and their shadows worked wonders. See how that brightness shines through their bodies! *Gazing on the face of Stephen,* he says, *they seemed to see the face of an angel.* But that was nothing to the glory shining like lightning within. What Moses bore on his face, they carried in their souls, but to a much higher degree. The mark on Moses was more tangible; but this was incorporeal. Dimly glowing bodies catch fire from brighter ones close by and pass on to others their own incandescence. All that resembles what happens to the faithful. In this way they detach themselves from the world and have their converse only in the things of heaven.

Responsory   *Ps 113:1.3.5*

When Israel came forth from Egypt, the house of Jacob from an alien people, † the sea fled at the sight, the Jordan turned back on its course.
V. Why was it, sea, that you fled, that you turned back, Jordan, on your course? † The sea fled . . .

Alternative Reading

From a sermon by John Henry Newman *(Parochial and Plain Sermons V, 138-140)*

We cry Abba, Father, through the Spirit sent into our hearts

If Christ is our sole hope, and Christ is given to us by the Spirit, and the Spirit be an inward presence, our sole hope is in an inward change. As a light placed in a room pours out its rays on all sides, so the presence of the Holy Ghost imbues us with life, strength, holiness, love, acceptableness, righteousness. God looks on us in mercy, because he sees in us "the mind of the Spirit," for who so has this mind has holiness and righteousness within him. Henceforth all his thoughts, words, and works, as done in the Spirit, are acceptable, pleasing, just before God; and whatever remaining infirmity there be in him, that the presence of the Spirit hides. That divine influence, which has the fullness of Christ's grace to purify us, has also the power of Christ's blood to justify.

Let us never lose sight of this great and simple view, which the whole of scripture sets before us. What was actually done by Christ in the flesh eighteen hundred years ago is in type and resemblance really wrought in us one by one even to the end of time. He was born of the Spirit, and we too are born of the Spirit. He was justified by the Spirit, and so are we. He was pronounced the well-beloved Son, when the Holy Ghost descended on him; and we too cry Abba, Father, through the Spirit sent into our hearts. He was led into the wilderness by the Spirit; he did great works by the Spirit; he offered himself to death by the eternal Spirit; he was raised from the dead by the Spirit; he was declared to be the Son of God by the Spirit of holiness on his resurrection: we too are led by the same Spirit into and through this world's temptations; we, too, do our works of obedience by the Spirit; we die from sin, we rise again unto righteousness through the Spirit; and we are declared to be God's sons — declared, pronounced, dealt with as righteous — through our resurrection unto holiness in the Spirit.

Or, to express the same great truth in other words: Christ himself vouchsafes to repeat in each of us in figure and mystery all that he did and suffered in the flesh. He is formed in us, born in us, suffers in us, rises again in us, lives in us; and this not by a succession of events, but all at once: for he comes to us as a Spirit, all dying, all rising again, all living. We are ever receiving our birth, our justification, our renewal, ever dying to sin, ever rising to righteousness. His whole economy in all its parts is ever in us all at once; and this divine presence constitutes the title of each of us to heaven; this is what he will acknowledge and accept at the last day. He will acknowledge himself — his image in us — as though we reflected him, and he, on looking round about, discerned at once who were his: those, namely, who gave back to him his image. He impresses us with the seal of the Spirit, in order to avouch that we are his. As the king's image appropriates the coin to him, so the likeness of Christ in us separates us from the world and assigns us over to the kingdom of heaven.

Responsory   Ps 43:3.2
Their own sword did not win them the land, nor their own arm give them victory. † It was your right hand, your arm, and the light of your face, for you loved them.
V. Our fathers have told us the story of the deeds you did in their days. † It was your . . .

THURSDAY   Year II

First Reading   2 Corinthians 4:5-18

Responsory   2 Cor 4:6; Dt 5:24
God has said: Let light shine out of darkness. † He has shone in our hearts that we might make known the glory of God shining on the face of Christ Jesus.
V. The Lord our God has shown us his glory and greatness, and we have heard his voice. † He has shone . . .

Second Reading   From a treatise by Saint Symeon the New Theologian (Traités Théologiques et Éthiques I, 10: SC 122, 252-254)

We receive the Word of God in our hearts

Every one of us believes in him who is the Son of God and son of Mary, ever-virgin and mother of God. And as believers we faithfully welcome his gospel into our hearts, confessing in words our belief, and repenting with all our soul of our past sins. Then immediately, just as God the Word of the Father entered the Virgin's womb, so also in ourselves the word which we receive in learning right belief appears like a seed. You should be amazed when you hear of such an awe-inspiring mystery, and because the word is reliable you should receive it with full conviction and faith.

In fact we receive him not bodily, as the Virgin and Mother of God received him, but both spiritually and substantially. And the very one whom the chaste Virgin also received, we hold in our own hearts, as Saint Paul says: *It is God, who commanded light to shine out of darkness, who has shone in our hearts to reveal the knowledge of his Son.* In other words: he has become wholly substantial in us. And that he actually meant this, he made clear in the next verse: *But we contain this treasure in earthenware pots,* calling the Holy Spirit a treasure. But elsewhere he also calls the Lord Spirit: *The Lord is the Spirit,* he says. And he tells us this so that if you hear the words *the Son of God,* you should think of and hear the words *the Spirit* at the same time. Again, if you hear the Spirit mentioned you should join the Father to the Spirit in thought, because concerning the Father too it is said: *God is Spirit.* You are constantly taught that the Holy Trinity is inseparable and of the same substance, and that where the Son is the Father is also, and where the Father is the Spirit is also, and where the Holy Spirit is the whole of the deity in three persons is, the one God and Father with Son and Spirit of the same substance, "who is praised for ever. Amen."

So if we wholeheartedly believe and ardently repent, we receive the Word of God in our hearts, as has been said, like the Virgin, if of course we bring with us our own souls chaste and pure. And just as the fire of the deity did not consume the Virgin since she was supremely pure, so neither does it consume us if we bring with us chaste and pure hearts; on the contrary it becomes in us the dew from heaven, a spring of water, and a stream of immortal life.

Responsory   *Ps 88:2.9; Ps:5:2*
> Let my prayer come into your presence; incline your ear to my cry.
> † I call to you, Lord, all the day long; to you I stretch out my hands.
> V. Hearken to the sound of my cries, my king and my God. † I
> call . . .

Alternative Reading

From a sermon by Saint Augustine of Hippo (Enarr. in Ps. 38, 9: CCL 38, 410-411)

Everything has become new

Even if our outer being is decomposing, says Paul, *nonetheless our inner being is being renewed from day to day.* Therefore while we give our attention to sin, to mortality, to the seasons which come and go, to groaning and toil and sweat, to stages of life which, instead of remaining constant, follow on from one another, passing by without proper understanding from infancy to old age, let us recognize here on earth the old being, the old day, the old song, the Old Testament. But on turning to the inner being, to the things that are to be renewed in the place of those which will be changed, let us discover the new being, the new day, the new song, the New Testament. And, what is more, let us love that newness in such a way as not to fear the old regime when we have already got the new. Now, therefore, on today's track we are passing from old to new. This movement actually takes place when external things are done away with and internal things are being renewed. It is a process which lasts until whatever is external is done away with, until it pays its debt to nature, comes to the point of death, and is itself renewed in the resurrection. At that time everything will be well and truly new, what I mean is the things which are yet to come and which now exist only in hope.

You are, therefore, really doing something here and by now divesting yourself of the old and by running to meet the new. It was, therefore, while the psalmist was running toward the things which are new, and straining toward the things which are in front, that he said: *Lord, make known to me my end, and the number of my days which really exists, in order that I may know what I lack.* Look! He is still dragging Adam along, and in this guise is hurrying to Christ. *Look,* he said, *you have made my days old.* The old days derive from Adam. They are what you have made old. They are growing old every day, and at such a rate as to face annihilation one of these days. *And my substance is like nothing before you.* Before you, Lord, my substance is like nothing, before you who can see this, and when I see this, I see it before you, but I do not see it before other people like myself. For what am I to say? In what words am I to express the fact that, in comparison with what really is, what I am is absolutely nothing? But it is expressed within, it is felt within, you see. *Before you,* Lord, where your eyes are not where human eyes are. Where are your eyes? *My substance is nothing.*

Responsory   Ps 88:2.9; Ps:5:2

Let my prayer come into your presence; incline your ear to my cry.
† I call to you, Lord, all the day long; to you I stretch out my hands.
V. Hearken to the sound of my cries, my king and my God. † I call to . . .

FRIDAY   Year II

First Reading   2 Corinthians 5:1-21

Responsory   *2 Cor 5:18; Rom 8:32*
God reconciled us to himself through Christ, † and he gave us the ministry of reconciliation.
V. He did not spare his own Son but handed him over for the sake of us all. † And he gave . . .

Second Reading   From a sermon by Saint Augustine of Hippo
(Sermo 38, 2; CCL 41, 476-479)

The time for faith is hard

It is for the sake of the good things which God will only give to the good, and the bad things which will only be inflicted on the bad, that God wants us to believe that both these things will appear in the end. For what reward does faith receive, or what meaning is there in the word at all, if you demand to see now what you are going to receive in the future? Therefore you must not expect to see what you are to believe, you must believe what you are to see: believe, as long as you cannot see, to avoid being ashamed when you do see. So let us believe while it is time for faith, before it is time for seeing. As the Apostle says: *As long as we are in this body we live away from the Lord: for we walk by faith.* So we walk by faith as long as we believe what we cannot see: but we shall receive our sight, when we see the Lord face to face, as he is. The apostle John too separates the time for faith and the time for seeing, as he says in his letter*: Dear friends, we are God's children now, and what we shall be has not yet appeared.* That is the time for faith: look now at the time for seeing. *We know,* he continues, *that when he appears we shall be like him, because we shall see him as he is.*

The time for faith is hard, as everyone knows. It is hard, but that is the work for which we get our reward in the end. You must not be lazy over work for which you want a reward. For if you yourself hired a servant, you would not pay him before he had done anything for you. You would say to him: "I'll pay you when you've done the work." He would not say to you: "I'll do the work when you've paid me." It is the same with God. If you fear God you will not fail to honor your contract with him. Will God fail you on his side, when he orders you not to fail him on yours? Still, you might not be able to fulfill your promise. Even if you have no intention of playing him false, yet the weakness of human nature makes us helpless in the face of difficulties. What have we to fear from God, who cannot deceive us because he is truth, and at the same time has everything in abundance because he created everything?

So let us believe in God, my friends. This is the first commandment, this is the starting-point of our religion and our life: to have our hearts fixed in faith, and with our heart fixed in faith to live a good life, keep clear of all impostors and withstand all earthly evils; and as long as the one flatters and the other threatens, to face both with unshaken heart, so as to be neither defeated by the one nor broken by the other. Therefore if you have both self-restraint and patient endurance, when the good things of this world have gone their way and no evil will ever again be inflicted on you, you will possess everything good and nothing bad. What, then, were we told in the reading? *My son, if you enter God's service, you must be upright and reverent, and prepare your soul to be tested. Humble your heart and be patient, so that your life may grow at the last.* So that your life may grow, not now, but at the last: *so that your life may grow at the last.* Can we imagine how much it will grow? It will grow till it becomes eternal.

Responsory   Ps 5:7; Is 6:3

Through the greatness of your love I have access to your house. † I bow down before your holy temple, filled with awe.
V. Holy, holy, holy is the Lord of hosts; the whole earth is full of his glory. † I bow down . . .

Alternative Reading

From a commentary by Primasius of Hadrumetum (Commen. in Apocalyp. V:PL 68, 921-922)

All things new

Behold, I make all things new. This city is said to come down from heaven since the grace by which God made it is from heaven. This is why he says to it also in Isaiah: *I the Lord am your master.* It came down as its beginning, when in the era of this world the grace of God came down by means of the water of renewal in the Holy Spirit, who was sent down from heaven. From then onward its citizens ever increase. But when at the end God's judgment comes through his Son Jesus Christ, such will be the renewed brightness of the city through God's gift that no traces of age will remain. Our bodies will be made new, and pass into incorruption and immortality from corruption and mortality.

This is why God gives his promise: *And God shall wipe away every tear from their eyes, and death shall now be no more, nor mourning, nor crying, nor sorrow.* All this assuredly refers not to this life but to the next. In this life, the more holy a person is, and the more filled with holy desires, the more he weeps in prayer. So we read: *My tears have been my bread day and night,* and *Every night I shall wash my bed.*

And he said to me: These words are most faithful and true. And he said to me: It is done. These words are to be believed rather than explained, especially as he speaks of what has happened in such a way as to allow none to doubt what will happen.

I am Alpha and Omega, the beginning and the end. He bore witness to this at the beginning of the book of the Apocalypse, and here it was necessary to repeat it a third time, so that none may be thought to be God before him, as Isaiah says, nor after him.

To him that thirsts I will give from the fount of water of life gratis. From this fountain he waters unbelievers on their journey, and to those who complete it he offers drink from it in abundance in their native home. No pilgrims should falter through thirst in the desert of this world, for rain descends on them, and they are made citizens, and made continually drunk with the stream of God's delight. "Gratis" here has a double sense, meaning both freely and by grace, for, as Paul says, life everlasting is the grace of God.

He that shall overcome shall possess these things, and I will be his God, and he will be my son. Here he recounts the birth mentioned by Paul: *God has sent the spirit of his Son into your hearts, crying Abba, Father.* Now if they are sons and heirs, they are heirs of God and coheirs with Christ. They are saved through hope. Once they have through hope attained reality, God will be for the chosen the reward of eternal blessedness, so that being possessed by him they may possess him for ever.

Responsory   *Ps 5:7; Is 6:3*

Through the greatness of your love I have access to your house. † I bow down before your holy temple, filled with awe.

V. Holy, holy, holy is the Lord of hosts; the whole earth is full of his glory. † I bow down . . .

SATURDAY   Year II

First Reading   2 Corinthians 6:1—7:1

Responsory   *2 Cor 6:14.16*
What do righteousness and iniquity have in common? Is there a common ground between the temple of God and idols? † You are the temple of the living God.
V. Are you not aware that you are God's temple, and that his Spirit lives within you? † You are the . . .

Second Reading   From a homily by Ralph the Fervent
                        (Hom. In Epist. et Evang. Domini XXXV: PL155, 1788-1789)

We servants of Christ must not offend our neighbor in our speech

We give no offense to anyone, so that no fault may be found with our ministry, but that in every way we may show ourselves as God's servants. In this next chapter, my friends, the Apostle exhorts us, as God's servants, to show ourselves blameless. And though all who correctly administer the grace that God has given them may in a general sense be termed God's servants, yet it particularly refers to the servants of the Holy Church. So it is we, my friends, who are servants of the altar and stewards of God's word, whom the Apostle warns to show ourselves in every way as God's servants. For as, according to Solomon, an evil prince has wicked servants, so the opposite is appropriate, that a holy Lord should have holy servants. That is why he says himself: *You must be holy, because I am holy.* For a shameful servant greatly exasperates God. "But he says to the sinner: Why do you recite my commandments, and presume to speak of my covenant?" Therefore the Apostle mentions six ways in which we must particularly show ourselves as God's servants: in the avoidance of offense, the patient endurance of affliction, by doing good works, being good ourselves, preaching correctly, by the right use of prosperity and adversity.

So in the first place he warns us to show ourselves as God's servants by the avoidance of offense, when he says: *We give no offense to anyone, so that no fault may be found without ministry.* That is, so that we do not offend God through disobedience or negligence, nor our neighbor by provocation, bad words or bad example. Again, since all must take care not to offend God in the matter of obedience, this must apply particularly to us, Christ's servants, who must also intercede for the offenses of others. For if any of the people offend, the priest will pray for them. But if the priest offends, who will pray for him?

Let us also, my friends, take care not to offend God through carelessness, because, according to Jeremiah, cursed are those who do God's work carelessly. Eli certainly rebuked his sons, but because he was lukewarm and careless in doing so, he perished with them. This is a warning to some of us, my friends, who are lukewarm and negligent in our duty towards God, in preaching and correction, in prayer and reading and whatever else, since, according to John, Christ casts out the lukewarm. We servants of Christ must also take care not to offend our neighbor in our speech. That is, we must not be abusive, must refrain from swearing, not be disparaging, scurrilous or obscene, but rather our speech should be seasoned with the salt of wisdom, so as to give pleasure to our listeners.

Responsory   *Ps 37:1-3.16*

Do not fret because of the wicked, or envy those who do evil, for soon they will fade like the grass, and wither like green pasture.
† Trust in the Lord and do good, and you will live in the land and be secure.
V. The few possessions of the righteous are better than the wealth of the wicked. † Trust in . . .

EIGHTH WEEK IN ORDINARY TIME

SUNDAY Year II

First Reading 2 Corinthians 7:2-16

Responsory 2 *Cor 7:10, see 9*
The sorrow God sends us produces a repentance that leads to salvation, † but worldly sorrow brings death.
V. Our sorrow was used by God, and so we suffered no loss. † But worldly sorrow brings death.

Second Reading From a sermon by Cardinal John Henry Newman *(Parochial and Plain Sermons* V, 322-325)

Sorrow into joy

The gospel promises to turn all sorrow into joy. It makes us take pleasure in desolateness, weakness, and contempt. *We glory in tribulations also,* says the Apostle, *because the love of God is shed abroad in our hearts by the Holy Ghost which is given unto us.* It bids us take comfort under bereavement: *I would not have you ignorant, brethren, concerning them which are asleep, that you sorrow not, even as others which have no hope.* But if there be one sorrow, which might seem to be unmixed misery, if there be one misery left under the gospel, the awakened sense of having abused the gospel might have been considered that one. And, again, if there be a time when the presence of the Most High would at first sight seem to be intolerable, it would be then, when first the consciousness vividly bursts upon us that we have ungratefully rebelled against him. Yet so it is that true repentance cannot be without the thought of God; it has the thought of God, for it seeks him; and it seeks him, because it is quickened with love; and even sorrow must have a sweetness, if love be in it. For what is to repent but to surrender ourselves to God for pardon or punishment, as loving his presence for its own sake, and accounting chastisement from him better than rest and peace from the world?

Consider Saint Paul's account of the repentance of the Corinthians; there is sorrow in abundance, nay, anguish, but no gloom, no dryness of spirit, no sternness. The penitents afflict themselves, but it is from the fullness of their hearts, from love, gratitude, devotion, horror of the past, desire to escape from their present selves into some state holier and more heavenly. Saint Paul speaks of their *earnest desire, their mourning, their fervent mind toward him.* He rejoices, *not that they were made sorry, but that they sorrowed to repentance. For you were made sorry,* he proceeds, *after a godly manner, that ye might receive damage by us in nothing.*

On the other hand, remorse, or what the Apostle calls *the sorrow of the world,* works death. Instead of coming to the fount of life, to the God of all consolation, remorseful men feed on their own thoughts, without any confidant of their sorrow. They disburden themselves to no one: to God they will not, to the world they cannot confess. We are pent up within ourselves, and are therefore miserable. Perhaps we may not be able to analyze our misery, or even to realize it, as persons oftentimes who are in bodily sicknesses. We do not know, perhaps, what or where our pain is; we are so used to it that we do not call it pain. Still so it is; we need a relief to our hearts, that they may be dark and sullen no longer, or that they may not go on feeding upon themselves; we need to escape from ourselves to something beyond; and much as we may wish it otherwise, and may try to make idols to ourselves, nothing short of God's presence is our true refuge.

Responsory   *Ps 55:22; 37:5*
Entrust your cares to the Lord and he will support you. † He will never allow the righteous to stumble.
V. Commit your life to the Lord; trust in him and he will act. † He will never . . .

Alternative Reading

From a discourse by Pope Paul VI (Discourses, 18 July 1973)

Yes, Christians, and happy to be so

What does it mean to be a Christian? We would like each one of us to return in a critical spirit to this pressing question of our religious primer.

The apostolic catechesis exhorts us several times to make this introspective examination. We at once discover that our personality is the object of preceding and ineffable divine thought: God chose us in Christ before the foundation of the world. An intentional call to the divine plan of salvation, therefore, dominates our destiny. Our duty is to realize that we are called: Consider your call, brethren, Saint Paul wrote to the Corinthians, that we are, as Saint Peter writes, a chosen race, a royal priesthood, a holy nation, God's own people. The first dawning awareness of our Christian conscience should be that of possessing an immense fortune, of being raised to an incomparable dignity. Who does not remember the solemn and striking words of Saint Leo the Great: "O Christian, recognize your dignity"? We must feel ourselves Christians and happy at the same time. Yes, Christians, and happy to be so.

How often it is repeated and recommended to us: Be glad in the Lord; I repeat, be glad, says Saint Paul to the Philippians. A joy that nothing can spoil is a necessary element of the Christian psychology, even in adversities and tribulations: With all our affliction, I am overjoyed. And this joy is not diminished. On the contrary, it is enhanced in the very expression of humility, which is perfect in the recognized truth of the disproportion between the greatness of God and the littleness of the human creature: remember the "magnificat" of the Blessed Virgin. Nor is it extinguished; on the contrary it is born again in the painful confession of one's sins. Let the bones you have broken rejoice.

This awareness of existential bliss explains that the most faithful interpretation of our condition as Christians is to give thanks to God, as we do in the preface of the Mass, and as in the holy eucharist, which means precisely thanksgiving. We translate into sacramental language the fullness of our supernatural identity, operating in Christ himself: It is no longer I who live, but Christ who lives in me.

Responsory   *Ps 55:22; 37:5*
   Entrust your cares to the Lord and he will support you. † He will never allow the righteous to stumble.
   V. Commit your life to the Lord; trust in him and he will act. † He will never . . .

MONDAY   Year II

First Reading   2 Corinthians 8:1-24

Responsory   *2 Cor 8:9; Phil 2:7*
You are well aware of the generosity of our Lord Jesus Christ.
Though he was rich, he became poor for your sake, † so that
through his poverty you might become rich.
V. He emptied himself, assuming the condition of a slave. † So that
through . . .

Second Reading   From a letter by Saint Paulinus of Nola
                    (Ep. XXXII, 20-21: CSEL 29, 294-296)

Let us cheerfully give now to those in need

In the world judges who are bribed by presents from the
accused are condemned. But if any of you are worried about your
innocence in some sinful matter, and hasten to bring the price of
your salvation to our own judge, you must not be afraid to do
God's justice the insult of bribery, so to speak. Christ willingly
accepts the price of your salvation from you, because he prefers
mercy to sacrifice. But perhaps you will ask where to find him, and
how to bribe one whom you cannot see. Get up, shake off the sleep
of physical inertia. Raise your mind, weighed down as it is with
earthly thoughts, from dead cares, that is, from its physical connections. Lift up and direct your soul to the Lord, and you will
reach Christ. Working by his own precepts, you will see him in
every poor person, touch him in everyone in want, welcome him
in every stranger, for he declares that whatever is done in his name
to the least of his people is done to himself. Here is your answer to
how you are to see the invisible and understand the incomprehensible. So let us be poor now in this world, to be rich then in the next
world. Let us weep now, to rejoice then. Let us go hungry now, to
take our fill then. *You have the poor always with you,* he says. You
see that we have no excuse ever to put off doing good, since if we
have the will to do so the poor are right before our eyes.

So let us cheerfully give now to those in need, and to Christ in
the form of his own poor, so that we can share in the glory which
he will give them in abundance. For it is on that account that the
Lord himself gives the advice to *make friends for yourselves by*

means of unrighteous wealth. You see how the almighty Lord turns night into day and unrighteousness into righteousness: *so that when it is no longer any use to you*, he continues, *they may welcome you into an eternal home*. The human race is governed by a change of fortune between wealth and poverty, as the parable of the rich man in Hades and the poor man in the kingdom of heaven showed. It helps us to understand the intention of the creator of the universe, according to which he prepared the wealthy to be of use to the poor and the poor to be of use to the wealthy, so that the rich might provide the poor with nourishment and the poor provide the rich with righteousness. This, as the apostle said, was to make for equality. The eternal riches, which will recompense the poor in the next world for their poverty in this, will flow out freely to us in our own need, if we use our wealth in this world to help the poor. Therefore we must sow earthly seed in this world to reap a spiritual harvest in the next. The toil of our hands now on earth must earn rest then for our souls in heaven. Let present hope make future certainty. Let the house we build on earth be one to shelter us in heaven. May I feed the poor on earth, where I am rich and they are in need, so that they may feed me in heaven, where I shall be in want and they will have their fill. Take care over your spiritual trade, and if possible deny that we are greedy people, who sell land and farm out taxes to buy up the immunity of heaven together with eternity.

Responsory   *Ps 149:2-4*
Let Israel rejoice in its Maker; let the people of Zion exult in their king. † Let them praise his name with dancing, and sing psalms to him with timbrel and lyre.
V. For the Lord accepts the service of his people; he crowns the humble with victory. † Let them praise . . .

Alternative Reading

From the writings of Henry of Friemar (Tractatus de incarnatione Verbi I, 3)

Christ enriched us by his poverty
and endowed us out of his indigence

The same honor, the same worship that is paid to the divinity is paid to the humanity as well, inasmuch as it subsists in the divinity. And therefore God cannot confer a greater dignity upon a human being than to give it a share in the veneration due to himself. In his fourth book Damascene explains how latreutic worship can be paid to a creature: "As a lighted piece of charcoal is not simply wood but wood united to fire, so the flesh of Christ is not mere flesh but flesh united to the godhead." In that passage he speaks therefore of the flesh of Christ as divinized; because of this divinization there is a sharing in the honor and veneration due to God, as we are told in Hebrews: *And let all God's angels worship him*, and in Philippians: *At the name of Jesus let every knee bend in heaven, on earth, and beneath the earth.*

Thirdly, the eternal Word willed to stoop to such great poverty, in order that he might enrich us abundantly with heavenly gifts. Should one reflect on the manner in which he enriched us, one would find it wonderful indeed, since he enriched us by his poverty and endowed us out of his indigence. The Apostle teaches this in so many words in Second Corinthians: *Brethren*, he says, *you know the grace of our Lord Jesus Christ: that though he was rich he became poor for our sake, in order that we might be enriched by his poverty.* And it is truly marvelous that by his poverty and need he has enriched us in bodily as well as in spiritual ways.

He has enriched us in bodily ways, because there is nothing dearer, nothing more precious in the entire treasury of the Church than the mean and worthless rags in which not only the poor Christ but poverty itself is wrapped. Is there anything more precious than the stable manger in which Christ was laid? Is there anything more glorious than the fearful gibbet of the cross on which he suffered? Therefore Bernard rightly says in a sermon: The poverty of Christ "is our wealth; the Savior's rags are more precious than any purple; this manger is more glorious than the gilded thrones of kings, and the poverty of Christ is richer than all wealth and treasures."

His poverty has also enriched us spiritually, because by handing himself over for us and shedding his blood for us and by laying down for us the life he loved, he poured out all heavenly blessings upon us. For when the wallet of his body was pierced in five places it poured out upon us in abundance the heavenly treasure it contained, and gave us generously of it. This is clear from the fact that he unsealed five fountains in himself at which we might drink freely of heavenly blessings and might at our pleasure draw ceaselessly the water of saving grace. To this drinking we are generously invited in Isaiah: *Draw water with joy from the wells of the Savior.* Once we have tasted fully of this water, it utterly kills all passing thirsts in us, as John says clearly. May he grant us a taste for this water, who lives and reigns forever.

Responsory   *Ps 91:11-12; Heb 12:1*

He will charge his angels to guard you wherever you go; † they will bear you upon their hands that you may not strike your foot against a stone.
V. Since we are surrounded by so great a cloud of witnesses, let us run with resolution the race that lies before us, our eyes fixed on Jesus, the pioneer and perfecter of our faith. † They will bear . . .

TUESDAY   Year II

First Reading   2 Corinthians 9:1-15

Responsory   *Lk 6:38; 2 Cor 9:7*

Give to others and you will receive; good measure, pressed down, shaken together, and running over, will be poured into your lap. † For whatever measure you give to others will be the measure you receive.
V. Each person should give according to what he has inwardly decided, not grudgingly or under compulsion. † For whatever measure . . .

Second Reading   From a homily by Saint Leo the Great
                     (Tract. 16, 1-2: CCL 138, 61-62)

Prayer which is offered with good works is quickly heard by God

The sublime nature of God's grace lies in this, my dear friends, that daily in our Christian hearts all our desires are transferred from what is earthbound to what is heavenly. Yet it is still true that our present life is lived with the Creator's aid and is supported by his providence. It is the one and same Lord who bestows temporal blessings and who promises the eternal blessings. There is a correspondence between two duties which we have of giving thanks to God. First of all for the fact that we are carried along by the hope of future happiness to the fulfillment of this great preparation. It is faith which gives us speed. And secondly, we are to honor and praise God for the goods which we receive annually. It is he who from the creation has granted the earth's fruitfulness and who has established the cycles of fruit production in the various plants and seeds. He never abandons his decrees so that his kindly providence as Creator remains throughout the creation.

Whatever benefit the harvests, the vines and olives have brought to man's use, all of it flows from the generosity of God's goodness. In his delicate way he helps on the hesitant labors of the farmers by the varied nature of the elements. Thus it is that wind and rain, cold and heat, day and night, serve our needs. If the Lord did not grant increase with his habitual planting and watering, human reason by itself would not be able to carry through its tasks to the end. Consequently it is perfectly right and just that we should help others from the things which our heavenly Father has mercifully bestowed on us.

There are many who have no share in fields, vines, or olives. It is worthwhile remembering the poverty of these people so that, out of the plentifulness which God has given, they too may bless God with us for the fruitfulness of the earth. With the landowners they can also rejoice at having been given what is the common part of the poor and of the pilgrims; that barn is a truly happy one and worthy to have all its products multiplied from which the hunger of the poor and weak is satisfied, from which the pilgrim's need is satisfied and from which the sick man's desire is cared for. God's justice allows these people to labor under various disabilities so that he may reward the lowly for their patience and the merciful for their kindness.

The most effective form of intercession for sin is in almsdeeds and fasting; and prayer which is offered with such good works is quickly heard by God. As it is written, *The merciful man does good to his own soul*, and nothing is more personal than what we bestow on our neighbor. For the share of earthly commodities which is given to those in need becomes eternal wealth. The riches which are born of this kindness will not be diminished by use, nor subjected to any corruption. *Blessed are the merciful, for they shall have mercy shown to them by God*. God is the highest reward and the form of the commandment.

Responsory   *Is 55:8-9; Heb 11:2*

My thoughts are not your thoughts, nor are your ways my ways, says the Lord. † For as the heavens are high above the earth, so are my ways above your ways, and my thoughts above your thoughts. V. It was for their faith that the people of former times won God's approval. † For as the heavens . . .

WEDNESDAY   Year II

First Reading   2 Corinthians 10:1—11:6

Responsory   *2 Cor 10:3-4; Eph 6:16.17*

Though we live in this world, we do not rely solely on the resources of the world to do battle. † Our warfare is not waged with the weapons of this world.
V. We arm ourselves with the shield of faith and with the sword of the Spirit, which is the word of God. † Our warfare is . . .

Second Reading   **From a homily by Saint John Chrysostom**
                     (In Heb. 28, 7: Bareille XX, 407-408)

May we all partake of grace and charity in grace and charity

Saint Paul says: *I have espoused you to one husband, as it were a chaste virgin presented to Christ.* He did not say that just to young maidens but to the Church as a whole. For the soul that is pure keeps its maidenhood, even in the married state. It is unsullied and unspoiled, truly and admirably so. Virginity in the bodily sense is the counterpart and the shadow: yet this virginity Saint Paul speaks of is the real thing. Let us cultivate it: then we shall be able to behold the bridegroom with countenance unabashed and serene, and to enter in with our lamps brightly shining, our oil still not failing, even though we have earned it by melting down our gold to keep our lamps alight. This oil I speak of is our love for each other. If we share what we have with others, so earning oil for ourselves, then it will be forthcoming to us and we shall not need to say, when the hour comes, *Give us oil, for our lamps are going out.* And we shall not need to make supplication of others or to go off to the oil merchant, getting ourselves shut out — and having to hear that terrible sentence, as we knock on the door, the voice that says, *I know you not.* On the contrary, he will recognize us and we shall be admitted to the presence of the bridegroom. And going in to the bridal chamber, the spiritual inner sanctum, we shall enjoy blessings in abundance. For if an earthly bridal chamber is something so resplendent, the apartments so admirable, that, once inside, one cannot lack for contentment, then how much the more so is the heavenly one? The bridal chamber I speak of is heaven itself, the best repose that one can find: it is thither that we are bound. If the bridegroom's chamber can be so described, what of the bridegroom himself? And what shall I say of our ridding ourselves of our gold and finery to share it with those in need? Should you not be ready to sell yourselves into bondage, to become slaves instead of free men, to make yourselves fit to belong with the bridegroom, to become the beneficiaries of his integrity and steadfast love? Or, even without all that, merely to gaze upon his face would you not gladly endure any kind of trial? Merely to have sight of an earthly king, do we not often forgo what we have, even with no thought of heaven? What should we not be required to do, in order to count ourselves worthy to see him: and not only that, but to go before him with our lamps lit and to be close to him, indeed to be of his company? What labor should we not undertake for that? What trial should we not patiently endure? So therefore let us, I beseech you, have a great desire for those good things, for the bridegroom himself: let us be pure and spotless, fit for the spiritual espousal with our master the bridegroom. This way we can enter heaven without spot or wrinkle, or anything of the kind, and enjoy the blessings that have been promised us. May we all partake of them in grace and charity.

Responsory   *Ps 145:4-5.14*

One age shall proclaim your works to another, shall declare your mighty deeds. † People will speak of your splendor and glory, and tell of your wonderful works.

V. The Lord supports all who stumble and raises all who are bowed down. † People will . . .

THURSDAY   Year II

First Reading   2 Corinthians 11:7-29

Responsory   *Gal 1:11.12; 2 Cor 11:10.7*

The gospel which I preached to you is not a human message. † I did not receive it through any man, but from our Lord Jesus Christ who revealed it to me.

V. As surely as Christ's truth is in me, I have preached the Gospel to you. † I did not . . .

Second Reading   From a homily by Ralph the Fervent
                    (Hom. In Epist et Evang. Dom. 28: PL 155, 1765-1766)

Four kinds of preachers

Admonishing the Corinthians for having received false preachers, Saint Paul says: *You willingly put up with the unwise because unwise is what you are yourselves.* What is unwise about the unwise man is his thinking himself to be wise, so that he always wishes his own counsel to prevail, rather than anyone else's. After all, the first step towards true wisdom is to recognize one's own ignorance and agree to wiser counsel. But then, the wise must put up with the unwise and bear with them, with a view to correcting and enlightening them, not giving consent to their errors as the Corinthians did. For they received false preachers who put the law and the gospel on the same footing, as well as preaching other errors besides: and they acquiesced in their errors.

There are (sad to relate) people like the Corinthians in the Church today, who are more receptive to mountebanks and false preachers than to their own proper preachers; people who would rather hear flattery than admonition, speakers who fawn on them rather than those who speak the truth. As Solomon says: *Secret waters taste sweeter* to them, whereas according to the gospel, the true sheep know their own shepherd's voice and follow that, not someone else's, because they do not know the voice of another.

We can say, brethren, that there are four kinds of preachers. There are those who preach badly and live badly and are in fact heretics, who ought not to be listened to or imitated, but banned instead. Others preach badly out of ignorance, but otherwise live good lives, albeit lacking wisdom. They are to be imitated in their way of life generally, but not listened to. Others preach well and live well: these are real preachers, to be heeded and to be imitated. Others there are who preach well yet live evil lives: and they are to be heeded but not imitated; for of them it is said: *You shall observe and do whatever they tell you, but do not act according to their deeds.* For such is the authority behind doctrinal truth that it is to be heeded when preached, no matter how wrong-headed the preacher or whatever his intention in preaching. Hence the Apostle says: *Whether Christ is preached by honest intent or by chance, I rejoice.* Conversely, no matter how upright the preacher or for whatever reason it may be preached, pernicious doctrine is not to be heeded. Hence Saint Paul says: *Even if an angel of heaven should preach to you otherwise, let him be anathema.* Just who it was that the foolish Corinthians were tolerating, Saint Paul explains when he adds: *You are quite ready to let someone lead you back into slavery.*

There are people like this around today who take the simple-minded away from the freedom of virtue and back to the slavery of pleasure and carnal license, telling them that all things were created for men to make use of. Do not agree with them, brethren; for they who act intemperately in what is permissible gravitate to what is not. And only he who observes moderation and constraint in what he may ethically do avoids lapsing into what he may not.

Responsory   *Phil 2:12-13; Eph 3:20*

Work out your salvation with fear and trembling, for † God is at work in you, inspiring both the will and the deed for his own chosen purpose.
V. Glory be to him whose power, working in us, can do immeasurably more than we can ask or imagine. † God is at work . . .

Alternative Reading

From a sermon by Walter of Saint Victor (Sermo 3 de triplici gloriatione in cruce 2-4: CCCM 30, 250-252)

The incomparable treasure of our salvation

There are three reasons for our glory in the cross: it is a remedy, an example, and a mystery. When we speak of remedy, we are referring to the merit of Christ's passion and death. Christ himself was free from all sin and was the only free person among the dead. He owed no debt to death but *because of the great love with which he loved us.* Christ was obedient to his Father and accepted an unmerited death in the place of us sinners who have a debt to death. His merit was thus very great and he has accorded us his merit so that it might become for each of us that which he lacks. The merit is so great that it embraces the salvation of all. It is entirely normal that the *importance* of the merit should depend on the *immensity* of love. Since Christ's love is boundless, the merit of his death equally knows no bounds. If all the saints, from the beginning of the world through to the end of time, were free from all sin and were to die for the sake of justice, their deaths together would not be as meritorious as that which was merited by the single and unique death of the Savior once and for all. As Saint Paul contemplated the incomparable treasure of our salvation, he exclaimed: *As for me, the only thing I can boast about is the cross of our Lord Jesus Christ.* This means: Far be it from me to judge that glory and salvation may come from any other source except that of the power, efficaciousness and merit of our Lord's passion. For in this one remedy is our sole hope.

Now, in addition to the remedy, there is demanded of those who are capable of carrying it out that they should follow the example *because Christ suffered on our behalf that we should follow in his footsteps.* We should therefore glory in the cross on account of its power of example. Joyfully should we imitate this example just as the apostle Paul took pride in his sufferings. And it is our task to imitate his example of the passion not only to preserve its remedial effects but also to increase its crown of glory.

We refer the term "mystery of the cross" to its mystical significance. The cross has a quadrilateral shape. And the four-sided shape of the cross reveals something of the four-sided dimension of Christian charity. As Saint Paul says, *So that planted in love and built on love you will with all the saints have strength to grasp the breadth and length, the height and depth.* Those who recognize themselves as within this fourfold dimension may justifiably glory in the mystery of the cross, in the same way as those who possess a lively faith and have been born again in Christ may rightfully rejoice in the remedy of the cross. The one who really carries *the marks of Jesus on his body* is able to glory in the example of the cross.

Responsory   *Lv 20:7.26*
    Consecrate yourselves and be holy, for I am the Lord your God.
    Keep my laws and obey them, for † it is I, the Lord, who make you
    holy.
    V. You must be holy to me, because I, the Lord, am holy. † It is I . . .

FRIDAY   Year II

First Reading   2 Corinthians 11:30—12:13

Responsory   *2 Cor 12:9; 4:7*
    Willingly I boast of my weaknesses, that the power of Christ may
    rest upon me, † for my power is made perfect in weakness.
    V. We possess this treasure in earthen vessels to show that this
    surpassing power comes from God. † For my power . . .

Second Reading   From the writings of Saint Thomas More
                      (A Dialogue of Comfort Against Tribulation I, 6)

If God is with us, who can stand against us

Let us in tribulation desire God's help and comfort, and let us
remit the manner of that comfort to his own high pleasure, which
when we do, let us doubt nothing, but just as his high wisdom sees
better what is best for us, then we can see ourselves. So shall his
high sovereign goodness give us just that thing that shall in deed
be best. For else, if we will presume to stand to our own choice
(except it so be that God offers us the choice himself, as he did to
David in the choice of his own punishment, after his high pride
conceived in the numbering of his people), we may foolishly
choose the worst: and by the prescribing unto God our self so
precisely what we will that he shall do for us (except that of his
gracious favor, he rejects our folly) he shall for indignation grant
us our own request, and after shall we well find that it will turn us
to harm.

How many men attain health of body that were better for their
souls' health their bodies were still sick? How many get out of
prison that happen on such harm abroad, as the prison should have
kept them from? How many just have been loath to lose their
worldly goodness, have in keeping of their goodness soon after

lost their life? So blind is our mortality and so unaware what will fall, so unsure also what manner mind we will ourselves have tomorrow, yet God could not lightly do man more vengeance, than in this world to grant him his own foolish wishes. What will we poor fools have to secure us, when the blessed apostle himself in his sore tribulation praying thrice unto God, to take it away from him, was answered again by God, in a manner, yet he was but a fool in asking that request, but that the help of God's grace in tribulation to strengthen him was far better for him than to take his tribulation from him.

And therefore by experience perceiving well the truth of your lesson, he gives us good warning not to be bold of our minds, when we require aught of God nor to be precise in our asking, but refer the choice to God at his own pleasure. For his own holy spirit so sorely desires our will, yet as men might say, he groans for us, in such ways as no one can tell. *Nos autem*, says Saint Paul, *quid oremus ut oportet, nessimus, sed ipse spiritus postulat pro nobis gemitibus inenarrabilibus*. We, what we may pray for yet was beheld for us, can not our self tell: but the Spirit himself desires for us with unspeakable groans, and therefore I say for conclusion of this point, let us never ask of God precisely our own ease by delivery from our tribulation, but pray for his aid and comfort, by which ways he himself likes best, and then may we take comfort even of our request. For both be we sure that this mind comes of God, and also be we very sure that as he begins to work with us, so (but if our self flies from him) he will not fail to tarry with us, and then he dwelling with us, what trouble can do us harm? *If God be with us*, says Saint Paul, *who can stand against us?*

Responsory   Jn 8:12; Rom 13:12

I am the light of the world. † Anyone who follows me will not walk in darkness, but will have the light of life.

V. Let us cast off the deeds of darkness and put on the armor of light. † Anyone who follows . . .

Alternative Reading

From a sermon by Cardinal John Henry Newman (*Parochial and Plain Sermons* VII, 68-70)

The Church in union with the hermitage and the cell

Blessed is the man, says the psalmist, *whom you chasten, and teach him out of your law.* Even the best men require some pain or grief to sober them and keep their hearts right. Thus, to take the example of Saint Paul himself, even his labors, sufferings, and anxieties, he tells us, would not have been sufficient to keep him from being exalted above measure, through the abundance of the revelations, unless there had been added some further cross, some *thorn in the flesh,* as he terms it, some secret affliction, of which we are not particularly informed, to humble him, and to keep him in a sense of his weak and dependent condition.

This history of the Church after him affords us an additional lesson of the same serious truth. For three centuries it was exposed to heathen persecution; during that long period God's hand was upon his people: what did they do when that hand was taken off? How did they act when the world was thrown open to them, and the saints possessed the high places of the earth? Did they enjoy it? Far from it, they shrank from that which they might, had they chosen, have made much of; they denied themselves what was set before them; when God's hand was removed, their own hand was heavy upon them. Wealth, honor, and power, they put away from them. They recollected our Lord's words, *How hardly shall they that have riches enter into the kingdom of God.* And Saint James', *Has not God chosen the poor of this world, rich in faith, and heirs of the kingdom?* For three centuries they had no need to think of those words, for Christ remembered them, and kept them humble; but when he left them to themselves, then they did voluntarily what they had hitherto suffered patiently. They were resolved that the gospel character of a Christian should be theirs. Still, as before, Christ spoke of his followers as poor and weak, and lowly and simple-minded; men of plain lives, men of prayer, not *faring sumptuously,* or clad in *soft raiment,* or *taking thought for the morrow.* They recollected what he said to the young ruler, *If you will be perfect go and sell what you have, and give to the poor, and you shall have treasure in heaven, and come and follow me.* And so they put off their "elegant clothing," their "gold, and pearls, and costly array"; they "sold what they had, and gave alms;" they "washed one another's feet"; they "had all things common." They formed themselves into communities for prayer and praise, for labor and study, for the care of the poor, for mutual edification, and preparation for Christ; and thus, as soon as the world professed to be Christian, Christians at once set up among them a witness against the world, and kings and monks came into the Church together. And from that time to this, never has the union of the Church with the state prospered, but when the Church was in union also with the hermitage and the cell.

Responsory   *1 Jn 4:9.16b; Jn 3:16*
God's love for us was revealed when he sent his only Son into the world so that we might have life through him. † God is love, and whoever lives in love lives in God and God lives in him.
V. God loved the world so much that he gave his only Son, so that whoever believes in him should not perish but have eternal life. † God is love . . .

SATURDAY   Year II

First Reading   2 Corinthians 12:14—13:13

Responsory   *2 Cor 13:11; Phil 4:7*
Rejoice, strive for perfection and live in peace, † and the God of peace and love will be with you.
V. May the peace of Christ, which surpasses all understanding, keep your hearts in Christ Jesus. † And the God . . .

Second Reading   From the writings of Cardinal Jean Daniélou
                       (*The Lord of History*, 327-328)

Zeal springs from the love of God

All Paul really wanted was for Christ to possess the souls of men: so long as the Churches were faithful, he was perfectly happy, he asked no more than this; this was his reward and nothing else mattered. He was thus entirely free from the least tendency towards empire-building, and from any possessiveness in regard to particular souls and particular churches. In this way, Saint Paul's feeling was poles apart from clerical despotism, which is indeed a caricature of real apostolic zeal; for the latter requires us to love souls only for Christ's sake, and never for our own: it means that we may never do anything with the idea of keeping people to ourselves, because it consists in such a great love of souls as to make us happy in their welfare even when it is none of our doing. That is the essence and the specific character of disinterested love: we must be glad whenever any good influence is at work; there must be no monopolizing of a soul. The importance of this rule is capital, for the alternative is self-seeking, a hidden corruption to destroy the purity of apostolic zeal. But this is not by any means to say that a harmful influence should not be vigorously attacked: in this situation, the case is altered, for we have no right to acquiesce in the subjection of a soul which is under our care, or connected with us in any way, to bad influences. If it is our duty to be unselfishly glad of every good influence, it is just as much our duty to fight to save souls from what we know is bad for them. Christ's spouse must not turn adulteress: we sought to have that intuitive quickness of perception, that penetrating insight which will enable us to detect, almost to feel, an infidelity. For we know that the seducer is none other than Satan, who was once an angel of light, and who can use the outward appearance of goodness for his purpose of enticing a soul away from whatever is really good for it. Sometimes he will turn a soul back from the true course of its own perfection by the attraction of something else that is good in itself, but less perfect, and represents for that particular soul a real infidelity. We must be able to defend souls against themselves: it is all part of apostolic zeal.

Such zeal springs originally from the love of God, but it comes from the love of men too; for we know that the real happiness and full perfection of men consists in fidelity to their calling and to the love of God. We have to help others to be true to themselves, help them to persevere in their own main task and to obey God's call to each one of them. So doing, we shall further at one and the same time both the rightful claims of God upon each soul, and the best interests of the souls of men. If this is our aim, with a purely spiritual and holy motive, and also with some degree of supernatural intensity of purpose (for the love of God is a devouring fire) then we have spiritual zeal, which is apostolic and godly.

Responsory   *Mi 6:8; Acts 17:28*

The Lord has shown us what is good; † what he requires of us is
only this: to act justly, to love tenderly and to walk humbly with our
God.

V. He is not far from any one of us, for in him we live and move and
have our being. † What he requires . . .

NINTH WEEK IN ORDINARY TIME

SUNDAY   Year II

First Reading   Galatians 1:1-12

Responsory   *Gal 1:3-4.10*
Grace and peace be yours from God our Father and from our Lord
Jesus Christ, † who gave himself up to death for our sins.
V. If I were seeking to win the approval of men, I would not then
be what I am — a servant of Christ. † Who gave himself . . .

Second Reading   From a commentary by Saint John
                    Chrysostom (In Gal. 1: Bareille XVIII, 69-70)

Amen

Why does Saint Paul say that this is an *age* of depravity? Well,
he was but using the common idiom. For we also are accustomed
to say, "I have had a bad day," meaning, not the time itself, but the
events and the circumstances. So also Saint Paul, in referring to the
evil ways of his day and age, adopts the same usage: and he
declares that Christ has released us from our former sins and
indeed made us secure for the future. He indicated this in saying,
by giving himself for our sins, then adding the words *to remove us
from this present world of corruption*, so implying the security of the
world to come. The old law has proved inadequate for this world:
but grace has become effective for both worlds. That has come
about by the will of God our Father, he adds. The Jews thought
they were obeying God the lawgiver and were correspondingly
fearful at the thought of casting off the old ways and taking up with
the new; and indeed Saint Paul corrects this idea of theirs, saying
that their doing so is what God wants, it being pleasing to the
Father. And he does not just say "Father," but "our Father,"
constantly making the point to emphasize that Christ made his
Father our Father. Glory be to him for all ages. Amen. There is
something strange and unfamiliar about it. For that word "Amen"
we find, not indeed at the beginning, introducing the Epistle, but
only after much has been said. Then having shown that what he
had said constituted a substantial charge against the Galatians,

something self-contained and independent, he makes that the starting point. The gist of the complaint does not require much argument. For recalling the cross and the resurrection, the atonement for sin, the assurances for the future, the Father's decree, the Son's wish, grace, peace, and all his gifts, he concludes with a doxology, glorifying God.

It was not for this alone that Saint Paul wrote these words, but also because of his utter amazement at the magnitude of the gift, the abundance of grace; and that we might realize, all at once and in a moment of time, just what we are and what it is that God has done for us. Finding mere arguments inadequate, he breaks out in a cry of adoration, sending forth his praise, albeit unworthy, but yet reasonable, service, over the whole world.

Responsory   *1 Jn 4:16.7*

God is love, and those who live in love live in God, † and God lives in them.
V. Let us love one another, for love comes from God and knows God. † And God lives . . .

MONDAY   Year II

First Reading   Galatians 1:13—2:10

Responsory   *1 Cor 15:10; Gal 2:8*

By the grace of God, I am what I am. † His grace in me has not been in vain.
V. It was the power of God which made Peter an apostle for the Jewish people, and it was his power which made me an apostle for the Gentiles. † His grace in . . .

Second Reading   From the writings of Tertullian of Carthage
                        (*De Praes. Haeret*. 20, 7-22, 9: CCL 1, 202-204)

What Peter preached, so did Paul

When classifying things, we must of necessity consider their origins. Now, if we examine the many great churches that there are, we see that they all stem from the original church, which was founded by the apostles, and that they therefore constitute but one Church. Moreover, the reality of their writing is affected by three characteristics: by the peaceful relations which exist between the churches, by the mutual hospitality which Christians offer one another, and by the fraternal charity they all display. These are duties which no other society enjoins, but which are characteristic of the one faith all Christians have.

This being the case, we put forward the following argument. If our Lord Jesus Christ entrusted the mission of preaching to the apostles, then no one should be received as a preacher, unless Christ has ordained him. After all, no one knows the Father but the Son and those to whom the Son has revealed him. However, the Son does not seem to have revealed the Father to anyone except his apostles, whom he sent out with the command that they should preach what he had made known to them. The apostles, then, preached exactly what Christ had revealed to them and so the only way in which we can determine the content of that revelation — and this is the crux of the matter — is by consulting the churches which the apostles themselves established by their preaching, whether it was by word of mouth, as we say, or by letter as happened later on.

So then, it is perfectly obvious that any doctrine which accords with the teaching of the apostolic churches, which are the original wellsprings of the faith, must be held to be true, since it must contain the teaching which the churches received from the apostles, and which the apostles received from Christ and which Christ received from God. But, on the other hand, any doctrine which is at variance with the truth as taught by the churches and therefore by the apostles and by Christ and by God must be condemned out of hand as being false. All we have to do is to show whether our doctrine derives from the apostolic tradition; then anything different must ipso facto proceed from falsehood. Well, we have already outlined the text: because none of our teachings is at variance with the teaching of the churches founded by the apostles. We are in communion with them, and that is proof that we teach the truth.

This test is so simple that, if we applied it straightaway, there would be nothing further to discuss. So let us suppose that we cannot prove our position and so give our opponents the chance of invalidating our argument, if they can. They are crazy enough to say that the apostles did not know everything, they did not hand on all they knew to everyone. Either way they put the blame on

Christ, for choosing to send out apostles who were ignorant or else oversophisticated.

Now who in his right mind can believe that the disciples the Lord gave us as our teachers were ignorant of everything, especially as he kept them with him as his constant companions, whether he was traveling or teaching or sitting? Sometimes he would take them aside to explain anything that seemed obscure to them, for he would tell them that they were being granted the privilege of understanding divine mysteries, whereas the crowd was not. Was anything kept secret from Peter, so-called because he was the rock on which the Church was to be built? He received the keys of the kingdom of heaven together with the power of binding and loosing both in heaven and on earth! Was anything hidden from John, who was the Lord's best-loved disciple? After all, when he leaned his head against the breast of Jesus, the Lord revealed to him, and only him, that Judas was the traitor. And what is more, he entrusted him to Mary to take his place as her son. You might as well say that the disciples who were traveling to Emmaus after the resurrection were ignorant, although the Lord deigned to expound all the scriptures. Granted there was a time when he had said: *I have still a lot to tell you, but you cannot assimilate it now*, but he added *When the Spirit of truth comes, he will guide you to the fullness of truth.* These words of his prove that there was nothing the disciples in question did not know, since he had promised that they would attain to the fullness of truth with the help of the Spirit of truth; and the Lord kept his promise. Indeed, the descent of the Holy Spirit is attested by the Acts of the Apostles.

Responsory   *Ps 11:4-5.7*

The eyes of the Lord look down upon the world; his gaze tests humankind. † The Lord tests the just and the unjust; he hates all who love violence.

V. The Lord is just and loves justice; the upright shall see his face. † The Lord tests . . .

Alternative Reading

From a homily by Saint John Chrysostom (Quatrième homilie sur Saint
Paul: Bareille IV, 150-151)

The intensity of Paul's zeal

The blessed Paul who nowadays unites us, having enlightened
the whole world, was himself once blinded, at the very moment of
his calling. But his incapacity became the world's enlightenment.
For when he lost his sight it was God who incapacitated him, that
he might regain his sight with profit and with interest, the range
of God's power being thereby revealed. This foreshadowed also
what was to follow, through Paul's sufferings, which taught him
the manner of his preaching and that total abandonment of himself
which he would need to make so as to follow his divine Master
with his very eyes closed.

This is why Saint Paul himself cries out, saying, *If anyone among
you thinks himself wise, let him become a fool, that he may become
truly wise.* He could not have recovered his sight so completely if
he had not first been likewise incapacitated: and by discarding the
thoughts of his own that disturbed him he entrusted everything to
faith. But let no one who hears this think that this calling is a matter
of coercion: for Saint Paul could have gone back the way he came.
Many people there are who have seen other, greater miracles and
yet turned back. Both in the New and in the Old Testaments: Judas,
Nebuchaddnessor, Elymas the sorcerer, Simon Magus, Ananias
and Sapphira, the Jews generally: but not Saint Paul. Going by the
clear light, he followed the road and journeyed heavenward. If you
were to ask why he had been incapacitated, this is what he would
have said: You know of my record as an activist amongst the Jews,
how savagely I persecuted the Church, all the harm I did, how I
excelled in my Judaism far beyond most of my generation, an
extreme zealot for the traditions of our fathers.

Because, therefore, Saint Paul was so energetic and headstrong,
he needed all the stronger a leash, lest he be carried away by the
intensity of his own zeal and mistake the purport of the words
spoken to him. That is why, to restrain Paul's natural ardor,
Almighty God first lulls the waves of his impetuosity by incapaci-
tating him, only then conversing with him, to demonstrate the
unapproachable character of the divine wisdom and the super-

abundance of God's knowledge. And so Paul came to learn against whom it was that he had been at war, that one whom he could withstand neither when he chastised nor when he prospered. For it was not the darkness that incapacitated him but the superabundance of the divine light putting his own in the shade.

Responsory   *Ps 16:7-8; Mt 19:17*
I will bless the Lord who gives me counsel, who even at night directs my heart. I keep the Lord always before me: † since he is at my right hand, I shall stand firm.
V. If you wish to enter into life, keep the commandments. † Since he is . . .

TUESDAY   Year II

First Reading   Galatians 2:11—3:14

Responsory   *Gal 2:16.21*
A man is not justified by observing the law, but through faith in Jesus Christ. † We have believed in Christ Jesus so that we might be made holy not through the observance of the law but by faith in him.
V. If holiness comes through keeping the law, then Christ died in vain. † We have believed . . .

Second Reading   From the writings of Thomas Merton
(*The New Man*, 117-119)

Life in Christ

When we speak of "life in Christ," according to the phrase of Saint Paul, *It is now no longer I that live, but Christ lives in me*, we are speaking not of self-alienation but of our discovery of our true selves in Christ. In this discovery we participate spiritually in the mystery of his resurrection. And this sharing of the death and resurrection of Christ is the very heart of the Christian faith and of Christian mysticism.

I came, said Jesus, *that they may have life*. The life he came to bring us is his own life as Son of God. And because of his resurrection he received the power to communicate to us all his Spirit as the principle of our own life and the life of our own spirit. The uncreated image, buried and concealed by sin in the depths of our souls, rises from death when, sending forth his Spirit into our spirit, he manifests his presence within us and becomes for us the source of a new life, a new identity and a new mode of action.

This new life in us is an extension of Christ's own risen life. It forms an integral part of that new existence which he inaugurated when he rose from the tomb. Before he died on the cross, the historical Christ was alone in his human and physical existence. As he himself said, *unless the grain of wheat fall into the ground and die, it remains alone. But if it dies, it brings forth much fruit*. Rising from the dead, Jesus lived no longer merely in himself. He became the vine of which we are the branches. He extends his personality to include each one of us who is united to him by faith. The new existence which is his by virtue of his resurrection is no longer limited by the exigencies of matter. He can now pass through closed doors, appear in many places at once, or exercise his action upon the earth while remaining hidden in the depths of the Godhead: yet these are only secondary aspects of his risen life. The primary aspect of his risen life is his life in the souls of his elect. He is now not only the natural Christ, but the mystical Christ, and as such he includes all of us who believe in him.

Christ living in me is at the same time himself and myself. From the moment that I am united to him "in one spirit" there is no longer any contradiction implied by the fact that we are different persons. He remains, naturally and physically, the Son of God who was born of the blessed Virgin in Nazareth, who went about doing good, and who died on the cross, two thousand years ago. I remain the singular person that I am. But mystically and spiritually Christ lives in me from the moment that I am united to him in his death and resurrection, by the sacrament of baptism and by all the moments and incidents of a Christian life. This union is not merely a moral union, or an agreement of wills, nor merely a psychological union which flows from the fact that I keep him in my thoughts. Christ mystically identifies his members with himself by giving them his Holy Spirit.

Responsory   *Ps 20:7-8; 121:2*

Some put their trust in chariots or horses, but our trust is in the name of the Lord. † They will collapse and fall, but we shall rise and stand firm.

V. My help shall come from the Lord, the creator of heaven and earth. † They will collapse . . .

Alternative Reading

From the conferences of Columban (Sermo X, 2-4: PL 80, 248-249)

The day of the Lord

We ought to remember our Lord and Savior Jesus Christ saying, *Let him who wishes to make his soul safe lay it down; for he who has laid down his soul for my sake shall find it.* Thus we must gladly lay down whatever we love apart from Christ for Christ's sake; first the life by which the body is quickened in union with the soul, if so it should be needful, must be laid down by those who bear martyrdom for Christ; or if the opportunity of such blessedness is lacking, yet we shall not lack the mortification of our wills, so that he who lives, *let him not live to himself, but to him who for him died.* Thus let us live to him who while he dies for us is life; and let us die to ourselves that we may live to Christ; for we cannot live to him unless first we died to ourselves, that is, to our wills. Let us be Christ's and not our own; for we are not our own, for *we are bought at a great price*, and truly a great one, when the Lord is given for a slave, the king for a servant, and God for man. What ought we to render ourselves, if the creator of the universe for us ungodly men, yet his creation, is unjustly put to death? Do you think you ought not to die to sin? Certainly you ought. Therefore let us die, let us die for the sake of life, since life dies for the dead, so that we may be able to say with Paul, *I live, yet no longer I, but Christ lives in me,* he who for me has died; for that is the cry of the elect. But none can die to himself, unless Christ lives in him; but if Christ be in him, he cannot live to himself. Live in Christ, that Christ may live in you.

But you wonder how reason lives in such a man, that he should tell you to die to yourself and live to Christ, or, as it must be said more truly, to live to yourself; for he who dies for Christ's sake himself lives, and he who lives to himself dies. For he is subject to death, if he lives for his own wishes, according to that saying of the apostle, *For if you have lived after the flesh, you shall die.* Thus you see, my dearest friends, that we live in foreign lands, while even our life is not our own, and we ought not to live to ourselves, and it requires great violence to seek by toil and to maintain by enthusiasm what a corrupted nature has not kept. But yet, though blessedness is lost, it has not lost the choice of free will. Thence we now force the kingdom of heaven by strength and violence, and this we snatch somehow, as it were, from amidst our enemies' hands in the middle of the field of strife, and as it were in the bloodstained soil of battle, while we are too hardly assailed not only by our foes but by ourselves, while he loves himself ill, and in the act of loving hurts himself; for he loves well who hates, that is, disciplines himself heathily, but he who makes terms with his foes is not said to love himself aright. So it is a great misfortune, when a man hurts himself and does not know it. For while man is at feud with himself, it is not the gift of all so to pacify him that one should love himself truly.

So here we must fight and struggle with our vices, that we may be crowned elsewhere. For this time is a time of war; for no one should expect rest in warfare, for the reason that in warfare none sleeps, and none joins his rank at rest. Thus we must form rank against all that is vicious, luxurious, and foully fair. But it is enough for the contestants to defeat their foes; if you have conquered yourself, you are conqueror of all; yet if you are your own conqueror, you shall be found dead to yourself, alive to God; but when you hear the word "dead," with what boldness shall you enter before the judgment seat of Christ! Each man who seeks martyrdom for Christ makes himself the pleader of his cause, the prompter of his wish, and the avenger of his disesteem. For if he had truly taken up the cross of Christ, he would notice that none of these things is lawful for him, since Christ also gave an example in this, that none should seek his own, by saying, *Not as I will, but as you will*, and, *I came down, not to do my will, but the will of him who sent me.*

Let us not be proud, let us not be forward, and not free; but let us be lowly, gentle, kindly, courteous, that Christ, the lowly yet exalted king, may reign in us. But that we may love this saving death with some thrill of hope, let us hear its end. For who is really happier than he whose death is life, whose life is Christ, and reward his savior, to whom heaven is made low and paradise opens, to whom earth is heavenly and hell is closed, for whom the gates are opened and life has no ending, to whom God is Father and an angel his minister, who obtains long time for short, blessing for misery, eternity for change, joy for sorrow, triumph for lowliness, heaven for earth, and by a happy exchange, God for mortality? Therefore if we disdain present things and only seek what is to come, we change all these aforesaid conditions for the better. But if (may it not happen!) we reject the stronger in favor of the lower, we shall doubtless lose both. Wherefore let us thus seek life with Jesus, that we may keep his dying in us first; and may Christ our God deign to grant us this, who with the Father and the Holy Spirit is ever one God unto ages of ages. Amen.

Responsory   *Ps 141:1-2; 143:1*

I call to you, Lord; hasten to help me; hear my voice when I cry to you. † Let my prayer rise before you like incense, the raising of my hands like an evening sacrifice.

V. Lord, hear my prayer; listen to my plea. † Let my prayer . . .

Alternative Reading

From a treatise by Ildefonsus of Toledo (Liber de cognitione baptismi X-XI: PL 96, 115-116)

The three ways

The human race, having consigned its creator to oblivion, was given a law through which the creator of all things would be brought back to the thinking of the creature who stood to lose God. And through that very law it was said: *Hear, O Israel! the Lord your God is One.* That said, the superstitions whereby creatures were worshiped instead of the creator were cast aside and the one God truly to be worshiped was openly demonstrated.

Hence the passage of time in our history is divided up in three ways. The fourth and final order of things will be established in the age of the beatific state. The first age was most unhappy: the second, not so, but not completely happy either: the third, abundantly happy: and the fourth age, happily established in the felicity of utter, eternal bliss. The first age was most unhappy, because man, having been created in God's image and likeness but then subverted by his deceiver the devil, becomes subservient to the kingdom of sin and a worshiper of idols, paying the honor due in piety to this creator alone, not to him — but out of impiety to creatures instead. The second age finds man not completely happy, because though the law has now indeed been given for him to know God by, yet it could not bring him to a state of justice before God. *For if justification is from the law, then Christ has died in vain.* The law was given to make us understand, but not to forgive us our sins. For by it our sin is recognized as such and punished, but not put right.

The law was indeed given to be sanctioned by offerings and ceremonies, that they might be offered to God just as he himself had ordained, and not as the Gentiles made sacrifices to demons. This observance of the law, coming as it did from their knowing God, was of great benefit to the people of those times. But it did not bring utter contentment, for the very good reason that it did not bring anything to perfection. So a time had to come when the joy inaugurated through the letter of the law could be accomplished through understanding its spirit.

In this time of grace, making the third age, the state of man is abundantly joyful: for Christ, prefigured and anticipated by all those holy sacrifices, has been unreservedly made manifest. Now that light has followed on darkness, truth on uncertainty, manifest reality on hints, revelation on what lay hidden, the gospel on the law, the grace and favor of sons on the fear of slaves, we may say that everything foreshadowed by the letter has been followed by its manifestation in the spirit. And that is most welcome for its clarity.

The fourth state is the one not to be described, that of eternal bliss, where, with all its obstacles overcome, humankind is to praise God, secure in the tranquillity which belongs to what is incorruptible.

Responsory   *Zep 2:3; Ps 22:26*

Seek the Lord, all you in the land who live humbly, obeying his commands. † Seek integrity, seek humility.
V. The poor shall eat and be satisfied; those who seek the Lord shall praise him. † Seek integrity . . .

WEDNESDAY   Year II

First Reading   Galatians 3:15—4:7

Responsory   *Gal 3:27.28; Eph 4:24*
All of you who have been baptized in Christ have put on Christ.
Now there is neither Jew nor Greek; † you are all one in Christ Jesus.
V. You must put on the new man created in the image of God, in
true justice and in holiness. † You are all . . .

Second Reading   From the writings of Theodoret of Cyrus
                          (De Divina Providentia 10, 59-62)

Learn to praise the creator's goodness

Saint Paul says: *As long as the heir is a child he differs nothing
from a servant though he be lord of all. But he is under tutors and
governors until the time appointed by the father. So we also, when we
were children, were slaving at the elements of worldly knowledge. But
when the fullness of time arrived God sent out his Son born from a
woman, born under the law, that he might ransom those under the
law, that we might receive adoptive sonship.*

That God did not come to this decision as an afterthought but
had so decreed from the beginning of time, let the same witness
testify in his Epistle to the Corinthians: *We speak wisdom among the
perfect: yet not the wisdom of this world, neither of the princes of this
world whose power is to be abrogated. But we speak the wisdom of God
in a mystery, a wisdom which is hidden, which God ordained before
the world unto our glory: which none of the princes of this world knew.
For if they had known it they would never have crucified the Lord of
glory.* For it was not through envy of their happiness that they
afforded men this occasion for great good fortune, but through
ignorance of the end of the mystery they raved against the Savior
of our souls and unwittingly donated to us the loftiest blessings.
The mystery was hidden but ordained before the world.

Knowing this, and aware of the all-pervading providence of
God, and seeing his unlimited love for men and his immeasurable
mercy, stop raving against the creator, learn to praise his goodness,
repay his great blessings with words of gratitude. Offer the incense
of your praise to God. Defile not your tongue with blasphemy, but

make it an instrument of praise, fulfilling the purpose for which it was made. Reverence what can be seen of the divine plan and do not trouble yourself about what is hidden. Await a full knowledge of these things in the life to come. When we are divested of the passions we will attain to perfect knowledge. Do not imitate Adam who dared to pick forbidden fruit. Do not touch what is hidden, but wait patiently on a full knowledge of these things in God's good time. Attend to wisdom, saying: *Do not say: What is this, or what is that? For all things were made to supply a need.* From every source, then, collect occasions for praise and, combining these in one hymn, offer it in union with us to the Creator, the Giver of blessings, the Savior Christ, our true God, to whom be glory, adoration, and lofty praise for endless ages. Amen.

Responsory   *Ps 119:161-162; see Jn 6:63*
   Though princes persecute me without cause, I stand in awe of your word. † I delight in your word like one who finds a treasure.
   V. Your words are spirit, Lord, and they are life. † I delight in . . .

Alternative Reading

From a sermon by Meister Eckhart (Sermon 29; *Sermons and Treatises* I, 215-217)

The day is full, when there is no more day

If anyone were to ask me, Why do we pray, why do we fast, why do we do all our works, why are we baptized, why (most important of all) did God become man? — I would answer in order that God may be born in the soul and the soul be born in God. For that reason all the scriptures were written, for that reason God created the world and all angelic natures: so that God may be born in the soul and the soul be born in God.

Saint Paul says: *In the fullness of time God sent his Son.* Saint Augustine says what this fullness of time is: "Where there is no more time, that is the 'fullness of time.'" The day is full, when there is no more day. That is a necessary truth: all time must be gone when this birth begins, for there is nothing that hinders this birth so much as time and creatures. It is an assured truth that time cannot affect God or the soul by her nature. If the soul could be touched by time, she would not be the soul, and if God could be touched by time, he would not be God. But if it were possible for the soul to be touched by time, then God could never be born in her, and she could never be born in God. For God to be born in the soul, all time must have dropped away from her, or she must have dropped away from time with will or desire.

Another meaning of "fullness of time": if anyone had the skill and the power to gather up time and all that has happened in six thousand years or that will happen till the end of time into one present Now, that would be the "fullness of time." That is the now of eternity, in which the soul knows all things in God new and fresh and present and as joyous as I have them now present. I was reading recently in a book — who can fully understand it? — that God is now making the world just as on the first day, when he created the world. Here God is rich, and this is the kingdom of God. The soul in which God is to be born must drop away from time and time from her, she must soar aloft and stand gazing into this richness of God's, there is breadth without breadth, expanseless expanse, and there the soul knows all things, and knows them perfectly. As for what the masters say of the expanse of heaven, it would be unbelievable to say it. Yet the least of the powers of my soul is wider than the expanse of heaven. I do not speak of the intellect, which is expanseless expanse. In the soul's head, in the intellect, I am as near to a place a thousand miles away across the sea as to the spot where I am standing now. In this expanse and in this richness of God's the soul is aware, there she misses nothing and expects nothing.

Responsory   *Ps 119:161-162; see Jn 6:63*

Though princes persecute me without cause, I stand in awe of your word. † I delight in your word like one who finds a treasure.

V. Your words are spirit, Lord, and they are life. † I delight in . . .

Alternative Reading

From a commentary by Saint Jerome of Bethlehem (In epistolam ad Galatas II, 4: PL 26, 369-370)

The removal of the dividing wall

Because the promises were made to Abraham and his seed, meaning Christ, those who are Christ's children are his seed, and are also said to be Abraham's seed, as if by natural generation. Indeed, whenever our Lord is called Abraham's seed, the words are to be interpreted in the physical sense, of his being descended from Abraham. But whenever we take in our divine Savior's words, believing in him and in what we are told of the nobility of Abraham's race, to which the promise was made, then we are bound to understand the seed in a spiritual sense, as that of the faith and the Christian preaching. We should note also that when it is said of the Lord that "the promises were made to Abraham and his seed," meaning Christ, the promises are to be understood in the plural, whereas when it is said of those who are Abraham's seed through Christ, the promise is mentioned in the singular, as here: *You therefore are the seed of Abraham, heirs according to the promise.* For it was fitting that what was said of Christ alone but standing for a plurality should be said of many in the singular. It goes on:

But I say, as long as the heir is a small child he is in no way different from a servant or slave, since though Lord of all he is nevertheless under supervision and wardship until his father decides otherwise. Here, the heir is a small child, indeed in no way different from a servant or slave: though Lord of all he is under supervision and wardship until his Father shall decide otherwise. That means, the entire human race till the coming of Christ and, to be more specific, till the end of the world. For just as everyone there is was somehow formed in the first man, Adam, and even though not yet born is to die, so also everyone, even those born before Christ's coming, are brought to life in the second Adam. So it happened, that we might come to observe the law in our forbears and that they might be saved by grace like their posterity. This understanding of it is in keeping with the mind of the Catholic Church and its maintaining the unity of divine providence, as embracing both the Old and the New Testament, making no distinction based on time between all those united in the human conditions. We are all of us built into one structure resting on the apostles and prophets, held together by Christ our Lord as cornerstone. He has made both parts into one by removing the dividing wall: and he has eliminated the enmity of the one people for another in his own flesh, replacing the harshness of the old law with the sweet reason and equity of the gospel teachings.

Responsory   *Ps 119:137.138.142; 7:12*
Lord, you are just indeed, you have imposed your will with justice.
† Your justice is an eternal justice, and your law is truth.
V. God is a just judge, slow to anger, but he threatens the wicked
every day, people who refuse to repent. † Your justice . . .

THURSDAY   Year II

First Reading   Galatians 4:8-31

Responsory   *Gal 4:28.31; 2 Cor 3:17*
We are like Isaac, children born of the promise, not children born
of the slave, but of the free woman. † Christ has set us free to be
free men.
V. The Lord is the Spirit, and where the Spirit of the Lord is, there
is freedom. † Christ has set . . .

Second Reading   From a letter by John the Solitary
                         (To Hesychius, 25-30: Sebastian Brock, *The Syriac Fathers in Prayers
                         and the Spiritual Life*, 87-89)

Be free

Be both a servant, and free: a servant in that you are subject (to
God), but free in that you are not enslaved to anything — either to
empty praise or to any of the passions.

Release your soul from "the bonds of sin"; abide in liberty, for
Christ has liberated you; acquire the freedom of the new world
during this temporal life of yours. Do not be enslaved to love of
money or to the praise resulting from pleasing people.

Do not lay down a law for yourself, otherwise you may become
enslaved to these laws of yours. Be a free person, one who is in a
position to do what he likes. Do not become like those who have
their own law, and are unable to turn aside from it, either out of
fear in their own minds, or because of the wish to please others; in
this way they have enslaved themselves to the coercion of their
own law, just when Christ had released them from the coercion of
the law!

Do not make hard and fast decisions over anything (in the future), for you are a created being and your will is subject to changes. Decide in whatever matter you have to reach a decision, but without fixing in your mind that you will not be moved to other things. For it is not by small changes in what you eat that your faithfulness is altered: your service to the Lord of all is performed in the mind, in your inner man; that is where the ministry to Christ takes place.

Do not be tied down to anything, or let anything enslave you. Release yourself from worry about the world by means of the freedom of the new life. There are ninety-nine commandments which have been dissolved and annulled by God, and do you want to establish your own law? There are many people who are more careful not to let their own law be broken, than all other laws.

Be free, therefore, and free yourself from every kind of destructive slavery, for unless you become free, you cannot be a worker for Christ; for that kingdom in the heavenly Jerusalem, which is free, does not accept children of slavery. The children of a free mother are themselves free, and are not enslaved to the world in anything.

Responsory   *Ps 119:97.105.135; 19:11*

Lord, how I love your law! Your word is a lamp for my feet, a light for my path. † Let your face shine on your servant and teach me your decrees.

V. By them your servant is instructed; in keeping them there is great reward. † Let your face . . .

Alternative Reading

From a letter to Diognetus (I, 9-10)

A sweet exchange

Once the measure of our sin had become full and overflowing, and it was perfectly clear that nothing but punishment and death could be expected as the wages of sin, the time came which God had foreordained. Henceforth he would reveal his goodness and grace — and Oh! how exceeding great is God's love and friendship for all. Instead of hating us and rejecting us and remembering our sins, he was compassionate and patient and took upon himself our sins. He gave us his own Son for our redemption. For us who were sinful, he gave up the Holy One; for the wicked the Innocent One; the Just One for the unjust; the Incorruptible One for corruptible ones; and for us mortals the Immortal One. For, what else but his righteousness could have concealed our sin? In whom, if not in the only Son of God, could we lawless and sinful people have been justified? What a sweet exchange! What an inexplicable achievement! What unexpected graces! that in One who was just the sin of many should be concealed, that the righteousness of One should justify many sinners. In the former time he proved the inability of our nature to obtain life, and now he has revealed a Savior capable of saving the incapable. For both these reasons he wanted us to believe in his goodness and to look upon him as guardian, father, teacher, adviser, and physician, as our mind, light, honor, glory, strength, and life, and to have no solicitude about what we wear and eat.

This faith, if only you desire it, you can have, and, first of all, the knowledge of the Father. For, God loved men and women, and for their sake made the world and made all things on earth subject to them. He gave them their reason and their mind. Them alone he allowed to look up to heaven. He fashioned them in his own image. To them he sent his only-begotten Son. To them he promised the kingdom which is in heaven and he will give it to those who love him. And with what joy do you think you will be filled when you come to know these things? And how you will love him who first loved you so much! And, when you love him, you will be an imitator of his goodness. And do not be surprised that a human being may become an imitator of God. He can do so because God wills it. You know there is no real happiness in getting the better of your neighbors, in wanting to have more than weaker people, in being rich and able to order your inferiors about. It is not in such ways that a person can imitate God, for these things are no part of his greatness. On the other hand, anyone can be an imitator of God, if he takes on his own shoulders the burden of his neighbor, if he chooses to use his advantage to help another who is underprivileged, if he takes what he has received from God and gives to those who are in need — for such a one becomes God to those who are helped. When you have faith, you will see that God rules in heaven, even though you are on earth; you will begin to speak of the mysteries of God; you will love and admire those who suffer because they refuse to deny God; you will condemn the deceit and error of the world as soon as you realize that true life is in heaven, and despise the seeming death in this world, and fear the real death which is reserved for those who are to be condemned to eternal fire which shall torment forever those who are committed to it.

Responsory   *Ps 119:97.105.135; 19:11*
Lord, how I love your law! Your word is a lamp for my feet, a light for my path. † Let your face shine on your servant and teach me your decrees.
V. By them your servant is instructed; in keeping them there is great reward. † Let your face . . .

FRIDAY   Year II

First Reading   Galatians 5:1-25

Responsory   *Gal 5:18.22.23-25*
If you are led by the Spirit, you are not under the law. † The signs of the Spirit's presence are love, joy and peace.
V. Since we live by the Spirit, let him direct our lives. † The signs of . . .

Second Reading   From a homily by Saint Gregory Nazianzen
(Oratio 7, 23-24: PG 35, 786-787)

That we may all be made one in Christ

Could I but mortify my own earthbound members! Could I but wear them all out in the spirit, advancing along that narrow path in which few walk, not the broad and easy road! For assuredly it is a great and resplendent future that awaits us, and the hope of it is beyond our deserving: *What is man, that you should bear him in mind?* What indeed is this new mystery in which I am involved? I am at once small and great, lowly and exalted, mortal and immortal, a sojourner on earth and a citizen of heaven. Under the one aspect my place is with this world here below, under the other it is with God; on the one hand with the flesh, on the other with the spirit. My destiny is to be buried with Christ, with Christ to rise again, to be Christ's co-heir, to become God's son, nay God's self: see to what point the developing argument has advanced us!

I could almost be grateful for the calamity that has led me to think along these lines; it has but increased my longing to be risen and gone hence. This is what that great mystery means for us, this is what is willed of us by God, who for our sake assumed man's nature and became poor that he might set our fallen humanity upright, rescue his image from defacement, and fashion us anew: that we may all be made one in Christ, who becomes in each and all of us, completely, all that he is in himself, so that *henceforth we are no longer male and female, barbarian and Scythian, slave and freeman*, for these terms betoken only fleshly characteristics, but wear about us only the sign-manual of God, by whom and for whom we were created, so plainly stamped with his image as to be identifiable from his likeness alone.

Ah, could we but be what we hope to be according to the great generosity of our bountiful God, who asks for little but lavishes great gifts, both now and in the world to come, on those who give him their true and heartfelt love! Then indeed should we, for our love towards him, for our hope in him, *bear all things, endure all things*, rendering him out thanks for everything, whether favorable or unfavorable, pleasant or painful, commending to him our own souls and the souls of those who, better equipped for their journey along life's highway, have reached their lodging before us.

Responsory   *Ps 76:4; Hb 3:2*
You are awesome, O Lord, more majestic than the everlasting mountains. † Who can stand when your anger is roused?
V. Lord, I have heard of your fame; I stand in awe of your deeds. † Who can stand . . .

Alternative Reading

From the writings of Thomas Merton (*The New Man*, 164-166)

Love's very life is spontaneity

The morality of the New Testament all flows from the central fact of our liberation from the law by the death of Christ. The essence of this morality is its freedom. Its first obligation is that we preserve our liberty. How? By keeping the great commandment which resumes and includes all the others. *For the whole law is fulfilled in one word: you shall love your neighbor as yourself.*

Clearly, love is impossible without freedom. Love that is not free is not even love. Love's very life is spontaneity. Therefore all the negative aspects of Christianity can be summed up in the obligation to *stand fast and not be caught again under the yoke of slavery.* Slavery, in this context, means servitude under a legal system, bondage to the "elements of this world" — to ceremonial and moral prescriptions which can do nothing, of themselves, to bring men to interior and spriritual fulfillment. *If you are led by the Spirit, you are not under the law.* But there is a far worse law — the "law of the flesh" with a worse slavery, beating down the spirit of man *so that you do not what you would.* Both these servitudes, from which we must keep ourselves free by the practice of a truly Christian life, involve and immersion and absorption in what is below us. The first imprisons us within ourselves in a fear that barricades itself behind legalism and superstition. The second, while seeming to liberate us from ourselves, weakens and stultifies our being in the confusion of fleshly licence. It places a barrier between us and the very ones who share our licence. True communion belongs to the spiritual order. It cannot be consummated merely in the flesh.

Weakness and fear are the elements that guide an enslaved spirit, whether its servitude be that of frank licentiousness or of apparent severity. *Perfect love,* however, *casts out fear.* And unless fear be cast out, we cannot find ourselves because we will not even face ourselves. The truth that is in us remains the object of our greatest anxiety. We strive to keep it hidden from ourselves precisely because the truth will make us free, and we prefer to be slaves. Freedom brings with it too much responsibility — more than we can face by ourselves. But the Easter mystery tells us where we can find the strength to face it.

Once we enter again into contact with our own deepest self, with an ordinate self-love that is inseparable from the love of God and of his truth, we discover that all good develops from within us, growing up from the hidden depths of our being according to the concrete and existential norms laid down by the Spirit who is given us from God. This mystical spontaneity (which begins with the free option of faith and grows with our growth in charity) sets the tone for our whole moral life. It is the inward promulgation of God's new law of charity in our hearts.

Responsory   *Ps 41:1; Gal 6:2*

Blessed are those who are concerned for the poor and the weak; †
the Lord will save them in time of trouble.
V. Bear one another's burdens, and so fulfill the law of Christ. † The
Lord . . .

SATURDAY   Year II

First Reading   Galatians 5:25—6:18

Responsory   *Gal 6:8; Jn 6:63*

A man can only reap what he has sown. If you sow in the field of
selfishness, it will bring you a harvest of death and decay; † if you
sow in the field of the Spirit, you will reap a harvest of life everlasting.
V. It is the Spirit that gives life; the flesh is of no avail. † If you sow . . .

Second Reading   From a sermon by Saint Augustine of Hippo
                     (Sermo 160, 4-5: PL 38, 875-876)

What chalice is that, unless it be that of humility and suffering?

*Far be it from me to boast, except it be in the cross of our Lord Jesus
Christ.* He could have said, in the wisdom of our Lord Jesus Christ:
and he would have spoken the truth. Or he could have said, in the
majesty — and again spoken the truth. But in fact he said: in the
cross. Where the worldly-wise philosopher is abashed, there the
apostle finds his treasure: by not despising the unprepossessing
outer husk he gets through to the precious center. *Not for me*, he
says, *to boast, save in the cross of Christ.* You have borne a fine
burden; and there is everything you sought: what there was of
significance hidden there, that you have now revealed. What help
did he get? *Through whom*, he says, *the world is crucified and I to
the world.* When could the world have been crucified to you, except
when he through whom the world was made was crucified for
you? *He who boasts, then, let him make his boast in the Lord.* What
Lord? Christ crucified. Where there is humility, there also is majesty; where there is weakness, there also is strength; where there
is death, there is life. If you wish to arrive at the latter, do not
despise the former.

You have heard about the sons of Zebedee, in the gospel. They sought the high places of preferment, asking that one of them might sit at the right hand of the great chief, and the other on his left. They were asking for great rank indeed: but because they relented, Christ called them from where they wished to go to that place whither they must go. What does he say, to those who sought such eminence? *Can you drink of the chalice that I am to drink?*

What chalice is that, unless it be that of humility and suffering? As he is about to drink it and change our infirmity in his own person, he says to the Father: *Father, if it might be so, (grant) that this cup might pass from me.* Changing those people into his own likeness who refused to drink his cup and instead sought the high places, ignoring the path of humility, he says this: *Can you indeed drink the cup which I am to drink?* You who seek Christ exalted and glorified, go back to Christ crucified. You wish to reign and to be glorified in Christ's resting place. But first learn to say: *It is not for me to glory, except in the cross of our Lord Jesus Christ.*

This is the Christian teaching, the precept of humility, the commendation of humility: that we should not glory, save in the cross of Christ. For it is not saying much if you glory in Christ's wisdom: but in Christ's cross, it is. Where the impious revile you, there the pious soul makes his boast; where the proud man reviles him, there the Christian makes his boast. Do not be ashamed of Christ's cross: you have taken the mark of it on your brow, as it were in an embarrassing place. Remember what you have on your brow, for all to see, and be not in fear of idle tongues.

Responsory   *Ps 18:7-8; 118:105*

The law of the Lord is perfect; it revives the soul. † The precepts of the Lord are right; they gladden the heart.

V. Your work is a lamp for my feet, and a light for my path. † The precepts . . .

Alternative Reading

From a sermon by Isaac of Stella (Sermo XXXI, in dominica I Quadragesimae 2: PL 207, 202)

On the pre-eminence of charity

Why is it, brethren, that we are so little concerned to find opportunities for rendering each other saving help, whereby we might give the more assistance where we see the greater need and bear each other's burdens as brethren should? Teaching this lesson, the blessed Apostle says: *Bear one another's burdens, and so fulfill Christ's law*; and again elsewhere: *Bearing with one another in charity*. For that in itself is what the law of Christ is.

When I observe something in my brother which seems an incorrigible fault, whether it be by some necessity of nature or from bodily or moral weakness, why should I not bear patiently with him, giving him my generous support, as it is written: *Their children are carried around on their shoulders and dandled on their knees*? Is it because I am lacking that charity which suffers all things, is patient in bearing its burden, and kind in loving? After all, this is the law of Christ, of him who truly bore our infirmities by his passion and will support our sorrows with his compassion, loving those whom he has carried, carrying those whom he has loved. Anyone who assails his brother in need, who sets a trap for his weakness, of whatever kind, is beyond question subject to the devil's own law and is carrying it out. So let us be compassionate, one to another, lovers of fraternity, bearing with weaknesses but giving our vices no quarter.

For every piece of discipline which positively furthers the love of God and the love of one's neighbor for his sake, no matter what observances or habits may accompany it, is the more acceptable to God. For it is that same charity for which all things have to be done or not done (as the case may be); changed or else left unchanged. It is both the beginning from which and the end to which all things should really be directed. Nothing incurs blame or guilt which truly is done for love and in the love which he himself thinks fit to bestow on us, he whom without it we cannot please and without whom we can do nothing; he who lives and reigns God through the undying ages. Amen.

Responsory   *Ps 18:7-8; 118:105*

The law of the Lord is perfect; it revives the soul. † The precepts of the Lord are right; they gladden the heart.

V. Your work is a lamp for my feet, and a light for my path. † The precepts . . .

TENTH WEEK IN ORDINARY TIME

SUNDAY Year II

First Reading Philippians 1:1-11

Responsory *Phil 1:9.10: see 6*
May your love grow ever deeper in knowledge and all discernment
† so that, perceiving always what is best, you may act blamelessly
and with a clear conscience.
V. I am sure that the one who began this good work in you will
continue to perfect it until the day of Christ Jesus, † so that, perceiving . . .

Second Reading From a homily by Saint John Chrysostom
(Phil. 1, 3: Bareille XVIII, 459-460)

He who began a good work in you will bring it to completion

I am sure of this, Paul says, *that he who began a good work in you
will continue it till the day of Jesus Christ*. Notice how he also teaches
them to be humble. For after bearing witness to their great achievement, to prevent them from feeling humanly proud of themselves,
he immediately tells them to attribute both past and future achievements to Christ. How did he do this? By not saying: "I am sure that
you will finish what you have begun," but: *He who began a good work
in you will bring it to completion*. He did not deny them their success,
for he said: I am glad of your partnership, that is, because they were
good workers. But he denied that such success was theirs alone, saying
it belonged principally to God. For he is speaking of God when he
says: *I am confident that he who has begun a good work in you will
continue it till the day of Jesus Christ*. He says: *I am convinced of this
not only with regard to you but to your descendants*. And this indeed
is no small praise, to tell people that God works in them.

For if God is no respecter of persons, which is certainly true,
but looks at our aims before taking part in our achievements, it is
clear that we ourselves are responsible for drawing him to us. So
in that way too Paul has not denied them praise, since if God
worked in us indiscriminately nothing would have prevented him
working in the Gentiles and the whole of humanity as well, if he

moved us like lumps of wood or stone and desired no cooperation from ourselves. So when Paul says: *God will bring it to completion*, this too is to their praise, since they had attracted the grace of God to work with them in their efforts to transcend human nature. And this is also praise in another way, due to the very fact that their achievements were beyond human capacity but needed the help of God. Then if God is going to complete the work, their labor will still be great, but we must be confident as we shall easily accomplish everything with God to help us.

Responsory   *Ps 103:8-9.13-14*

The Lord is merciful and loving, slow to anger and full of compassion. He will not always reprove us; his wrath will come to an end.
† As tenderly as a father treats his children, the Lord treats those who stand in awe of him.
V. He knows what we are made of; he remembers that we are dust.
† As tenderly as . . .

MONDAY   Year II

First Reading   Philippians 1:12-26

Responsory   *Phil 1:20.21*

I know that I shall never be put to shame, because my hopes and expectations have never been disappointed. I fully trust that now as always † Christ will be glorified in me, whether I live or die.
V. For to me life is Christ, and death is gain. † Christ will be . . .

Second Reading   From a sermon by Saint Columban
(Instructio VIII, 1-2: PL 80, 244-246)

The journey's end must always be wished and longed for by travelers

It is natural for travelers to hasten toward their native land, and natural too that they should have trouble on the way and safety at home. So let us who are on the way to it hasten toward our native land; for our whole life is like a single day's journey.

And therefore let us devote ourselves to divine rather than human affairs, and like exiles be always sighing for our native land and longing for it. For the journey's end must always be wished and longed for by travelers, and so because we ourselves are travelers and exiles in the world we should always be thinking of the journey's end, that is, the end of our life, for our journey brings us to our native land. But, there, all who have been traveling the world get different lots according to their merits. The good travelers come home because they love the journey. Let us not love the journey to our native land, so that we do not lose our eternal home, for that is the kind of home we have, and which we must love. Let this, then, be our constant aim: to live our way like travelers, exiles, visitors to the world, without clinging to any worldly ambitions or longing to fulfill any worldly desires, but to fill our minds entirely with heavenly and spiritual images, singing in thought and deed: *When shall I come and appear before the face of my God?* For *my soul thirsts for the strong and living God.* And saying with Paul: *I long to die and be with Christ.*

Let us realize that although *We are exiles from the Lord as long as we are in the body,* we are present in the sight of God. Therefore spurning all laziness, putting away all lukewarmness, let us do our best to please him who is present everywhere. Then, with a good conscience, we may pass happily from our journey in this world to the holy and eternal home of our eternal Father, from the present to the absent, from sorrow to joy, from transitory to eternal, from earth to heaven, from the region of the dead to that of the living. And then we shall see, face to face, the world of heaven and the king of kings, our Lord Jesus Christ, ruling his kingdom with right government, to whom be glory for ever. Amen.

Responsory   *Ps 146:5-7; 118:8-9*
  Happy are those who are helped by Jacob's God, whose hope is in the Lord their God. † It is he who keeps faith forever, and is just to those who are oppressed.
  V. It is better to take refuge in the Lord than to trust in human help; better to take refuge in the Lord than to rely on princes. † It is he who . . .

Alternative Reading

From a homily by Saint John Chrysostom (Phil 3: Bareille XVIII, 485-487)

To live well or badly depends on ourselves

Do not think of me as being robbed of this life, Paul says, since even when living in the world I would not lead a worldly life but the life that Christ wished me to live. Indeed, could he live a worldly life who thought no more of wealth and luxury than of hunger and thirst, who despised danger as much as health and security? He who had no worldly possessions, and was often willing to throw away his life if necessary, never trying to save it, could he live a worldly life? By no means.

Christ is my life, Paul says. If you will examine my life, you will find that true. And death is gain. Why? Because I shall be united more truly than ever to him; and so death is a better life. Those who intend to kill me will do nothing terrible to me, since they will convey me to my real life and set me free from this unbefitting one. What then? Since you are here you do not belong to Christ. Most certainly I do. But if there is fruitful work for me while living in the body, I do not know that I have any choice. To forestall the question: So if heaven is life, why does Christ leave you on earth? Paul says: There is fruitful work here. Therefore it is possible to use even this present life in case of need, without at the same time leading a worldly life like the great majority.

Paul tells you this to prevent you from thinking that life is not worth living, and from saying: "If we are no use here, why not destroy ourselves, why not kill ourselves?" That would be wrong, he says, it is possible to gain even in this world, if we live in accordance with the other world rather than this.

How great was his philosophy! How well he banished desire for this present life, without at the same time condemning this life! For in saying that death is gain he banished desire; but in saying that while living in the body there is fruitful work to be done, he showed that this present life too is necessary. In what way? If we use it in case of need and make it bear fruit, since if it is useless, it is no longer life. Even with the trees, for instance, we dislike the unfruitful as much as the dead ones, and throw both on the fire. For once again life itself is something neutral and indifferent, but to live well or badly depends on ourselves.

Responsory   *Ps 146:5-7; 118:8-9*
   Happy are those who are helped by Jacob's God, whose hope is in
   the Lord their God. † It is he who keeps faith forever, and is just to
   those who are oppressed.

V. It is better to take refuge in the Lord than to trust in human help; better to take refuge in the Lord than to rely on princes. † It is he who . . .

Alternative Reading

From the writings of Richard Rolle (*The Fire of Love*, 120-122)

Spiritual song

Nothing is better than mutual love, nothing sweeter than holy charity. To love and be loved is the delightful purpose of all human life, the delight of angels and of God, and the reward of blessedness. If then you want to be loved, love! Love gets love in return. No one has ever lost through loving good, if he has persisted in love to the end. On the other hand he does not know what it is to rejoice who has not known what it is to burn with love. So no one is ever more blessed than the man who is transported out of himself by the vehemence of his love, and who through the greatness of God's love experiences for himself the sweet song of everlasting praise. But this does not happen to a man overnight unless he has been converted to God, and has made remarkable efforts, and has rejected every desire for worldly vanity. Normally God infuses his own indescribable joy into those who love him. For a mind ordered and clean receives from God its thoughts of eternal love. Thinking has been cleansed when it is surging up into spiritual song. Purity of heart deserves to have the sound of heaven; and so as to maintain the praise of God with joy the soul is kindled with divine fire, and made glad with ineffable sweetness.

A man who gives up this world completely and attends closely to reading, prayer, meditation, watchings, and fastings will gain purity of mind and conscience, to such an extent that he would like to die through his supernal joy, for he longs *to depart and to be with Christ.* But unless his mind wholeheartedly cleaves to Christ, and he longs for him constantly and deliberately in all his thoughts, thoughts which are wholly loving and in intention unending, thoughts upon which he meditates unceasingly wherever he sits or wherever he goes, seeking interiorly to love only Christ, he will certainly not know any heavenly song, or sing joyfully to Jesus, or sound his praises either mentally or aloud.

Responsory   *Ps 146:5-7; 118:8-9*

Happy are those who are helped by Jacob's God, whose hope is in
the Lord their God. † It is he who keeps faith forever, and is just to
those who are oppressed.
V. It is better to take refuge in the Lord than to trust in human help;
better to take refuge in the Lord than to rely on princes. † It is he ...

TUESDAY   Year II

First Reading   Philippians 1:27—2:11

Responsory   *1 Pt 2:24; Heb 2:14; see 12:1*

Christ bore our sins on the cross so that we might die to sin and live
a life of holiness. † Through his death he broke the power of the
devil, the prince of death.
V. Our faith rests on Jesus, who endured the cross for the sake of
the joy that lay before him. † Through his death ...

Second Reading   From a sermon by Blessed Guerric of Igny
                      (Sermo 1 in Ramis Palmarum 1-2: PL 185, 127-130, 55-58)

I will serve you, says God

*Let this mind be in you which was in Christ Jesus, who, although
he was by nature God.* . . . This is for the hearing of the wicked and
runaway slave, man I mean, who although he was by nature and
rank a slave and bound to serve, refused to serve and tried to
appropriate freedom and equality with his Lord. Christ was by
nature God; equal to God not through robbery but by birth because
he shared omnipotence, eternity and divinity. He nevertheless
dispossessed himself and not only took the nature of a slave,
fashioned in the likeness of men, but also carried out the ministry
of a slave, lowering his own dignity and accepting an obedience to
the Father which brought him death, death on a cross.

But reckon it as too little for him to have served the Father as a
slave although his Son and co-equal unless he also served his own
slave as more than a slave. Man was made to serve his creator. And
what could be more just than that you should serve him by whom
you were created, without whom you cannot exist? And what
could be more blessed or more sublime than to serve him? To serve

him is to reign. "I will not serve," man says to his creator. "Then I will serve you," his creator says to man. "You sit down, I will minister, I will wash your feet. You rest; I will bear your weariness, your infirmities. If you are ill and afraid to die I will die for you so that from my blood you may make yourself medicine that will restore life."

O detestable pride of man who scorns to serve, pride that could not be reduced to humility by any other example than the servitude, and such servitude, of its Lord. And would that it could so be humbled, that even now it would feel and show gratitude for such great humility and goodness. But I seem still to hear the same Lord in Isaiah complaining of the ingratitude of his worthless slave in the words: "I have not made you serve me with offerings, I have not made you toil to provide me with incense. Yet you have made me serve with your sins, you have made me toil with your iniquities. And what toil? Even to exhaustion, hunger and thirst. Yes, even to sweat, a sweat of blood which ran down on to the earth; yes, even to death, death on a cross. You then, who stand idle the whole day, attend and see if there is any toil like my toil.

Indeed you have toiled hard, my Lord, in serving me. It was only just and fair that at least for the future you should rest and your slave, if only because it is his turn, should serve you.

How happy we shall be, O my brethren, if in this we listen to Saint Paul's advice: "Let this mind be in you which you have known to have been first in Christ Jesus." That is, let no one be lifted up above himself, but rather brought down below himself. Let him who is greater serve others; if anyone is injured let him be the first to make satisfaction in common; let everyone obey even to death. These are the footsteps, brethren, in which we may follow Christ in the form of a slave, and come in the end to see him in the form of God, in which he lives and reigns for ever and ever. Amen.

Responsory   *Ps 106:45; 89:34*

For their sake he remembered his covenant; † in his boundless love he relented.

V. I will never violate my covenant, nor go back on the promise I have made. † In his . . .

WEDNESDAY   Year II

First Reading   Philippians 2:12-30

Responsory   *2 Pt 1:10.11; Eph 5:8.11*
Strive all the more to confirm God's choice and calling of you.
† Then you will generously be granted entrance into the kingdom
of our Lord and Savior Jesus Christ.
V. Live as children of light and take no part in the empty works of
darkness. † Then you will . . .

Second Reading   From a sermon by Saint Augustine of Hippo
(Sermo 13, 2-3: CCL 41, 177-179)

You should give thanks for having been made in his image

Serve the Lord in fear, and exalt him with trembling. Exalt him, it
says, not yourself, him from whom you are what you are, both
because you are a man and because you are made just, if indeed
you already are. If you think that your being man comes from him
but your being just comes from yourself, you are not serving the
Lord in fear, nor exalting him with trembling: you are exalting
yourself in presumption. And what else should then befall you
than the logical consequence? *Lest the Lord's anger be kindled and
you stray,* he says, *from the way of righteousness.*

These are the Apostle's words: *Work out your salvation with fear
and trembling.* Why, then, with fear and trembling, if it is within
my power to work out my salvation at all? The reason is this: *For
it is God working within you even so.* So with fear and trembling be
it: for what the humble man secures with his petition, the proud
man loses with his. If, then, it really is God working within us, why
those words *Work out your salvation* — your *own* salvation? Because he so works in us that we also work: *Be my helper,* the
psalmist says. The man who summons up a helper is calling
himself a worker. But the good will, he says, is mine. That is true:
but what of the will that grants all that and stirs it up? Do not take
my word for it, but refer to Saint Paul. *For it is God,* he says, *whose
effect on you is that you resolve on and perform the acts of a good will.*

What, then, were you claiming as your own? Why should you
want to walk proudly and go astray? Return to your first resolve,
and realize your lack of virtue; and that you may become good

yourself, call upon him who is that already. For what pleases God in you is that alone which you have received from God — and not anything you have from yourself, for that is displeasing to him. If you consider your assets, what are they but what you have received? And if you have received all that, why brag about it as though you had not? He stands alone, only able to give. For him who has no superior, there can be no donor, no benefactor. Granted that you are his inferior, for that very reason you should give thanks for having been made in his image even so, that you may yet be found in him, you who have gone astray inside yourself. For there you could only lose yourself and you do not know how to find yourself, unless he who made you seeks you out.

Responsory   *Ps 113:4.6-7*
High above all nations is the Lord, yet he stoops from the heights to look down upon heaven and earth. † He lifts up the lowly from the dust, the needy from the dung-heap.
V. He has pulled down princes from their thrones and exalted the lowly. † He lifts up . . .

THURSDAY   Year II

First Reading   Philippians 3:1-16

Responsory   *Phil 3:8.10; Rom 6:8*
I have counted all things worthless so that I might gain Christ. † I wish to know Christ and the power of his resurrection, and to be one with him in his sufferings.
V. We believe that if we die with Christ, we shall also live with him. † I wish to . . .

Second Reading   From a sermon by Saint Augustine of Hippo
                       (Sermo 169, 16-18: PL 38, 925-926)

Limping along the road is better than running off it

I do not claim to have yet succeeded. Do not be deceived in me, Paul says: for I know myself better than you know me. If I am unaware of my failings, the same thing holds good for merits as well. *I lay no claim*, then, *to having succeeded. One thing*, indeed, I do not think I have within my grasp. I have many things: but one thing I have not yet secured. *One thing I have sought of the Lord; and this I will implore.* What is that? What did I implore? Why, *that I may dwell in the Lord's house all the days of my life.* To what purpose? *That I may contemplate the delight of the Lord.* That is what the Apostle says he has not yet obtained: and to the extent of being without it he is still falling short of perfection, meaning maturity.

So what am I to do? *What is past, I forget, attending rather to what lies ahead.* I still follow, *to gain the palm to which God is calling me on high, in Christ Jesus.* I follow the path, still plodding along, step by step, still on the way, still exerting myself, not yet having arrived. If only you also would do this, then, pondering what lies ahead, forgetting what is past, not looking back lest you remain where your gaze rests. Remember Lot's wife. *As many of us as are perfect, are mature, let us well understand this.* Saint Paul had already said, I am not perfect, and so he adds, *As many of us as are perfect, let us well understand this. I do not claim to have reached my goal. It is not that I have already received the reward, that I am yet mature and made perfect in Christ.* And he adds the words already quoted, *As many of us as are made perfect, let us well understand.* Perfect in one respect not in another: perfect as wayfarers are, but not yet arrived at their destination. And that you may see that he means perfect as wayfarers, on the road, not possessors, hear what follows. (Again that verse:) *As many of us as are perfect, let us realize this, and should you take anything amiss,* let no one mislead you into thinking that you are anything of yourselves. He who thinks himself to be of any consequence when he is not, that man deceives himself. He who thinks himself knowledgeable on some matter does not yet understand the nature of knowledge. Hence, *If your attitude is wrong on some point,* in your childlike simplicity God will show you where. But let us persevere in the way we have taken. That God may show us where our ideas are at fault, let us not remain at the spot we have already reached, but go on from there instead. You realize that we are travelers on a road. You may say, what sort of travelers? Well, briefly, the sort that make progress in virtue and understanding (as well), for fear it happen that you fall short of understanding and go the wrong way, sluggishly. It is progress that you should aim for, criticizing yourselves constantly with candor, without guile or illusion, flattery, without fear or favor. For there is no one within you, before whom you need either feel abashed or make your boast. There is one there, indeed: but humility is what pleases him — and it is he who will try to test you. You should do that yourselves. Never feel pleased with yourself, if you wish to improve on what you are; for where you take pleasure, there you will linger. Say, This is far enough, this is good enough and you are lost. Instead, always take the *next* step, keep going, keep moving forward; do not stop on the way, do not go back, do not turn aside. He who does not advance stays where he is; he who returns to the spot he has left is going backwards; he who rebels is turning aside. Limping *along* the road is better than running *off* it.

Responsory   *Sir 42:15-16; 43:28*

By the words of the Lord his works come into being, and all creation obeys his will. † As the sun as it shines looks upon all things, so the work of the Lord is full of his glory.

V. Where can we find the power to praise him, since he is greater than all his works? † As the sun . . .

Alternative Reading

From a sermon by Saint Augustine of Hippo (Homilies on the Gospel of John 98, 7)

Do not abandon the foundations

When addressing those who seemed to themselves to be already perfect, the blessed apostle first said that he himself was imperfect, and then he added: *Let us, as many as are perfect, be thus minded, and if in anything you are of a different mind, the Lord will reveal this also to you.* And lest perhaps they encounter seducers who might try to turn them away from the faith by promising knowledge of the truth, and lest they think that this was what the apostle meant when he: *the Lord will reveal this also to you*, he immediately added: *Nevertheless, let us walk in that which we have reached.* If, then, you come to an understanding that is not contrary to the rule of the Catholic faith, to which you have come as to the way leading you to the fatherland, and if your understanding is such that you to have no doubts at all, then add to the building but do not abandon the foundations.

The more knowledgeable ought to teach the uninstructed without saying that Christ, the Lord of all, and the prophets and apostles, who were far greater than they, were lying in any way.

You must be on guard not only against chatterers and seducers of the mind who talk fictitious and lying nonsense and who in their silliness promise as it were a proud knowledge that is against the Catholic rule of faith which you have accepted. Flee also, as from a plague more perilous than others, those who discourse truly about the immutability of the divine nature or about incorporeal creatures or the creator and who prove what they say by means of documents and utterly certain arguments, but at the same time try to turn you away from the one mediator between God and humanity. That is the kind of person the apostle meant when he said: *When they knew God, they did not glorify him as God*. For what does it profit to have a true understanding of the immutable good but not possess him by whom we are delivered from evil?

Let the warning of the most blessed apostle not slip from your hearts: *If anyone preaches to you a gospel other than that which you have received, let him be anathema*. He does not say "more than you have received," but *other than you have received*. For if he had said the former, he would have spoken in a way prejudicial to himself, since he wanted to go to the Thessalonians in order to supply what was lacking in their faith. But one who thus supplements adds what was missing; he does not take away what was there. On the other hand, one who transgresses the rule of faith does not advance on the way; he departs from the way.

Responsory   *Sir 42:15-16; 43:28*

By the words of the Lord his works come into being, and all creation obeys his will. † As the sun as it shines looks upon all things, so the work of the Lord is full of his glory.

V. Where can we find the power to praise him, since he is greater than all his works? † As the sun . . .

FRIDAY   Year II

First Reading   Philippians 3:17—4:9

Responsory   *Eph 4:17; 1 Thes 5:15-18*

I urge you in the Lord's name to stop living as the pagans live with their worthless concerns. Always seek to do what is best for one another and for everyone; † for this is what God wants you to do in Christ Jesus.

V. Rejoice always, pray constantly, and always give thanks.† For this is . . .

Second Reading   From a sermon by Cardinal John Henry Newman *(Sermon on the Subjects of the Day, 278-282)*

This is the very definition of a Christian — one who looks for Christ

The first great and obvious characteristic of a Bible Christian, if I may use that much abused term, is to be without worldly ties or objects, to be living in this world, but not for this world. Saint Paul says, *our conversation is in heaven,* or in other words, heaven is our city. We know what it is to be a citizen of the world; it is to have interests, rights, privileges, duties, connections, in some particular town or state; to depend upon it, and to be bound to defend it; to be part of it. Now all this the Christian is in respect to heaven. Heaven is his city, earth is not. Or, at least, so it was as regards the Christians of scripture. *Here,* as the same apostle says in another place, *we have no continuing city, but we seek one to come.* And therefore he adds to the former of these texts, *from whence also we look for the Savior, the Lord Jesus Christ.*

This is the very definition of a Christian — one who looks for Christ; not who looks for gain, or distinction, or power, or pleasure, or comfort, but who looks *for the Savior, the Lord Jesus Christ.* This, according to scripture, is the essential mark, this is the foundation of a Christian, from which everything else follows; whether he is rich or poor, high or low, is a further matter, which may be considered apart; but he surely is a primitive Christian, and he only, who has no aim of this world, who has no wish to be other in this world than he is; whose thoughts and aims have relation to the unseen, the future world; who has lost his taste for this world, sweet and bitter being the same to him; who fulfills the same apostle's exhortation in another epistle, *Set your affection on things above, not on things on the earth, for you are dead, and your life is hid with Christ in God. When Christ, who is our life, shall appear, then shall you also appear with him in glory.*

Hence it follows that watching is a special mark of the Scripture Christian, as our Lord so emphatically sets before us: *Watch, therefore, for you know not what hour your Lord will come.*

And Saint Peter, who once suffered for lack of watching, repeats the lesson: *The end of all things is at hand; be therefore sober, and watch in prayer.* And accordingly, prayer as Saint Peter enjoins in the last text is another characteristic of Christians as described in scripture. They knew not what hour their Lord would come, and therefore they watched and prayed in every hour, lest they should enter into temptation. *They were continually in the temple praising and blessing God.*

This habit of prayer, then, recurrent prayer, morning, noon, and night, is one discriminating point in Scripture Christianity, as arising from the text with which I began, *our conversation is in heaven.*

In a word, there was no barrier, no cloud, no earthly object, interposed between the soul of the primitive Christian and its savior and redeemer. Christ was in his heart, and therefore all that come from his heart, his thoughts, words, and actions, savored of Christ.

Observe this well, my brethren; religion, you see, begins with the heart, but it does not end with the heart. It begins with the conversion of the heart from earth to heaven, the stripping off and casting away all worldly aims; but it does not end there; it did not end there in the Christians whom scripture describes, whom our Lord's precepts formed: it drew up all the faculties of the soul, all the members of the body, to him who was in their heart.

Responsory   *Ps 18:7-8; 118:105*

The law of the Lord is perfect; it revives the soul. † The precepts of the Lord are right; they gladden the heart.
V. Your work is a lamp for my feet, and a light for my path. † The precepts . . .

SATURDAY   Year II

First Reading   Philippians 4:10-23

Responsory   *Phil 4:12-13; 2 Cor 12:10*

I know what it is like to be rich and what it is like to be poor. I have eaten well and gone hungry, have experienced poverty and plenty. † With Christ's help I can do all things.

V. For the sake of Christ I am content with my weaknesses and frustrations. † With Christ's help . . .

Second Reading   From the writings of Meister Eckhart
                     (Talks of Instructions 18)

Let nothing touch your mind with power and love but God alone

You need not worry about food and drink, as to whether they seem too good for you, but train your ground and your mind to be far above such things. Let nothing touch your mind with power and love but God alone — it should be exalted above all else. Why? Because that would be a feeble kind of inwardness that the outward dress could correct. Rather should the inward correct the outer, if it rests entirely with you. But if it just comes to you, you can from your ground accept it as good, just as you would put up with it if it were different, and would be glad and willing to endure it. The same applies to food, friends and relations and to whatever else God gives you or takes from you.

And that I consider better than anything, that a man should fully abandon himself to God when he would cast anything upon him, be it disgrace, trouble or whatever kind of suffering it might be, accepting it with joy and gratitude, allowing oneself rather to be led by God than plunging into it oneself. So just learn all things gladly from God and follow him, and all will go well with you. In that way you can well take honor or comfort, but in such a way that, if discomfort and dishonor were to be a man's lot, he would likewise be able and willing to bear them. *Then* they may rightly and legitimately feast, who would have been as ready and willing to fast. And that is doubtless why God spares his friends much great suffering; for otherwise his measureless good faith would not permit this, seeing that so much great profit resides in suffering, and he would not and ought not to deprive them of any good thing. He is satisfied with the good will, otherwise he would not omit any suffering, on account of the innumerable benefits suffering brings.

And so, so long as God is satisfied, rest content: and when something different pleases him in regard to you, be also content. For a man should inwardly be so wholly for God with all his will, that he should worry little about the way or about works.

Responsory   *Ps 118:33.34; Ps 18:8*

Teach me the demands of your statutes — and I will keep them to
the end. † Train me to observe your law, to keep it with my whole
heart.

V. The precepts of the Lord are right, they gladden the heart. † Train
me . . .

ELEVENTH WEEK IN ORDINARY TIME

SUNDAY Year II

First Reading Isaiah 44:21—45:3

Responsory *Is 44:24.22*
Return to me, for I have redeemed you. † Raise a glad cry, you heavens.
V. I formed you to be a servant to me. † Raise a glad . . .

Second Reading From a commentary by Saint John Chrysostom (In Ps. 125, 1: Bareille IX, 491-493)

We leap for joy

When the Lord returned the captives to Zion, we were like people who are comforted. If it was a comfort for them to be released from a barbaric nation, how much more should we not be glad and leap for joy at being set free from sin, and preserve that joy always, never destroying or disturbing it by falling again into the same faults?

Then our mouths were filled with joy and our tongues with gladness. Then they will say among the nations: the Lord has done great things for them. The Lord has done great things for us. To rejoice at deliverance from captivity helps not a little to inspire people with nobler sentiments. But who, you may ask, would not rejoice at this? The ancestors of these people did not. When they were released from Egypt and set free from slavery, they were so ungrateful that in the midst of all their benefits they did nothing but grumble, and were angry and embittered and perpetually distraught. But we are not like that, says the psalmist; we leap for joy.

Let us learn the reason for their joy. We do not only rejoice, they say, because of our deliverance from terrible suffering, but because it will make the whole world know God's care for us. For as the psalmist says: *Then they will say among the nations: The Lord has done great things for them. The Lord has done great things for us.* There is no repetition here; the words are meant to describe their joy. The first saying is that of the nations, the second is their own. Notice this too: they did not say "He saved us," or "He delivered us," but "He did great things for us," for they wanted to show the incredible event in all its wonder.

Can you not see that this people gave a lesson to the whole world when they were carried off into captivity as well as when they returned? For their return preached its own message. News of them went round everywhere and made God's love for humankind known to everyone, because the wonderful things he had done for them were truly great and incredible. Cyrus himself, who had them in his power, set them free without anyone asking him because God made him relent.

Responsory   *Ps 68:3; 1 Cor 2:9*
    The righteous shall rejoice before God, † they shall exult and dance for joy.
    V. Eye has not seen, nor ear heard, nor human heart conceived what God has prepared for those who love him. † They shall . . .

MONDAY   Year II

First Reading   Ezra 1:1-8; 2:68—3:8

Responsory   *Ezra 1:2-3*
    All the kingdoms of the earth the Lord, the God of heaven, has given to me, and he also charged me † to build him a house in Jerusalem.
    V. Everyone went up. † To build him . . .

Second Reading   From a commentary by Saint Bede of England
                          (In Esdram et Nehemiam: PL 91, 812-813)

Let us build a house to the Lord

Whoever is among you of all his people, may his God be with him, and let him go up to Jerusalem which is in Judah and rebuild the house of the Lord.

A great faith shines out in these words of King Cyrus, and a great love. He understood that the people of Israel, above all other nations, was the people of God, and he gave leave to all without exception who wished to return to their native land to do so as free men. He acknowledged that the Lord God who dwelt in heaven dwelt also in Jerusalem and could go up with each one of those returning from Babylon to Jerusalem. Is it not clearer than daylight that he believed this God to be non-corporeal, unrestricted by place, a spirit, present everywhere; whom he acknowledged dwelt in Jerusalem and its temple yet without doubting that he held sway simultaneously in the kingdom of heaven; whom he believed reigned in heaven yet was with his faithful on earth, guiding their hands and hearts to accomplish what was good and salutary? For the rest, all the words of this text are full of spiritual significance.

For who does not easily recognize that it is only those whom God is with who can pass from sinfulness to sanctity — from captivity in Babylon to freedom in Jerusalem? *Without me*, Christ says, *you can do nothing*. Can anyone fail to see here a reference to the spiritual ascent, the "going-up" to Jerusalem? Those who really desire to please God must necessarily lift up their hands to higher things, long for what is divine and transcend the display of this world and its attractions through their love of eternal reality. We are reminded that Jerusalem is in Judah, so that we who through disregard of God were once held captive by the Chaldeans and thereafter freed from malign spirits, may return to the vision of peace and light by our recognition of God's love. And there let us build a house to the Lord God of Israel — in the unity of catholic peace, in the acknowledgment of our sinfulness and God's loving-kindness and grace. Let us prepare our hearts so that he himself may deign to dwell in them and enlighten them by his presence. But let us also take care to set the hearts of our neighbors alight, so that they too may praise their creator and engage in the works of love. Indeed, either way we build a house to the Lord: whether we commit ourselves to the pursuit of holiness or, by our words and example, inspire those whom we can to walk in the way of holiness.

Responsory   *Ps 113:1.3.5*

When Israel came forth from Egypt, the house of Jacob from an alien people, † the sea fled at the sight; the Jordan turned back on its course.

V. Why was it, sea, that you fled, that you turned back, Jordan, on your course? † The sea fled . . .

TUESDAY   Year II

First Reading   Ezra 4:1-5.24—5:5

Responsory   *Ezra 1:2-3*
All the kingdoms of the earth the Lord, the God of heaven, has given
to me, and he also charged me † to build him a house in Jerusalem.
V. Everyone went up. † To build him . . .

Second Reading   From a commentary by Saint Hilary of
                      Poitiers (In Ps. 126, 3-8: CSEL 22, 615-619)

God's house and temple

*Unless the Lord build the house for himself, they labor in vain who
build it.* The hearing of the psalm, then, is not restricted to the days
of Solomon, but is to be understood also as appropriate to those of
Haggaeus. Either labor, whether Solomon's building or Haggaeus', is in vain, it says. For of the city built by Zorababel, today
there remain only the ashes from the conflagration and the ugly
sight of ruin and devastation. These seats of kings, where the
builders thought to restore the glory of the eternal kingdom, have
undergone further destruction as the seat of every other kingdom,
one after another, has been overthrown. For it to endure, then, a
house ought to be built by God; for unless it be built by the Lord,
it will not last.

As to which house is God's we are to understand that this can
be ascertained from how long it is built to last. So it is that houses,
in the sense of buildings, do not bespeak an infinite God as their
owner; neither can his unlimited power be confined in some place,
the omnipotence that made all things. As the Apostle bears witness: *The God who made the world and everything in it, he who is
Lord of heaven and earth, dwells not in temples made by the hands of
men.*

Is there, then, no repose in God, no dwelling place for him?
Some people might suppose that he who is nowhere ought to be
non-existent. So let us hear his own testimony about his rest and
his dwelling place. This is what he says: *This is my resting place for
ever; here will I live, for I have chosen it.* Now it is Zion that he chose:
but is that the place about which the lament in this prophecy is

being made? *Unless the Lord build the house* (it says) *they labor in vain who build it.* Zion, where the temple stood, has been turned upside down. So where is the Lord's seat and eternal dwelling place now? What precisely is that temple which is fit for his habitation? It is the one of which it was said: *You are a temple of God; and the Spirit of God dwells in you.* This is God's house and his temple; it is full of the teaching and the power of God, a becoming residence for the holiness of the divine love. To this, the same prophet bears testimony: *Thy holy temple, wonderful in its proportions.* The holiness of men, their judiciousness and self-restraint — *that* is the temple of God.

The house, then, must be built by God. Any house made by the works of men will not endure; neither can any based on the maxims of this world stand its ground; neither can our vain labors and useless worry have any lasting effect. The construction and the maintenance must be otherwise. The beginnings must not be made on water and shifting sands, but foundations laid on the prophets and the apostles. Then living stones must serve to build it up; the cornerstone to keep it in place and hold it together; the interlocking pieces making up the whole man, built on the scale of Christ's body, to be adorned by the beauty and elegance of spiritual graces. What is built by God, that is to say his teachings, will not fall down. Israel, once made captive after the abundance and prosperity of the nations, will now secure the building of this house. This house is itself growing, into more houses, so as to build up the faithful at every turn and to beautify and extend that blessed city in each one of us.

Responsory   Ps 43:3.2

Their own sword did not win them the land, nor their own arm give them victory. † It was your right hand, your arm, and the light of your face, for you loved them.
V. Our fathers have told us the story of the deeds you did in their days. † It was your . . .

WEDNESDAY   Year II

First Reading   Haggai 1:1—2:10

Responsory   *Hg 1:8; Is 56:7*
Go up into the hill country and build a house; † and I will take
pleasure in it, says the Lord.
V. My house shall be called a house of prayer for all nations. † And
I will . . .

Second Reading   From the writings of Jacques Bossuet
(Élévations sur les Mystères, Oeuvres Complètes VII, 183-185)

The second temple

Because the coming of Jesus Christ was prepared from the
beginning of the world, and the whole of the law was, so to speak,
pregnant with it and quite ready to bring it to birth, God left his
holy people without prophets and without prophecies for four or
five hundred years. He wanted to give them this time to think them
over and long for the Savior. Just before he put an end to the
prophecies, that is, in the days of Daniel, Haggai, Zechariah and
Malachi, he revealed the divine mysteries more clearly than ever
before.

Haggai had said these memorable words in praise of the second
temple: *Once again, in a little while*: for what was four hundred
years or so in comparison with so many thousands of centuries in
which the people had waited for the Savior? *Once again, then, in a
little while, I shall shake heaven and earth, and fill with splendor this
house newly rebuilt*, namely, the second temple, *says the Lord of
hosts, the almighty God. The splendor of this second house will be
greater than that of the first; and I shall establish peace in this place,
says the Lord of hosts.*

If it is the outward magnificence of the temple that ought to
claim our attention, the splendor of the first temple, under the
wealthy rule of Solomon, Jehoshaphat, Hezekiah, and the other
kings, is without question the greatest. Far from the second temple
having an equal magnificence, those who were rebuilding it and
had seen the first could not keep back their tears as they saw how
inferior it was to the first. It is true that in course of time the second
temple achieved great splendor in the East: people saw the gifts of

kings being taken there; and I do not know if Herod, who rebuilt it, did not rise to the magnificence of Solomon in doing so. But after all and be that as it may, there is nothing there worth *shaking heaven and earth* about: and such a vast movement ought to end in something greater than earthly riches. This, then, is *the vast movement of heaven and earth*: it heralds the expected appearance of Christ in this second temple. Another prophet of the same time explains it: *I am sending my messenger,* Malachi says, speaking in the name of the Lord, *to prepare the way before me: and it is then that the Lord will come to his temple, the Lord whom you seek, and the messenger of the testament* or covenant, *whom you desire. There he is coming, the Lord says.* Nothing is left in doubt: there is nothing new left to do.

Responsory   *Ps 88:2.9; Ps:5:2*
Let my prayer come into your presence; incline your ear to my cry.
† I call to you, Lord, all the day long; to you I stretch out my hands.
V. Hearken to the sound of my cries, my king and my God. † I call . . .

THURSDAY   Year II

First Reading   Haggai 2:11-24

Responsory   *Hg 2:6.7.9*
I will shake the heavens and the earth, † and the treasures of all the nations will come in.
V. The glory of this house will be great; I will give peace in this place. † And the treasures . . .

Second Reading   From the writings of Cardinal Jean Daniélou
                        (*The Presence of God,* 20-25)

The two temples

The glory of the Lord dwelt in the temple until the coming of the incarnation. but from that day it began to dwell in Jesus. The very word that Saint John uses to describe the incarnation — *dwelt among us* — is that which indicates the dwelling of God in the temple. And the presence of God which overshadows the Virgin is the same cloud whose presence showed that Yahweh dwelt in the tabernacle.

Thus the manhood of Jesus became the new temple and "the place where your honor dwells." It is this that Christ proclaimed to the Samaritan woman when he told her: *The hour will come, when you shall neither in this mountain, nor yet at Jerusalem, worship the Father, when the true worshipers shall worship the Father in spirit and in truth.* That is to say, not that they will not worship in any temple, but that they will worship in the true temple of the Spirit, as opposed to the figurative temple of the flesh. This is why Christ was able to reply to the Pharisees who accused him of misunderstanding the temple: *In this place is one greater than the temple.* From that time, the temple of stone might be destroyed; it would be of no importance since after three days the true temple was to be finally established. And indeed, three days after the veil of the temple was rent, the temple of the new law, the glorified manhood of Jesus, was raised up forevermore.

But between these two moments, between the appearance of the new temple at the incarnation and the end of the old temple at the passion, there was a unique period during which the two temples existed side by side, and the mystery of their connection, of their joint construction, was shown in a marvelous light. This encounter between the reality and the figure, a living and historical encounter, took place for the first time at the presentation. This was truly a unique moment in the sequence of periods. Up till then, there had been only a figurative temple, an image of that which was to come, a sign also of the promise to David. But here we see at once the figure and the reality, the promise and the gift. It is in the very heart of the figure that the reality was manifested, in the heart of the promise that the gift was conveyed.

To carnal eyes, there is a child in the temple; to the eyes of Simeon, unsealed by the Holy Spirit, this child is more than the temple. He is the one for whom the temple has kept ceaseless vigil. The temple is now rendered useless.

The temple was only a shadow. Now the light is come; all the candles are lighted in the hands of the faithful. "Soon shall the angel of the covenant come into the temple." The riddle is suddenly unraveled before Simeon's eyes; he grasps this connection between the figure and the reality which is the whole meaning of scripture. Israel had lived by scripture without fully possessing the key — and here today it is given to her. Israel may disappear: *Nunc dimittis*. Simeon holds in the palms of his hands, in the midst of the temple, the master of the temple.

Responsory   *Ps 5:7; Is 6:3*

Through the greatness of your love I have access to your house. † I bow down before your holy temple, filled with awe.
V. Holy, holy, holy is the Lord of hosts; the whole earth is full of his glory. † I bow down . . .

FRIDAY   Year II

First Reading   Zechariah 1:1—2:4

Responsory   *Zec 1:16; Rv 21:23*

I turn to Jerusalem in compassion; † there my house shall be rebuilt.
V. The city had no need of the sun or the moon for light, for its lamp was the Lamb. † There my house . . .

Second Reading   From a homily by Saint Gregory the Great
(Hom. 2 in Ez. 1, 5: CCL 142, 210-212)

The heavenly Jerusalem is built as a city

For precisely because that vision of inward peace is made up of a community of saints as its citizens, the heavenly Jerusalem is built as a city. Even while, in this earthly life, its citizens are lashed by whips and subjected to oppression, its stones are being quarried every day.

It is also the city, namely, the holy Church, which is to reign in heaven but is still toiling on earth. It is to its citizens that Peter says: *And you are being built up like living stones.* Paul also says: *You are God's land, God's building.* Clearly the city already has its great building here on earth in the lives of the saints. In a building, of course, one stone supports another, since they are placed one on top of another, and one supporting another is itself supported by another. So in the same way, in the holy Church, every member both supports and is supported by the other. For neighbors give each other mutual support, so that the building of love may rise through them. Hence too Paul's instruction to us: *Bear each other's burdens, and in that way you will fulfill the law of Christ*; and he proclaims the virtue of this law, saying: *It is love which fulfills the law.*

For if I neglect to support you in the way you live, and you pay little attention to supporting me in mine, how will the building of love rise among us? He alone who supports the whole fabric of the holy Church supports us in our good ways and our faults as well. But in a building, as we have said, the supporting stone is itself supported. For just as I already support the ways of those whose behavior in the matter of good works is still unformed, so I too am supported by those who have surpassed me in the fear of the Lord, and yet have supported me, so that I myself should learn to support through being supported. But they have also been supported by their predecessors.

However the stones placed at the top of the building to finish it off, though supported of course by others, have no one to support in turn. For those, too, who are born at the Church's end, that is, at the end of the world, will certainly be supported by their predecessors, to dispose them to behave in a way that leads to good works; but when they have none to follow them who could profit by them, they have no more stones to support for the building of the faithful above them. So for the time being they are supported by us, and we are supported by others. However it is the foundation that carries the entire weight of the building, because our Redeemer alone supports the lives of all of us together. As Paul says of him: *For no one can lay any foundation other than the one that has been laid, which is Christ Jesus.* The foundation supports the stones and is not supported by the stones, because our Redeemer supports us in all our troubles, but in himself there was no evil demanding support.

Responsory   *Ps 37:1-3.16*

Do not fret because of the wicked, or envy those who do evil, for soon they will fade like the grass, and wither like green pasture.
† Trust in the Lord and do good, and you will live in the land and be secure.
V. The few possessions of the righteous are better than the wealth of the wicked. † Trust in the . . .

Alternative Reading

From a commentary by Carroll Stuhlmueller (*Rebuilding with Hope*, 56-57)

God's initiative in repentance

The prophetical imperative, *return to me, says the Lord of hosts, and I will return to you, says the Lord of hosts*, seems to condition our return to grace upon our own human initiative. Yet at once this position is challenged by the thrice repeated formula, *thus says the Lord of hosts*, as though we never would have thought of it, had the Lord not drummed the idea into us! We are reminded of the penitent woman in Luke 7:36-50, whose return to grace, Jesus declared, was due to her love: *her sins, which are many, are forgiven, for she loved much.* Yet the bold initiative of the sinful woman, entering an august and forbidding assembly of law-abiding people, meant that she had been observing the kind and compassionate Jesus and may have even heard him say: *I have not come to call the righteous, but sinners to repentance.*

The strong love of God, attracting us to a new confidence in divine compassion and forgiveness, appears magnificently in what is the centerpiece of the book of Exodus. Exodus is probably Israel's most important book of covenant and law, and at its center these three chapters provide an exceptional method for interpreting law. We first observe Moses' shattering the tablets of the law at the sight of Israel's idolatry, then his intense desire to see the face of the Lord in all its glory, and finally the awesome moment, when Moses stood atop Mount Sinai with a new set of tablets in his arms and heard the Lord passing by and declaring: *The Lord, the Lord, a God merciful and gracious, slow to anger, and abounding in steadfast love and faithfulness, keeping steadfast love for thousands, forgiving iniquity and transgression and sin, but who will by no means clear the guilty, visiting the iniquity of the fathers to the third and the fourth generation.*

Such blinding glory thereafter emanated from Moses' face that he had to wear a veil over it except when conversing with God.

Law is to be interpreted from the setting of the Lord's *steadfast love and faithfulness for thousands of generations*, and in this way does it lead to a mystic union with God. This contemplative wonder of faith and this loving bond with God must subsist within liturgy, otherwise liturgy will degenerate into idolatry. This vision of God's luminous compassion "will by no means clear the guilty." Sin is rightly understood as an evil act that brings its own fallout of sorrow and guilt. Unless sin is called by its right name, forgiveness and compassion become meaningless. Yet punishment, extending *to the third and the fourth generation,* is surpassed by compassion *for thousands of generations.* It is the faith-perception of such a God, already suffused within Israel, which first beckons toward repentance and anticipates any initiative on our part to return to the Lord. God's anger toward the sinful is swallowed up within God's compassion for the repentant sinner.

Responsory   *Ps 37:1-3.16*

Do not fret because of the wicked, or envy those who do evil, for soon they will fade like the grass, and wither like green pasture. † Trust in the Lord and do good, and you will live in the land and be secure.

V. The few possessions of the righteous are better than the wealth of the wicked. † Trust in the . . .

SATURDAY   Year II

First Reading   Zechariah 2:5-17

Responsory   *Zec 2:8-9*

Run, tell this to that young man: † People will live in Jerusalem as though in open country, because of the multitude of men and beasts in her midst.

V. I will be for her an encircling wall of fire. † People will live . . .

Second Reading   From a commentary by Saint Cyril of Alexandria (In Zachariam Prophetam: PG 72, 40)

The whole world was made splendid by the preaching of the gospel

Be delighted and rejoice, daughter of Zion, because I am coming and shall dwell among you, says the Lord. And many nations will flee for refuge to the Lord in that day and become his people, and they will dwell in your midst.

Even from this you may understand that the Savior's coming will be the occasion of the sublimest joy for those on earth. For of necessity he commanded the spiritual Zion to be delighted and glad, since she is the Church of the living God, or rather she is the holiest multitude of those saved through faith. And he promised he would come, and would certainly live among her people.

For Saint John tells us: *He was in the world*, and *the Word who was God* did not hold aloof from his created beings. But it was he who gave life to those partaking of life, and who also sustains all things for their own well-being in life. But *the world refused to recognize him*, for it "worshiped created things." Yet he came among us when, assuming our own likeness, he was born of the Holy Virgin. When too he *appeared on earth and lived among men and women*. And holy David will also bear witness, saying: *God, our God, will come visibly, and will not keep silence*. Then too he became visible to the Gentiles.

For it was no longer only the Israelites who were being taught by the old commandment. But rather the whole world was made splendid by the preaching of the gospel, and the Lord's name became great among all the nations and in every land. For he was *the expectation* of the nations, as the prophet says. And *every knee* will bow to him *in heaven, on earth and in hell, and every tongue confess that Jesus Christ is Lord, to the glory of God the Father*. For the nations ran together in faith toward him, and dwelt with him in the holy spiritual Zion, coming from the ends of the earth. And they understood clearly that God loved the world so much *that he gave his only Son so that all who believed in him should not perish but have eternal life*. For the Father sent his Son to us from heaven, as savior and redeemer, so that we should believe in him and see in him the Father. And so that looking at him, the exact image of the Father from whom he was born according to nature, we should think of the original.

Responsory   *1 Cor 10:11-12; Is 48:15*

These things happened as warnings and were written down for our instruction. Therefore † let those who think they are standing firm be careful or they may fall.

V. I myself have spoken and called him, brought him and prospered his plans. † Let those who . . .

TWELFTH WEEK IN ORDINARY TIME

SUNDAY   Year II

First Reading   Zechariah 3:1—4:14

Responsory   *Rv 11:4, see 3*
These are the two olive trees and two lampstands † that stand in
the presence of the Lord of the earth.
V. The Lord shall select his two witnesses to prophesy. † That stand
in . . .

Second Reading   From a commentary by Saint Cyril of
Alexandria (In Zachariam Prophetam: PG 72, 64-65)

Emmanuel

*This is the word of the Lord concerning Zerubbabel: Not by great
power, nor by force, but by my Spirit, says the Almighty Lord.* This
is the same as saying that all that Zechariah had just seen would
come to completion at the appointed time, not as the achievement
of human power, nor by physical force, but by the power of the
Holy Spirit, and as at a sign from God.

For the Only Son was made human like ourselves. However,
he did not engage in physical combat to set up the Church as a light
to the world. Nor did he wield arms in a literal sense, drawing up
the two nations in warlike battlelines around him. He did not even
provide the lampstand with spiritual lamps, but by the force of the
Holy Spirit he first appointed apostles in the Churches, next prophets and evangelists and the rest of the holy assembly, filling them
full of God's gifts and enriching them with the Spirit in abundant
profusion.

So it was neither by great power nor by the physical strength
of Christ but by the power of the Spirit that Satan was despoiled,
and the whole horde of hostile powers fell with him, and that the
Israelites and those who formerly "worshiped created things
rather than the creator" were called through faith to knowledge of
God. Lamps were revealed in the Churches too, the saints who
shone out together with the lantern, that is, Christ. For they be-

came, as Paul writes in his great wisdom, *stars in the universe, holding fast to the word of life.*

Again, the fact that it was not by human hand but by his own powers as God that Emmanuel saved the world he solemnly affirmed through the mouth of Hosea. These are his words: *but I shall have mercy on the children of Judah, and I shall save them — not by bow and arrow, sword, war, chariots, horses or horsemen, but by the Lord their God.* But he gave the clearest message to Zerubbabel, of the tribe of Judah, and at that time placed in the position of king of Jerusalem. For in case he thought that the splendid and marvelous achievements foretold for him meant wars, and it was fighting that would begin at the appointed time, the Lord had to drive such unsound human thoughts out of his mind, and instead commanded him to understand that it was by activity worthy of God and not by human power that Christ would bring such things to a conclusion. And then we remember saying that in himself Zerubbabel signified Christ, since he was of the tribe of Judah and a king, but he was also this in conjunction with Jesus the son of Jehozadak, so that Emmanuel might be understood as both king and high priest at once in the same person.

Responsory   *Ps 55:22; 37:5*

Entrust your cares to the Lord and he will support you. † He will never allow the righteous to stumble.

V. Commit your life to the Lord; trust in him and he will act. † He will never . . .

MONDAY   Year II

First Reading   Zechariah 8:1-17.20-23

Responsory   *Zec 8:7.9; Acts 3:25*

Thus says the Lord: I will rescue my people from the lands of the east and the lands of the west. † Let your hands be strong, you who hear these words proclaimed by the prophets.

V. You are the children of the prophets, heirs of the covenant God made with our fathers. † Let your hands . . .

Second Reading   From the writings of Walter Hilton
(*The Ladder of Perfection* II, 3)

This is the way

There was a man that would go to Jerusalem, and because he did not know the way, he asked another man, who he believed knew the way better than him. When he asked him whether he would come to Jerusalem or not, the man answered that he could go no further without great pains and hardships, saying the way is long and perilous, and full of great thieves and robbers, and many other hindrances that come to pass to a man along the way. Nevertheless, there is one way, if one takes and sticks to it, that I am sure one will come to that city of Jerusalem, and never lose one's life, nor be slain, nor die by default. Though he would often be robbed and beaten, and suffer much pain along the way, his life will be safe.

Then said the pilgrim, "So I may have my life saved, and come to the place that I covet, I care not what mischief I suffer in going."

That other man answered and said, "Lo, I set you in the right way. This is the way, and see that you bear in mind all that I tell you. Whatsoever you see, hear, or feel, that would hinder you in the way, stick not at it, willingly consent not to it, abide not with it, behold it not, like it not, fear it not, but still go forward holding on your way, and ever think and say with yourself that you would rather be at Jerusalem. Jerusalem is, as much as to say, a sight of peace, and beholds contemplation in perfect love of God, for contemplation is nothing else but a sight of God, which is very peace.

The beginning of the highway, in which you shall go, is reforming in faith, and grounded humbly on the faith and on the laws of holy Church as I have said before. For trust assuredly, though you have sinned up to now, if you are now reformed by the sacrament of penance, after the law of holy Church, you are on the right way. Now then, since you are in the safe way, if you hurry along in your going and make a good journey, it behooves you to hold these two things often in mind: *Humility and Love*; and often say to yourself, *I am nothing, I have nothing, I covet nothing, but one*. Humility says, *I am nothing, I have nothing*; Love says, *I covet nothing, but one*, and that is Jesus.

And if you do all this, then you shall resolve in your heart fully and wholly that you will be at Jerusalem, and at no other place but there; that is, your heart shall have wholly and fully nothing but the love of Jesus and the spiritual sight of him in such manner as he shall please to show himself; for to that end only are you made and redeemed, and he it is that is your beginning and your end, your joy and your bliss.

Responsory   *Ps 149:2-4*
Let Israel rejoice in its Maker; let the people of Zion exult in their king. † Let them praise his name with dancing, and sing psalms to him with timbrel and lyre.
V. For the Lord accepts the service of his people; he crowns the humble with victory. † Let them praise . . .

Alternative Reading

From a commentary by Saint Cyril of Alexandria (In Zachariam prophetam: PG 72, 109-111)

The Church worships in spirit and in truth

These are the Lord's words: I shall return to Zion and dwell in Jerusalem. Then Jerusalem will be called the true city, and the mountain of the almighty Lord the holy mountain.

God fills the universe, and the universe is full of his ineffable nature. However, sometimes he is said to abandon sinners, not that he departs from them in a spatial sense (it would be silly to think that), but by no longer wishing to pay attention to them, and thinking them no longer worthy of mercy or love. That is his way of showing his anger, we say. The result was that Israel turned to false worship, and Jerusalem became unfaithful.

So the God of the universe as it were abandoned them, and exposed them to the evils that followed from his turning away. But when he at last had mercy on them, he said: "I shall return," that is, I shall give up being angry, and show how much my care is worth and rebuild my house. For when he had as it were turned away, the holy mountain, that is, the temple in Jerusalem, no longer seemed to be a holy place, at least to those who saw it burnt down. So when it was raised again and God had decided to dwell in it, worship would once more be revived within it. Then Jerusalem would be called the true city, no longer offering worship to artificial gods and images with false names as it did before, but serving the one, by nature true God properly, through its decision to live an upright life in future, in ready obedience to all God's commands.

With good reason you could apply such sayings to the Word, who was born for us in our own likeness. Although he was in the form of and in complete equality with the Father, *he emptied himself, taking the form of a servant, and was born as a human being. And he became poor for us, so that through his poverty we might be rich.* Therefore although long ago God rightly turned away because of Adam's transgression, and the fact that *from youth onward the human mind was prone to evil,* he turned back to us as if out of his own innate kindness at last, and dwelt in the Church, and made a city and a holy dwelling-place out of his consecrated people. For he spoke somewhere of a chosen place, and obviously the Church, saying: *Here I shall dwell for it is the place I have chosen.* Blessed David also says in the psalm: *Glorious things are spoken of you, city of God.* The prophet Isaiah told us about this too, when he said: *In the last days the mountain of the Lord will be revealed, and the house of God will be seen on the highest mountain raised far above the hills, and all nations will come to it.* For the Church of Christ is in a commanding position, and as if it stood on a mountain it is known to everyone everywhere. Then it is also called "true," certainly not because it worships symbols and foreshadowings, but rather because it has received the truth, which is Christ, it also worships in spirit and truth.

Responsory   *Ps 91:11-12; Heb 12:1*

He will charge his angels to guard you wherever you go; † they will bear you upon their hands that you may not strike your foot against a stone.

V. Since we are surrounded by so great a cloud of witnesses, let us run with resolution the race that lies before us, our eyes fixed on Jesus, the pioneer and perfecter of our faith. † They will bear . . .

TUESDAY   Year II

First Reading   Ezra 6:1-5.14-22

Responsory   *Mt 9:13; Hos 6:6.4*

Go and learn the meaning of these words: † I want a loving heart
more than sacrifice, knowledge of my ways more than holocausts.
V. Your love is like the morning cloud, the dew that swiftly fades
away. † I want a . . .

Second Reading   From a commentary by Saint Bede of England
                      (In Esdram et Nehemiam Allegorica expositio II, 7: PL 91, 858)

The sacrifice of the passover hints at the glory of the resurrection

And they celebrated the feast of unleavened bread, etc. Now the
Apostle teaches us how we must celebrate the feast in spirit, when
he says: *Let us therefore keep the feast, not in the old leaven, nor in
the leaven of malice and iniquity, but in the fresh leaven of sincerity
and truth.* Seven days of celebrating go into that: for throughout
our time in this world, however many days it may run, we are to
live our lives in sincerity and truth, and indeed in every kind of
sacrifice and offering. For our blessed Lord himself tasted death
for a time at Eastertide, only to vanquish it by the eternal power of
his resurrection. And our celebration of Easter here and now can
be taken to represent symbolically our resurrection. Hence just as
the building of the temple stands for the present condition of Holy
Church, so the dedication of it symbolizes the life that is to come,
consisting in the rejoicing of the holy souls who have left the life
of the body behind. The sacrifice of the passover hints at the glory
of the resurrection, when no longer will all the elect need to be
refreshed by the flesh of the spotless Lamb — that is, our Lord and
our God — in the sacrament, as believers; for they will be refreshed
indeed by seeing him as he is in very truth. Wherefore in this
passover all priests and levites, all the congregations of the people,
all those who had joined them from among the Gentiles, are held
to have been of the world, all brought into one, as it were; for truly
then will the Lamb of God have taken away the sins of the world.
And as Saint John the Apostle said: *The blood of Jesus the Son of God
cleanses us of all sin.* Then there will be true unity, for God will be
all in all. Then the true feast of unleavened bread will be celebrated

with rejoicing with no leaven of malice or wickedness remaining among the elect, but all clinging in truth and in sincerity of heart, to the vision of God. And all this will come to pass, not in seven days of this changing world, but in that one day of eternal life within the courts of the Lord which is better than thousands, and in the light of the holy Spirit whose sevenfold grace the prophet commends to us.

Responsory   *Is 55:8-9; Heb 11:2*
My thoughts are not your thoughts, nor are your ways my ways, says the Lord. † For as the heavens are high above the earth, so are my ways above your ways, and my thoughts above your thoughts.
V. It was for their faith that the people of former times won God's approval. † For as the . . .

WEDNESDAY   Year II

First Reading   Ezra 7:6-28

Responsory   *Canticle 8:6-7; Jn 15:13*
Love is as strong as death; its flames are like a blazing fire. † Deep waters cannot quench love.
V. There is no greater love than this: to lay down your life for your friends. † Deep waters cannot quench love.

Second Reading   From the letters of Gregory of Nyssa
(De Virginitate 24: PG 46, 414-416)

Crucified with Christ

You have been crucified with Christ; offer yourself to God as a pure priest

Look at the man who has reached perfection, and boldly embark on that noble voyage with the inspiration of the Holy Spirit, guided by Christ, your pilot, at the joyful helm.

For if there is danger in a single contact with sin, and for that reason you think it unsafe to aim too high, how much harder it is if you make sin a perpetual habit, and therefore have no part at all in the purer life. How will you obey the voice of the crucified, you who live thus? He died to sin, and you flourish in it. He commanded you to follow him, as he carried the cross on his body like a trophy of victory over the devil, but you have refused to be crucified to the world and spurn mortification of the flesh. You defy Paul's summons: *to offer yourself as a living sacrifice, holy and well-pleasing to God.* You conform to the world, instead of being renewed in mind and thence transformed; far from walking in this new way of life, you are still busy following the old unregenerate ways.

You do not serve God as a priest, although anointed for the very purpose of offering a gift to God — but not something completely alien, or a counterfeit presented from the external world. It must be truly yours, the gift of your inner self, which ought to be as perfect and blameless as the sacrificial lamb, free of all blemish and shame. How will you make such an offering to God, when you disobey the law which prohibits an impure man from being a priest. If you desire God to appear to you, why do you not listen to Moses, who exhorted the people to abstain from marriage so as to make room in their hearts for the sight of God?

If, however, it means so little to you to be crucified with Christ, to offer yourself as a sacrifice to God, to become a priest of God Most High, and to be thought worthy of God's great manifestation, we can think of nothing more sublime to tell you, since even the consequences of these seem unimportant to you. For after we have been crucified with Christ, we go on to live and reign with him in glory; and our self-offering to God leads to a change in our nature and dignity from that of man to that of angel.

Responsory   *Ps 145:4-5.14*

One age shall proclaim your works to another, shall declare your mighty deeds. † People will speak of your splendor and glory, and tell of your wonderful works.
V. The Lord supports all who stumble and raises all who are bowed down. † People will speak . . .

Alternative Reading

From a commentary by Saint Bede of England (In Esdram et Nehemiam Allegorica expositio II, 9: PL 91, 860-861)

Peace

Just as Zorobabel and Jesus stand for our Lord and Savior, who releases our race from captivity by his grace and himself makes his dwelling in us, building himself up there by sanctifying us and taking possession of us; so also Ezra the priest and nimble scribe openly proclaims the same Lord, *who has not come to abolish the law but to bring it to perfection.* For he, the Lord, could truly be called a scribe of God's law or a nimble scribe in the law of Moses, having given Moses the law himself through an angel. He it was who taught the holy prophets all truth, by the grace of his Spirit, he who was soon to touch with his love the minds of all his chosen ones, kindling in them the understanding of his Father's will and the urge to accomplish it. Wherefore promising the grace of the New Covenant the prophet says: *And this is the covenant I have made with the house of Israel since those days, says the Lord; I shall make my laws in their minds, and on their hearts shall I write them.* The psalmist touchingly recalls the man who wrote that, when he says: *My tongue is the pen for a scribe nimbly writing.* The prophet's tongue indeed was the scribe's busy pen; for whatever the Lord taught by inwardly enlightening him without any delay in time, *that* he himself revealed in time to men, outwardly, by means of the spoken ministry. Ezra, whose name means "helper," clearly shows this in his own person. For it is through him alone that the congregation of the faithful can be released from their tribulations and is to be (as it were) conducted from the Babylonian captivity to the liberty of Jerusalem, from the confusion of vice to the peace and serenity of virtue, step by step according to their merits.

The resemblance to Ezra was kept up even in his deeds. For it was not the least part of the people that he led back from captivity to Jerusalem, bringing at the same time both the money and the vessels consecrated to God, for the glory of his temple, while purging the same people of their alien wives by his authority as mediator. All of which reveals to the thoughtful reader what deeds the Lord has wrought in his holy church and what is to be done. We too shall take pains to make clear the message, so that they may be understood by those even less thoughtful than we. For Ezra's going up from Babylon, the children of Israel and the sons of the priests and Levites with him, represents the merciful dispensation of our redeemer, whereby he appeared in the flesh, and his entering into the confusion of this world, being free himself from the confusion brought by vice, so that when returning he might bring us with him, freed from all confusion, to the tranquillity of eternal peace. We have received a pledge of that eternal peace in the Church as it now is: for as the Lord says, *My peace I leave you; my peace I give unto you.*

Responsory   *Phil 2:12-13; Eph 3:20*

Work out your salvation with fear and trembling, for † God is at work in you, inspiring both the will and the deed for his own chosen purpose.

V. Glory be to him whose power, working in us, can do immeasurably more than we can ask or imagine. † God is at . . .

THURSDAY   Year II

First Reading   Ezra 9:1—10:5

Responsory   *Bar 2:16; Dn 9:18; Ps 80:20*

Look down from your holy dwelling place, O Lord, and think of us. Turn your ear towards us, my God, and listen; † open your eyes and look on our distress.

V. O Lord of hosts, restore us; let your face shine upon us, and we shall be saved. † Open your eyes . . .

Second Reading   From a homily by Saint Leo the Great
                             (Tract. 43, 1-4: CCL 138A, 251-255)

Cast your cares upon the Lord, and he will sustain you

The Apostle exhorts us to *put off our old self with its actions and to be renewed day by day* through a holy way of life, for *you are the temple of God* he says. If we are the temple of God then, and the Holy Spirit dwells in our hearts, we must be very watchful to see that our hearts are not an unworthy dwelling for so great a guest.

When dealing with houses made by hands, people exercise a praiseworthy diligence and make sure to repair quickly any damage done by the rain or wind or the simple passage of time. So we too must constantly take care not to let anything disordered or unclean be found in our souls. For although our edifice will not last without the help of its builder, and the structure cannot remain intact without the watchful care of its maker, yet we are living matter and spiritual stones, and therefore the author of our being works in such a way that the person being renewed must collaborate with him. We must not, then, be disobedient to the grace of God nor separate ourselves from that Good without which we are unable to be good. If we find anything impossible or extremely difficult in what we are commanded, we must not only look to our own powers but have recourse to him who commands. God issues his commands with the intention of rousing our desire and giving us the help we need. Therefore, as the prophet says, *Cast your cares upon the Lord, and he will sustain you.* Is there anyone so proud and arrogant, so sure of his own purity and integrity, as to think he needs no renovation? Such an attitude is mistaken, and the person who believes himself to be invulnerable amid the temptations of life has become excessively conceited.

The believer has no doubt that divine providence is at work always and everywhere. He knows that the outcome of human affairs does not depend on the power of the stars for that power is non-existent, and that everything is ordered by the utterly equitable and merciful judgment and will of the supreme king. Nonetheless, things do not always work out as we desire, and the cause of the wicked often triumphs over that of the just. It is only too likely, then, that even generous souls may be disturbed and driven to wrongful complaints. Therefore, since few have such solid strength as not to be shaken by any shifts of circumstance and since prosperity no less than adversity leads many believers astray, we must be diligent in healing the wounds we receive because of our human weakness.

Responsory   *Jn 8:12; Rom 13:12*
I am the light of the world. † Anyone who follows me will not walk in darkness, but will have the light of life.
V. Let us cast off the deeds of darkness and put on the armor of light. † Anyone who follows . . .

FRIDAY   Year II

First Reading   Nehemiah 1:1—2:8

Responsory   *1 Tm 6:11-12; 2 Tm 2:10*
Seek after integrity and holiness, faith and love, patience and gentleness; † fight the good fight of faith and take hold of eternal life.

V. I will bear all things for the sake of God's chosen, that they may obtain salvation. † Fight the good . . .

Second Reading   From a homily by Saint Augustine of Hippo
(Enarr. in Ps. 146, 4-5: CCL 40, 2124-2125)

Seeing God

The Lord is rebuilding Jerusalem, and calling the exiles from Israel back. So the Lord is rebuilding Jerusalem and recalling its exiled people; for the people of Jerusalem are the people of Israel. There is an eternal Jerusalem in heaven, where the citizens are also angels. What, then, does Israel mean? Seeing God. So all the citizens of that city rejoice at seeing God in that great and splendid heavenly city. God himself is their theatre. But we are exiles from that city: banished for our sins, to prevent us remaining there, and burdened with mortality, to prevent us returning there. God has noted our exile, and he who rebuilds Jerusalem has reinstated the sinners. How did he reinstate them? *By calling the exiles from Israel back.* For sin had made them exiles. God took pity on these and searched for them, since they were not seeking for him. Where did he look? Whom did he send to set us free from our captivity? He sent the Redeemer, as the apostle tells us: *God shows his love for us, by the fact that when we were still sinners Christ died for us.*

So he sent his Son, our Redeemer, to set us free from our captivity. "Take a purse with you," he said, "and put the price of the prisoners in it." For he clothed himself in a mortal body, and there was the blood which was shed for our redemption. With that blood he called the exiles from Israel back. Yet if he called back exiles long ago, why should he want to call back exiles today? If the exiles were called back to be shaped into a building by the craftsman's hand, why should those be called back whose own turbulence caused them to fall out of the craftsman's hand? *He heals those who have a contrite heart.* That is why the exiles from Israel are called back: to be healed through a contrite heart. Those who have failed to mortify their heart are not healed. What does it mean: to mortify our heart? *If you had wanted a sacrifice, I should certainly have given you one; but you take no pleasure in burnt offerings.* What then? Are we to remain without the oblation of sacrifice? Listen to what he wants you to offer, as he goes on to say:

The sacrifice acceptable to God is a contrite spirit; God will not despise a contrite and humble heart. So *he heals those who have a contrite heart;* for he comes near them to heal them; as it is said elsewhere: *The Lord is near to those who have a contrite heart.* Such are the people he heals; but their healing will only be perfect at the end of their mortal life, when this corruptible body will put on incorruptibility, and this mortal body will put on immortality.

Responsory   *1 Jn 4:9.16b; Jn 3:16*
God's love for us was revealed when he sent his only Son into the world so that we might have life through him. † God is love, and whoever lives in love lives in God and God lives in him.
V. God loved the world so much that he gave his only Son, so that whoever believes in him should not perish but have eternal life.
† God is love . . .

SATURDAY   Year II

First Reading   Nehemiah 2:9-20

Responsory   *Neh 2:19-20*
It is the God of heaven who will grant us success. † We, his servants, shall set about the rebuilding.
V. What is this that you are about? † We, his servants . . .

Second Reading   From a commentary by Saint Bede of England
(In Esdram et Nehemiam Allegorica expositio III, 16-17: PL 91, 886)

The sadness of the just will have been turned into joy

When Sanballat the Horonite and Tobiah the servant, the Ammonite, heard this it displeased them greatly. The heretics are displeased, and all the Church's enemies likewise, every time they observe the chosen ones taking pains over the Catholic faith or the correction of behavior, whereby the walls of Holy Church are repaired. For we should take proper note of the great diversity of men and their affairs: indeed, we mentioned earlier that those who remained from the captivity in Judea had been in great affliction and humiliation; but also that Nehemiah kept up a long fast, with prayer and tears, because the walls of Jerusalem were broken down and its gates burnt with fire. And now on the other hand it was the enemies of this same holy city that were saddened and fallen into great affliction, because they understood that its buildings were to be restored and at the same time the citizens to be raised beyond the threat of enemies assailing them. From which we gather that even in this life the Lord's words can apply, where he said: *Amen, amen, I say to you, that you will weep and cry, and the world will rejoice while you are sad*. But then he added: *but your weeping will be turned to joy*. For when the world which rejoiced is weeping, the sadness of the just will have been turned into joy. Then it will be seen that Holy Church prospers and that those who had erred by sinning have returned to the fold, as penitents.

I came to Jerusalem and remained there three days. He goes round observing various parts of the devastated city, carefully noting the details of the damage and how it may be put right. So likewise, men of spiritual insight have quite frequently to get up in the night (as it were) and scrutinize with the expert's eye the state of holy Church, while others rest. They do this, vigilantly inquiring how they may be chastised to amend and set to rights those things which by the onslaughts of vice have become tarnished or dislodged. But the wall of Jerusalem lies where it has been knocked down; and the faithful wallow in worldly pleasures and baseness. The gates are eaten away by fire now that those who should have shown others the way in to the true life have forsaken the office of teaching the truth and are stagnating in the general inactivity, pursuing the hobbies of the moment.

And I said to them: You know the afflictions we suffer. These words hardly need explanation: they are easily understood in the spiritual sense. The holy doctors, all of them enlivened with zeal for God, are in the greatest affliction as long as they observe that Jerusalem, the vision of peace, which the Lord gives us with his commendation, is forsaken by reason of antipathy and dissension; and as long, also, as they see the gates of strength, which, as Isaiah says, praise should occupy, thrown down and had in contempt, while the gates of hell are upstanding. Wherefore they endeavor, by recruiting the servants of the word into one combined effort, to rebuild by faith and good works what seems to have been damaged and in part destroyed.

Responsory   *Mi 6:8; Acts 17:28*

The Lord has shown us what is good; † what he requires of us is
only this: to act justly, to love tenderly and to walk humbly with our
God.

V. He is not far from any one of us, for in him we live and move and
have our being. † What he requires . . .

Alternative Reading

From a commentary by Saint Cyril of Alexandria (In Michaeam
prophetam 3, 35-36: PG 71, 689-703)

Mount Sion, mother of the firstborn, where we shall be together with Christ

Behold I am laying a stone for the foundations in Zion, a tested
stone, a precious cornerstone; and he who has faith in it will not be
put to shame. The builders of Zion rejected the tested and precious
stone, *but now it is in place as the cornerstone.* For Christ has become
king of both the Gentiles and the Jews, whom he has created into
a single new man, making peace through the cross, and joining
them in spiritual union to form a cornerstone. For it is written: *The
whole multitude of believers were united in heart and soul.*

Through sanctification and faith they have become similar in form
to that most precious cornerstone, and so Saint Peter wrote well and
wisely: *You yourselves, like living stones, must be built up into a spiritual
house, to be a holy temple and a dwelling place for God in the Spirit.*

*And in the last days the mountain of the Lord's house will be
revealed.* We can see in these prophetic words a clear reference to
the future Church of the Gentiles. For Israel in the flesh had, as it
were, ceased to exist, the sacrificial rites of the law had come to an
end, the priests of the house of Levi had abandoned their office,
and lastly the famous temple itself had been destroyed by fire and
Jerusalem demolished. This was the moment when Christ proclaimed the Church of the Gentiles, as if in the last days, that is, at
the consummation of our age; for it was then that he became man.
The prophet speaks of the Church as a mountain, *which is the house
of the living God.* It soars aloft, because there is nothing whatsoever
earthbound in the Church. It is raised on high by the knowledge
of the precepts of God; and the very mode of life of those justified
by Christ and sanctified by the Spirit is made sublime.

Our care is Christ; we shall find his teachings to be the true path, and we shall walk as if in his company, not only in the present and the past but for ever and ever. These words are true. For those who suffer with Christ now will live in unity with him for the rest of time, sharing his glory and reigning with him. Christ is the care of those who put their love for him before all else, turning away from the aimless distractions of this world, preferring to seek righteousness and what is pleasing to him, and to excel in virtue. Saint Paul was one such man. Therefore he writes: *I have been crucified with Christ. It is no longer I who live my life, but Christ who lives in me.*

Yet the prophet shows that Israel could not entirely lose hope. The people were indeed crushed and rejected, or rather cast off, because of their utter disregard for God. They fought against him, with shameless and profane idolatry, and were liable in no small degree to charges of blood-guilt. For they had killed the prophets, and in the end they crucified the very Savior and Redeemer of the world. But, for the sake of their fathers, the remnant were pitied and saved, to become great people.

For it is true and right to consider this holy multitude whom Christ has justified as a very great people. The things that distinguish them, and should make them a cause of wonder, are goodness of mind and nobility of heart, that is, sanctification, hope in Christ, faithful sonship, admirable virtues and marvellous endurance, submission to Christ's rule and devotion to his teaching. *For we have one teacher, Christ.* And the prophet's Mount Zion is the heavenly Jerusalem, mother of the first-born, where we shall dwell in unity with Christ.

Responsory　　　　　　　　　　　　　　　　　　　　*1 Jn 4:16.7*

God is love, and those who live in love live in God, † and God lives in them.

V. Let us love one another, for love comes from God and knows God. † And God lives . . .

THIRTEENTH WEEK IN ORDINARY TIME

SUNDAY   Year II

First Reading   Nehemiah 3:33—4:17

Responsory   1 Cor 9:19.22; Jb 29:15-16
Though I am not bound to anyone, I became a slave to all. To the
weak I became weak. † I became all things to all men that I might
at least save some.
V. I was eyes for the blind and feet for the lame; I was a father to
the poor. † I became all . . .

Second Reading   From a sermon by Blessed Guerric of Igny
(Sermo 3 de Resurrectione Domini 3.5: SC 202, 250.256-258)

Keep awake that the morning light may rise upon you

Keep awake, brethren, intent upon your prayers; keep awake,
careful how you carry out your duties, all the more so since the
morning of that unending day has dawned, which saw the doubly
welcome, serene, eternal light, return to us from the dead, and the
morning rising caused the sun to shine with a new brightness. *It is
now time for you to wake out of sleep; it is far on in the night; day is
near.* Keep awake, I say, that the morning light may rise upon you,
no other than Christ, *who will reveal himself, sure as the dawn;*
prepared to enable those who are on the watch for him, to relive
once more the mystery of his resurrection in the morning. Then
indeed you will sing with joyful heart: *The Lord is God; he has given
light to us. This is the day which the Lord has made; let us rejoice and
be glad in it;* the day, that is, when he will allow the light which he
has hidden with his hands to shine upon you, telling you, his
friend, it is his to give, and that you may raise yourself up to receive
it.

Sluggard, how much longer are you going to sleep? Yes, how
much longer are you going to slumber on? Scripture says, *A little
sleep, a little slumber, a little folding of the hands in rest;* otherwise,
while you are asleep, unaware of it, Christ will have risen from his
tomb; and when, resplendent, he passes by, you will not deserve
to see even his back. Then, when it is too late, you will utter

lamentations of repentance, and say with the ungodly, *Because we have wandered from the way of truth, neither the light of righteousness has shone upon us, nor has the sun of understanding risen upon us.*

But, for you who fear my name, says the prophet, *the sun of righteousness shall rise.* And the man *who lives an upright life, his eyes shall see the king in his splendor.*

This undoubtedly refers to happiness in the life to come; but, as Christ's resurrection clearly proves, it is also granted to us in due measure for our consolation in this life.

So let us all rouse up and requicken our spirits, whether to watch in prayer or to work with a will, so that our renewed and lively zest may show that, once again, we have received a share in Christ's resurrection. Indeed the chief sign of a man's return to life is vigorous and energetic action. Moreover, he will make a perfect return to life, if he dies to the body and opens his eyes to contemplation. However, his understanding will be undeserving of this until he increases his love by frequent longings and ardent desires, to render himself capable of something so sublime.

Life begins to return when prayer increases love; it reaches perfection when the understanding receives the light of contemplation. Strive, then, brethren, to mount ever higher on the ladder of the virtues, the means whereby we grow in holiness of life, so that, as the apostle says, you may finally arrive at the resurrection of Christ from the dead: he who lives and reigns for ever and ever. Amen.

Responsory   Ps 11:4-5.7

The eyes of the Lord look down upon the world; his gaze tests humankind. † The Lord tests the just and the unjust; he hates all who love violence.

V. The Lord is just and loves justice; the upright shall see his face. † The Lord tests . . .

MONDAY   Year II

First Reading   Nehemiah 5:1-19

Responsory   *Ps 77:14-16*
What god so great as our God? † You are the God who works
wonders.
V. You have shown your power to the nations; with your strong
arm, you have redeemed your people. † You are the . . .

Second Reading   From a sermon by Saint Cyprian of Carthage
(attributed to Cyprian: PLS 1, 51-52)

A Christian is one who imitates Christ in everything

God's will is what Christ did and taught: it means humility in
behavior, steadfastness in faith, modesty in words, justice in deeds,
mercy in good works, discipline in daily life; to be incapable of
doing injury to anyone, but able to bear the injury done to rejoice
at the prosperity of our neighbor as if we ourselves had deserved
to prosper, to think of another's loss as our own loss, and another's
gain as our own gain. It is to love a friend not for the world's sake
but for God's, to put up with and even love an enemy, to do
nothing to anyone which you would not want to suffer yourself,
to refuse no one what you rightly want given to you; to help your
neighbor in time of trouble not only according to your means, but
willing to be of use to him even beyond your means, and to keep
the peace with your brothers. It is to love God with all your heart,
to love him as Father but fear him as Lord; and to put nothing
before Christ, for he has never put anything before us.

But all who love the name of the Lord will be glorified. Let us
be unhappy here, so as to be happy afterwards. Let us follow the
Lord Jesus Christ. *Those who say they believe in him must live in the
same way as he lived.* Christ, the Son of God, came not to reign, but
though king he shunned the kingdom; he came not to rule, but to
serve. He became poor to make us rich; he took blows for us, so
that we ourselves should feel no pain when scourged.

Let us imitate Christ. Christian is a name that stands for justice,
kindness, and integrity. A Christian is one who imitates and follows Christ in everything, who is holy, innocent, undefiled, and
chaste. There is no place in the heart of a Christian for malice, but

only for devotion and goodness. A Christian is one who follows the life of Christ, who is merciful to all and ignorant of injustice. A Christian is one who forbids the poor to be disparaged in his presence, who helps the unfortunate, mourns with those who mourn, feels another's pain as if it was his own, and is moved to tears by the tears of others. A Christian's house is open to all, no one is ever shut out. The poor are always welcome at his table; everyone knows that Christians are really good, and no one is left with any sense of injustice. A Christian is one who serves God diligently day and night, whose soul is sincere and immaculate, whose conscience is faithful and pure, whose mind is wholly on God, and who despises worldly possessions so that he may acquire heavenly ones.

Responsory   *Ps 16:7-8; Mt 19:17*

I will bless the Lord who gives me counsel, who even at night directs my heart. I keep the Lord always before me: † since he is at my right hand, I shall stand firm.

V. If you wish to enter into life, keep the commandments. † Since he is . . .

TUESDAY   Year II

First Reading   Nehemiah 7:72—8:18

Responsory   *Dt 6:4; 7:9; 6:5*

Hear, O Israel, and carefully keep what the Lord has commanded you, † and you will know that the Lord your God is a faithful God, true to his promises and merciful to all who love him.

V. You shall love the Lord your God with all your heart and with all your soul and with all your strength. † And you will . . .

Second Reading   From the writings of Saint Augustine of
                          Hippo (Conf. XI, 2, 3—3, 5: CSEL 33, 282-284)

Give me what I love; for I love indeed,
and this love you have given me

Yours is the day, yours the night, a sign from your sends minutes speeding by; spare in their fleeting course a space for us to ponder the idden wonders of your law: shut it not against us as we knock. Not in vain have you willed so many pages to be written, pages deep in shadow, obscure in their secrets; not in vain do harts and hinds seek shelter in those woods, to hide and venture forth, roam and browse, lie down and ruminate. Perfect me too, Lord, and reveal those woods to me. Lo, your voice is joy to me, your voice that rings out above a flood of joys. Give me what I love; for I love indeed, and this love you have given me. Foresake not your gifts, disdain not your parched grass. Let me confess to you all I have found in your books, Let me hear the voice of praise, and drink from you, and contemplate the wonders of your law from the beginning when you made heaven and earth to that everlasting reign when we shall be with you in your holy city.

Have mercy on me, Lord, and hearken to my longing; for I do not think it arises from this earth, or concerns itself with gold or silver or precious stones, with splendid raiment or honors or positions of power, with the pleasures of the flesh or with things we need for the body and for this our life of pilgrimage; for all these things are provided for those who seek your kingdom and your righteousness. Look and see, O my God, whence springs desire. The unrighteous have told me titillating tales, but they have nothing to do with your law, O Lord; and see, that law is what stirs my longing. See, Father, have regard to me and see and bless my longing, and let it be pleasing in your merciful eyes that I find grace before you, so that the inner meaning of your words may be opened to me as I knock at their door. I beg this grace through our Lord Jesus Christ, your Son, the man at your right hand, the Son of Man whom you have made strong to stand between yourself and us as mediator. Through him you sought us when we were not seeking you, but you sought us that we might begin to seek you. He is the Word through whom you made all things, and me among them, your only Son through whom you called your believing people to be your sons by adoption, and me among them; through him, then, do I make my plea to you, through him who sits at your right hand to intercede for us, for in him are hidden all treasures of wisdom and knowledge. And they are what I seek in your books. Moses write of him; Christ told us to himself, and he is the Truth.

Let me listen, so that I may understand how you made heaven and earth in the beginning. Moses wrote that statement; he wrote it and went away, and made his passover, his passing from you to you; and so he is not here face to face with me now. If he were, I would take hold of him and ask him and in your name implore him to open these mysteries to me. I would bend my bodily ears to the sounds that broke from his mouth.

But since I cannot question him, who spoke truthfully because you, O Truth, had filled him, I beg you yourself, O Truth, my God, to pardon my sins, and as you granted that servant of yours the grace to say those things, grant also to me the grace to understand them.

Responsory   *Ps 20:7-8; 121:2*
Some put their trust in chariots or horses, but our trust is in the name of the Lord. † They will collapse and fall, but we shall rise and stand firm.
V. My help shall come from the Lord, the creator of heaven and earth. † They will collapse . . .

WEDNESDAY   Year II

First Reading   Nehemiah 9:1-2.5-21

Responsory   *See Dn 9:4; Rm 8:28*
The Lord our God is strong and faithful, true to his promises and merciful to those who love him, † and to all who keep his commandments.
V. For those who love God, everything works together for good. † And to all . . .

Second Reading   From the writings of Nicolas Cabasilas
                        (*Vita in Christo* VI, 13: PG 150, 681-683)

There is no other name by which we must be saved

That we may be able always to pay attention to Christ, and be zealous in this at all times, let us call on him who is the subject of our thoughts at every moment. And of course those who call upon him need no special preparation or special place for prayer, nor a loud voice. For he is present everywhere, and is always with us; he is even nearer to those who seek him than their very heart.

It is fitting, then, that we should firmly believe that our prayers will be answered. We should never hesitate on account of our evil ways, but take courage because he on whom we call is *kind to the ungrateful and the wicked.* In fact he is so far from ignoring the entreaties of the servants who have offended him, that before they had called on him or even thought of him, he had already called them himself by his coming to earth — for he said, *I came to call sinners.*

Then if that was the way he sought those who did not even want him, how will he treat those who call on him? And if he loved us when we hated him, how will he reject us when we love him? It is just this that Paul's words make clear: *If, when we were enemies, we were reconciled to God by the death of his Son, how much more, when we are reconciled, shall we be saved by his life.*

Again, let us think about the kind of supplication we make. We do not pray for the things that friends are likely to ask for and receive, but rather for such things as are specifically prescribed for those who are called to account, servants who have offended their master. For we do not call upon the Lord in order that he may reward us, or grant us any other favor of that kind, but that he may have mercy on us. Who, then, are likely to ask for mercy, forgiveness, remission of sins and things of that sort from God who loves humanity, and not go away empty-handed? Those who are called to account, if indeed *those who are well have no need of a physician.* For if human beings are at all in the habit of calling upon God for mercy, it is those who are worthy of mercy, in other words sinners.

So let us call on God with our voice and in mind and thought, so that we may apply the only saving remedy to everything through which we sin, for in the words of Peter: *there is no other name by which we must be saved.*

Responsory   *Ps 141:1-2; 143:1*

I call to you, Lord; hasten to help me; hear my voice when I cry to you. † Let my prayer rise before you like incense, the raising of my hands like an evening sacrifice.

V. Lord, hear my prayer; listen to my plea. † Let my prayer . . .

THURSDAY   Year II

First Reading   Nehemiah 9:22-37

Responsory   *Dt 10:17; 1:17*
   The Lord your God is the God of gods, the great God, mighty and
   awesome. † He has no favorites and accepts no bribes.
   V. You will listen to the lowly as well as the great and have no fear
   of any man, for judgment belongs to God. † He has no . . .

Second Reading   From the writings of Saint Clement of
                      Alexandria (Ex lib. Stromatum 7, 7: PG 9, 450-451. 458-459)

All our life we must honor God

We are commanded to worship and honor this same person,
whom we believe to be the Word, our Savior and ruler, and
through him the Father. Nor must we confine our worship to
special days, but offer it perpetually throughout our lives and in
every way.

The chosen race, justified by the commandment, declared:
Seven times a day I praise you. So he who possesses true knowledge
honors God, that is, thanks him for his gifts of spiritual knowledge
and right conduct, in no specific place or appropriate sanctuary,
still less at certain feasts or on definite days, but everywhere and
all his life, whether in solitude or with others of his own faith.

Now the presence of some good man, because it inspires respect and reverence, is always an influence for the better on those
who chance to meet him. Then surely one who is always in the
presence of God, through spiritual knowledge and a life of ceaseless thanksgiving, cannot help but become a better person in every
way, in deed, word, and thought. Such is the man who is convinced
of God's presence everywhere, refusing to believe that he is enclosed in any specific place. Then because of this conviction of ours
that God is present everywhere, our whole life becomes a celebration. We praise God as we till the fields or sail the seas, and in all
the other ways of life in which we employ our skills. Thus he who
possesses true knowledge draws closer to God, and is always
serious and always happy. He is serious because his attention is
concentrated on the divine being, and happy because of his con-

tinuous awareness of the blessings which God has given to mankind.

Yet petitionary prayer is not superfluous, even though we receive blessings without asking for them. Both thanksgiving and prayer for the conversion of his fellowmen are required of the true Christian. That is the very way in which our Lord prayed. First he gave thanks because he had fulfilled his earthly ministry. Then he prayed that as many as possible might receive true knowledge so that thanks to that knowledge they might set out on the road to salvation, and by their salvation glorify God, and so that he who alone is good, and alone is the Savior, might be recognized through his Son for all eternity. And yet, the faith of one who believes that he will receive what he has need of is in itself a kind of prayer, stored up within the spirit.

But if prayer is an opportunity for communion with God, like any other opportunity of approach to God we must not neglect it. The sanctity of the man who possesses true knowledge is combined with God's blessed providence, and in the voluntary profession of Christian faith shows forth the perfection of God's kindness to men. For that sanctity in a way corresponds to providence and is a return of affection on the part of God's friend.

God is not compelled to do good, but chooses to reward those who of their own free will turn to him. For the care that God takes of us is not at all like the menial service that an inferior being bestows on a superior; on the contrary, it is out of pity for our weakness that the dispensations of providence are active in our concerns. There is the same relationship between a shepherd and his sheep, a king and his subjects, as well as between ourselves and the rulers to whom we owe obedience, those who hold their appointed offices as a duty which God has entrusted to them. So the true worshipers and servants of the divine being are those who offer him the most free and the most royal service, arising both from a devout mind and from spiritual knowledge.

Responsory   *Zep 2:3; Ps 22:26*

Seek the Lord, all you in the land who live humbly, obeying his commands. † Seek integrity, seek humility.

V. The poor shall eat and be satisfied; those who seek the Lord shall praise him. † Seek integrity . . .

FRIDAY   Year II

First Reading   Nehemiah 12:27-47

Responsory   *Dt 4:1; 31:19.20; Ps 81:9*
Give heed, O Israel, to the commands of the Lord, and inscribe them
in your heart as in a book; † I will give you a land where milk and
honey flow.
V. Listen, my people, to my warning; O Israel, if only you would
listen to me. † I will give . . .

Second Reading   From a homily by Saint John Chrysostom
                         (In Matth. XXV, 3: Bareille XII, 40-42)

Give thanks to God

Let us give thanks to God throughout our lives. For how wrong
it would be, if every day we enjoyed his blessings in deed, and yet
in word gave him no return, and that too when an offering of
gratitude would but increase our advantage. For God needs nothing from us, but we need everything from him. So our thanks are
of no profit to him, but they make us more worthy of him. For if
the memory of their kindness towards us deepens our love for our
fellow men, how much more will the perpetual memory of the
Lord's goodness to us make us more eager to keep his commands.

For the best safeguard of a kindness is to remember it with
everlasting gratitude. That is why that awe-inspiring and life-giving sacrament which we celebrate at every gathering is called the
eucharist. It is the commemoration of many blessings and the
culmination of divine providence, and teaches us to give thanks
always.

For if to be born of a Virgin was a great miracle, and the amazed
evangelist wrote of it: *All this happened,* what can we say of the
Lord's sacrifice? For if the Lord's birth was called *all this,* what
should we call his crucifixion, the shedding of his blood, and his
giving himself to us as a spiritual feast? Therefore we must give
thanks to him continuously, and let thanksgiving be the motive of
all we do and say. And let us give thanks not only for our own
blessings, but for those of our neighbors too. Thus we shall be able
to rid ourselves of envy, and increase our love and make it more

sincere. For to continue to envy those on whose behalf we give thanks to the Lord will be impossible.

Therefore the priest too, when that sacrifice is set before him, bids us give thanks for the whole world, for the old dispensation and the new, for all that was done for us before and all that awaits us hereafter. For this sets us free from earth and turns us towards heaven, and makes angels out of men. Even the very angels, in heavenly choirs, give thanks to God for his goodness to us, as they sing: *Glory to God in the highest, and on earth peace to men in whom he is well pleased.*

But what is this to us who are not on earth and are not men? It means a great deal, for it teaches us so to love our fellow-servants that we rejoice in their good fortune as if it were our own. It is for that reason that Saint Paul in all his letters gives thanks for the blessings of the whole world. So let us too give everlasting thanks for all the gifts, large or small, that are given both to ourselves and to others.

Responsory   *Ps 119:161-162; see Jn 6:63*

Though princes persecute me without cause, I stand in awe of your word. † I delight in your word like one who finds a treasure.
V. Your words are spirit, Lord, and they are life. † I delight . . .

SATURDAY   Year II

First Reading   Isaiah 59:1-14

Responsory   *1 Pt 2:9.10; Dt 7:6.8*

You are a people God has made his own; once you were not his people, but now you are the people of God. † In the past you knew nothing of God's mercy, but now you have received mercy.
V. Because he loved you, the Lord chose you and brought you out from the land of slavery. † In the past . . .

Second Reading   From the writings of Julian of Norwich
                    (*Revelations of Divine Love* 78)

We still need to recognize our sin and weakness

In his merciful way our Lord shows us our sin and weakness by that light, lovely and gracious, which shines from himself. Our sin is so vile and horrible that in his courtesy he will not show it to us except under the light of his mercy and grace. It is his will that we should know four things: first, that he is the ground of our life and existence; second, that he protects us by his might and mercy all the time we are in sin among the enemies out to wreck us — we are in so much the greater danger since we give them the opportunity they want, being ignorant of our own need; third, how courteously he protects us, making us know when we are going astray; fourth, how loyally he waits for us, with unvarying affection; he wants us to turn to him, uniting with him in love, as he is with us.

So it is that with this gracious information we are able to view our sin positively and not despairingly. For, indeed, we must face it and by such sight be made ashamed of ourselves, and humbled for our pride and presumption. We have got to see that of ourselves we are nothing but sin and wretchedness. We can estimate from the little our Lord shows us how great is the total we do not see. For in his courtesy he limits the amount we actually see: we could not stand the sight of what in fact it is, so vile and horrible it is. And by this humiliating knowledge, through our contrition and his grace we shall break with everything that is not our Lord. Then will our blessed Savior heal us completely, and unite us to himself. This break and healing our Lord intends for mankind generally. The man who is highest and nearest to God sees himself as sinful and as needy as I am; and I who am the least and most lowly of all who are to be saved can be comforted along with the highest. So has our Lord made us one in his charity.

When he showed me that I would sin, I was so enjoying looking at him that I did not pay much attention to this revelation, so our Lord in his courtesy refrained from further teaching until he gave me the grace and will to attend. By this I was taught that though we may be raised to contemplation by our Lord's especial favor we still need to recognize our sin and weakness. Without such knowledge we cannot be truly humble, nor indeed can we be saved.

I saw afterwards, too, that we may not always have this knowledge of ourselves, or of our spiritual enemies — they do not wish us so much good! If they had their way we should not know it till our dying day. We are greatly indebted to God then that he himself, for love's sake, wills to show it to us in this time of mercy and grace.

Responsory   *Ps 119:137.138.142; 7:12*

Lord, you are just indeed; you have imposed your will with justice.
† Your justice is an eternal justice, and your law is truth.
V. God is a just judge, slow to anger, but he threatens the wicked every day, people who refuse to repent. † Your justice . . .

FOURTEENTH WEEK IN ORDINARY TIME

SUNDAY Year II

First Reading   Proverbs 1:1-7.20-33

Responsory   *Rm 12:16; 1 Cor 3:18-19; 1:23.24*
Never allow yourself to be self-satisfied; if you pride yourself on
your worldly wisdom, you will have to unlearn it all before you are
truly wise; † worldly wisdom is foolishness in the eyes of God.
V. We preach a crucified Christ, and he is the power of God and the
wisdom of God. † Worldly wisdom is . . .

Second Reading   From the writings of Blessed Angela of
                      Foligno (Memorial, 190-191)

A way in which the soul knows that God is within it is by an
embrace which God bestows upon the soul. Never has a mother
embraced her son with such love, nor can anyone else on this earth
be imagined who embraces with a love that nears the indescribable
love with which God embraces the soul. God presses it to himself
with such tenderness and such love that I think that no one on earth
who has not had this experience can believe it. Since I, the brother
scribe, resisted her on this point — for I found it hard to believe —
Christ's faithful one responded: "One could perhaps believe something of it but not its full expression."

This embrace of God sets ablaze a fire within the soul with
which the whole soul burns for Christ. It also produces a light so
great that the soul understands the fullness of God's goodness,
which it experiences in itself, and which is, moreover, much greater
than the soul's experience of it. The effect then of this fire within
the soul is to render it certain and secure that Christ is within it.
And yet, what we have said is nothing in comparison to what this
experience really is.

I, the brother scribe, asked her, at this point, if the soul shed any
tears in this state. Christ's faithful one responded that the soul did
not then shed any tears, either of joy or of any other kind; for this
is another state, far superior to the one where the soul sheds tears
of joy.

In this state, God, likewise, produces in the soul such a super-abundance of joy that it does not know what more to ask for; more, if this state lasted, I would consider myself to be in paradise. This joy has an effect that can be observed in every part of the body. Everything bitter or injurious or whatever else one could be afflicted with becomes sweet. Moreover, I could not conceal the effects from my companion.

Then I, the brother scribe, questioned Angela's companion concerning this point. She told me that once while she and Angela were walking together along a road, the countenance of Christ's faithful one became white and radiant, then ruddy and joyful, and her eyes grew large and shone so brilliantly that she no longer seemed herself. This same companion also told me: "When I saw Angela in this state I was filled with sadness and feared that someone, a man or a woman, would meet us and notice her in this state. I told Angela, 'Why don't you at least try to cover your face? Your eyes seem to shine like candles.' "This companion, because she was shy and very simple, and still did not know all the gifts of grace Angela had been granted, then began to lament and beat her breasts with her fists, and said to Christ's faithful one: "Tell me why this is happening to you? Try to get out of sight or hide yourself somewhere, for we cannot walk around if you are in such a state." Out of her simplicity and ignorance, she then cried out: "Woe is me, what are we going to do?" Christ's faithful one, for her part, trying to console and reassure her, told her: "Do not fear, for even if we meet someone, God will help us." This happened not only once but so many times that her companion said she could not count them.

Christ's faithful one herself also told me: This joy lasted for many days, and certain joys I believe will never go away but will grow greater and find their total fulfillment in heaven. For now I am not without them in my life; hence when something sad happens to me I immediately recall the joys of that state and I am not troubled.

Responsory   *Ps 119:97.105.135; 19:11*

Lord, how I love your law! Your word is a lamp for my feet, a light for my path. † Let your face shine on your servant and teach me your decrees.
V. By them your servant is instructed; in keeping them there is great reward. † Let your face . . .

MONDAY   Year II

First Reading   Proverbs 3:1-20

Responsory   *Prv 3:11, 12; Heb 12:7*
Do not resent the Lord's correction, and take no offense when he
rebukes you; † for those whom he loves the Lord reproves, just as
a father chastises a favorite son.
V. God is treating you as his sons, for what son is there whom his
father does not discipline? † For those whom . . .

Second Reading   From a sermon by Cardinal John Henry
                        Newman *(Parochial and Plain Sermons VI, 40-42)*

What is meditating on Christ?

If it be so, that the Son of God came down from heaven, put
aside his glory, and submitted to be despised, cruelly treated, and
put to death by his own creatures — by those whom he had made,
and whom he had preserved up to that day, and was then uphold-
ing in life and being — is it reasonable that so great an event should
not move us?

Or, rather, may not so great a benefactor demand of us some
overflowing gratitude, keen sympathy, fervent love, profound
awe, bitter self-reproach, earnest repentance, eager desire and
longing after a new heart? Who can deny all this? Why then is it
not so? Why are things with us as they are?

For this one reason, if I must express my meaning in one word,
because you so little *meditate.* You do not meditate, and therefore
you are not impressed.

What is meditating on Christ? It is simply this, thinking habitu-
ally and constantly of him and of his deeds and sufferings. It is to
have him before our minds as one whom we may contemplate,
worship, and address when we rise up, when we lie down, when
we eat and drink, when we are at home and abroad, when we are
working, or walking, or at rest, when we are alone, and again when
we are in company; this is meditating. And by this, and nothing
short of this, will our hearts come to feel as they ought. We have
stony hearts, hearts as hard as the highways; the history of Christ
makes no impression on them. And yet, if we would be saved, we
must have tender, sensitive, living hearts; our hearts must be

broken, must be broken up like ground, and dug, and watered, and tended, and cultivated, till they become as gardens, gardens of Eden, acceptable to our God, gardens in which the Lord God may walk and dwell; filled, not with briars and thorns, but with all sweet-smelling and useful plants, with heavenly trees and flowers. The dry and barren waste must burst forth into springs of living water. This change must take place in our hearts if we would be saved; in a word, we must have what we have not by nature, faith, and love; and how is this to be effected, under God's grace, but by bodily and practical meditation through the day?

Saint Peter describes what I mean, when he says, speaking of Christ, *Whom having not seen you love*: in whom, though now you see him not, yet believing, you rejoice with joy unspeakable and full of glory.

Christ is gone away; he is not seen; we never saw him, we only read and heard of him. It is an old saying, "Out of sight, out of mind." Be sure, so it will be, so it must be with us, as regards our blessed Savior, unless we make continual efforts all through the day to think of him, his love, his precepts, his gifts, and his promises. We must recall to mind what we read in the gospels and in holy books about him; we must bring before us what we have heard in Christ; we must pray God to enable us to do so, to bless the doing so, and to make us do so in a simple-minded, sincere, and reverential spirit. In a word, we must meditate, for all this is meditation; and this even the most unlearned person can do, and will do, if he has a will to do it.

Responsory   *Is 55:6; Eccl 12:1*
Seek the Lord while he may be found; † call on him while he is near.
V. Remember your Creator in the days of your youth. † Call on him . . .

TUESDAY   Year II

First Reading   Proverbs 8:1-5.12-36

Responsory   *Prv 8:22; Jn 1:1*
In the beginning, before he made the earth, † the Lord created me.
V. In the beginning was the Word, and the Word was with God, and the Word was God. † The Lord created me.

Second Reading   From a sermon by Blessed Guerric of Igny
(In fest. Sancti Benedicti, Sermo 1: PL 185, 99-103)

Wisdom will be a mighty testing stone

Happy, scripture says, *are those who have found wisdom.* But it does not stop there. No; it continues: *and who are rich in prudence.* Solomon found wisdom but because he lacked prudence, because he was not careful enough in keeping watch over himself and guarding himself from pagan women, he not only lost wisdom but fell into the supreme folly of idolatry.

Some people, like Solomon, have been drawn away by the desires of the flesh; others through fickleness and inconstancy abandon wisdom when they encounter the slightest difficulty. These are the ones who believe for a while but in time of temptation fall away. As the scriptures say: *Wisdom will be to them as a mighty testing stone.* They protest: *This teaching is hard.* Yes, it is hard, but does that mean it is not true? The stone is hard, but does that mean it is not precious?

Now the stone referred to was Christ, a mighty stone, but not hard. He was the rock, but a rock that could be changed, and indeed is changed, into pools or fountains of water, whenever he finds faithful hearts that are gentle and humble into whom he can pour himself. For if those who were so quickly offended and drew back at the mere appearance of hardness had remained with the apostles, they might well have drunk with them from the Rock that followed them. They might have drunk from the streams of living water flowing copiously from the Rock that was struck on the cross so that today also the people and their cattle might drink. They might even have sucked *honey from the rock and oil from the flinty stone.*

Now to achieve the wisdom of remaining with Wisdom I think it most important not readily to let restlessness or some slight indisposition keep us away from any of the occupations of wisdom such as the divine office, private prayer, holy reading, our everyday tasks, or the rule of silence. Indeed, with regard to silence we share the prophet's promise: *In silence and hope shall be your strength.* For if in silence you devote yourself to holiness, heeding the saying of Jeremiah that *it is good to wait in silence for the salvation of the Lord,* then in the midst of the silence the all-powerful

Word will leap down to you from his royal throne. The waters of Shiloah which flow silently will inundate the valley of your calm and peaceful heart like a gently flowing stream. You will experience this not once but many times if holiness is the purpose of your silence, that is, if you meditate on holiness, keeping in mind the texts of scripture that I have placed before you, and not forgetting the all-seeing eye of God.

It is the fear of the Lord that makes us always mindful of this eternal eye, which unceasingly beholds and judges all things; it draws us back from any wrong action or thought, and teaches us instead to meditate upon holiness, restraining us so that we remain with wisdom.

May he enable us to share in these things who deigned to share in our nature, Jesus Christ, the Wisdom of God, who lives and reigns for ever and ever. Amen.

Responsory   *Ps 76:4; Heb 3:2*
You are awesome, O Lord, more majestic than the everlasting mountains. † Who can stand when your anger is roused?
V. Lord, I have heard of your fame; I stand in awe of your deeds.
† Who can stand . . .

Alternative Reading

From a homily by Saint Athanasius of Alexandria (Contra Arianos, Oratio 2, 78.81-82: PG 26, 312.319)

The Wisdom of God

The only and absolute wisdom of God is the creator and maker of all things. For as the psalmist says: *You have made all things in wisdom,* and: *The earth is full of your creation.* Then so that created things should not only be, but be good, God was content that his Wisdom should come down to the level of created beings. In that way a form and seeming image of him would be imprinted on all in common and each separately, to show that they were wise and works worthy of God. For just as our own word is an image of the Word who is the Son of God, so our wisdom is also an image of the Word who is himself Wisdom. Since it is through this image that we have the power to know and think, we become capable of receiving the creator Wisdom, and through him we are able to know his Father. For as Saint John says: *Whoever has the Son has*

the Father also; and: *Whoever receives me receives him who sent me.*
Then since there is such an image of Wisdom created in ourselves
and in all the works of creation, it is probably the true creator
Wisdom, assuming the attributes of his own image, who says: *The
Lord created me for the benefit of his works.*

*For since, in God's wisdom, the world did not know God by
wisdom, God chose to save the faithful through the simple message of
the gospel.* For God no longer wished to be known, as in former
times, through the image and foreshadowing of wisdom in created
beings. Instead he made the true Wisdom actually take flesh and
become man, and endure death on the cross, so that all the faithful
might in the future be saved through faith in him. He is of course
the same Wisdom of God who in the past revealed himself through
his own image in created beings, because of which he is also said
to be created, and revealed his Father through himself. But later it
was as the Word that he became flesh, as Saint John said, and, after
destroying death and saving our race, revealed himself even more
clearly and through himself his Father, when he prayed: *Grant
them to know you, the only true God, and Jesus Christ whom you have
sent.*

So the whole world is full of the knowledge of him. For we
know him as one, Father through Son, and Son from Father. And
the Father rejoices in the Son, and he rejoices in the Father with the
same joy, saying: *I was his delight; and every day I rejoiced in his
presence.*

Responsory   Ps 41:1; Gal 6:2
Blessed are those who are concerned for the poor and the weak;
† the Lord will save them in time of trouble.
V. Bear one another's burdens, and so fulfill the law of Christ. † The
Lord will . . .

Alternative Reading

From the writings of Saint Augustine of Hippo (Soliloquia I, 2-3: PL 32,
869-871)

God wisdom

God, who is loved by everything which is capable of loving,
whether it is done knowingly or unknowingly; God, in whom are
all things, but who is neither corrupted by the corruption of all

creation, nor hurt by its evil, nor deceived by its error; God, who has wanted only the pure to know what is true. You are God, father of truth, father of wisdom, father of true and complete life, father of blessedness, father of goodness and beauty, father of intelligible light, father of our awakening and enlightenment, father of the assurance which admonishes us to return to you.

I call upon you, God, truth, in whom and by whom and through whom all true things are true; God, wisdom, in whom and by whom and through whom all the wise are wise; God, true and complete life, in whom and by whom and through whom lives all that is truly and completely alive; God, blessedness, in whom and by whom and through whom all blessed things are blessed.

God, from whom to turn away is to fall, to whom to turn toward is to rise again, in whom to remain is to stand firm; God, from whom to go away is to die, to whom to return is to be alive again, in whom to dwell is to live; God, whom no one loses unless deceived, whom no one seeks unless admonished, whom no one finds unless cleansed; God, whom to forsake is to perish, whom to follow is to love, whom to see is to have; God, to whom faith calls us, hope encourages us, love unites us.

God, who converts us; God, who strips off of us that which is not, and clothes us with that which is; God, who makes us able to be heard; God, who strengthens us; God, who leads us into every truth; God, who tells us all good things, and neither drives us mad, nor allows anyone else to do so; God, who calls us back to the way; God, who leads us to the door; God, who causes it to be opened for those who knock; God who gives us the bread of life; God, through whom we thirst for that drink which will make us thirst no more; God, who shows to the world sin, justice, and judgment.

Now I love only you, I follow only you, I seek for only you, and I am ready to serve only you, because only you justly govern; I long to be under your rule. Command me, I beg you, and make any decree you wish, but heal and open my ears, so that I may hear your voice. Heal and open my eyes, so that I may see what is your will. Drive my madness from me, so that I may know you again. Tell me where I should look, so that I may see you; I hope to do all which you have commanded.

Responsory   *Ps 41:1; Gal 6:2*
Blessed are those who are concerned for the poor and the weak;
† the Lord will save them in time of trouble.
V. Bear one another's burdens, and so fulfill the law of Christ. † The
Lord will . . .

WEDNESDAY   Year II

First Reading   Proverbs 9:1-18

Responsory   *Lk 14:16-17; Prv 9:5*
A man once prepared a great banquet, and sent his servants to tell
the guests: † Come, all is ready.
V. Come, eat my bread and drink the wine which I have mixed for
you. † Come, all is ready.

Second Reading   From the writings of Prosper Guéranger
                       (*The Liturgical Year* II, 261-262)

The sevenfold sacraments

Our risen Jesus would have the sacraments be seven. As, at the
beginning, he stamped the creation of the visible world with this
sacred number — giving six days to work and one to rest — so,
too, would he mark the great spiritual creation. He tells us, in the
Old Testament, that Wisdom (that is, himself — for he is the eternal
Wisdom of the Father) will build to himself a house, which is the
Church; and he adds that he will make it rest on seven pillars. He
gives us a type of this same Church in the tabernacle built by
Moses, and he orders a superb candlestick to be provided for the
giving of light, by day and night, to the holy place; but there were
to be seven branches to the candlestick, and on each branch were
to be graven flowers and fruits.

When he raises his beloved disciple to heaven, he shows himself to him surrounded by seven candlesticks, and holding seven
stars in his right hand. He appears to him as a Lamb, bearing seven
burns (which are the symbol of strength), and having seven eyes
(which signify his infinite wisdom). Near him lies a book, in which
is written the future of the world; the book is sealed with seven
seals, and none but the lamb is able to loose them. The disciple sees

seven spirits, burning like lamps, before the throne of God, ready to do his biddings, and carry his word to the extremities of the earth.

Turning our eyes to the kingdom of satan, we see him mimicking God's work, and setting up a seven of his own. Seven capital and deadly sins are the instruments whereby he makes man his slave; and our Savior tells us that when satan has been defeated, and would regain a soul, he brings with him seven of the wickedest spirits of hell. We read in the gospel that Jesus drove seven devils out of Mary Magdalene. When God's anger bursts upon the world, immediately before the coming of the dread judge, he will announce the approach of his chastisements by seven trumpets, sounded by seven angels; and seven other angels will then pour out upon the guilty earth seven vials filled with the wrath of God.

We, therefore, who are resolved to make sure our election, who desire to possess the grace of our risen Jesus in this life, and to enjoy his vision in the next: Oh, let us reverence and love this merciful sevenfold, these admirable sacraments. Under this sacred number, he has included all the varied riches of his grace. There is not a want or necessity, either of souls individually, or of society at large, for which our Redeemer has not provided by these seven sources of regeneration and life. He calls us from death to life by baptism and penance; he strengthens us in that supernatural life by confirmation, the eucharist, and extreme unction; he secures to his Church both ministry and increase by holy order and matrimony.

It is to the soul which thus believes that the sacraments appear in all their divine beauty and power: we understand, because we believe. *Credite, et intelligetis!* It is the fulfillment of the text from Isaiah, as rendered by the Septuagint: Unless you believe, you shall not understand!

Responsory   *Ps 103:8-9.13-14*

The Lord is merciful and loving, slow to anger and full of compassion. He will not always reprove us; his wrath will come to an end.
† As tenderly as a father treats his children, the Lord treats those who stand in awe of him.
V. He knows what we are made of; he remembers that we are dust.
† As tenderly as . . .

THURSDAY   Year II

First Reading   Proverbs 10:6-32

Responsory   *Ps 37:30.31; 112:6.7*
The mouth of the just man utters wisdom, and his tongue speaks
what is right. † The law of God is in his heart.
V. The just man will be remembered for ever; he shall have no fear
of evil news. † The law of . . .

Second Reading   From a sermon by John Justus Landsberg
                        (In solemnitate Sancti Benedicti: Opera omnia III, 344-345)

Let us be ever aware of God's presence among us

Alas, beloved brethren! that there should be so many evils, so
many dangers inherent in our very speech! So many occasions of
harm being done by wicked tongues, whether in religion or in the
affairs of princes! If the loquacious man is a matter for alarm to the
wise man, where questions of state are concerned, how much again
in a monastery, or in the desert places, not to mention ruin to cities
or monastic communities, then, or disaster to souls and bodies. We
should take note how often dissension, envy, strife, indeed hatred
— all these can spring up even in small communities, simply from
idle talk going on day by day. Surely anyone can see this. Alas,
how it is that the young do this kind of harm, from being aroused
by evil talk, acquiring thereby bad habits of speech themselves
which often enough they can never afterwards abandon or correct.
It is for them of so little significance, alas, that Christ warns us, and
not just religious but Christians in general, that for every idle word
we utter account is to be rendered.

If of idle talk merely, whereby precious time comes to be lost
to no good purpose, the reckoning to be made of all mortals is so
strict, what are we to say of those full of pernicious talk, or
inquisitive talk, or of those who grumble or quarrel, and make a
habit of backbiting, or of licentious talk and detraction, or of those
who are full of arrogance and testiness, or hatred? Let us refrain,
then, dear brothers, from improper conversations; let us cut out
pointless talk: and even when we really need to speak let us not
linger long, lest we distance ourselves from Almighty God himself.
Let us be ever aware of God's presence among us, hearing every-

thing that passes, seeing all: let us not be downcast at the thought, surrounded by what is good; let us not drive him away. Let each one speak peace to his neighbor, pouring out words of consolation and comfort for his ears, not torrents of pestilential scurrility.

But if, after their talking, someone feels aware of hurt or loss (for the good of his conscience be it said), let him be humbled by the experience, making amends to whom amends may be due, whether by taking back what was said or by asking pardon, so that he may return to the peace of mind proper to prayer. May speaking to God be more pleasant for you than speaking to men, that you also may hear, through an inward instinct, what God is saying inwardly to you. May it be your merit to have waited in silence on God's good counsel. Resolve to avoid at each juncture the occasions for speaking, that you may lend an ear and a pure heart instead to God's inward promptings — which are liable, amidst the clatter of human speech, to go unheard and get blurred, or even driven out. O blessed silence, that God should find it worthy of his address, adding his voice! For it is in silence that he instructs the mind and instills compunction and remorse, softening the heart with tears, shedding his light, inflaming us with his love: and it is in silence that he refreshes us and inebriates the listener with the wine of his love. All this can escape a man's perception unless he travel far away, emptying himself out and making room for God in the silence and the solitude of his heart.

Responsory   *Ps 146:5-7; 118:8-9*

Happy are those who are helped by Jacob's God, whose hope is in the Lord their God. † It is he who keeps faith forever, and is just to those who are oppressed.

V. It is better to take refuge in the Lord than to trust in human help; better to take refuge in the Lord than to rely on princes. † It is he who . . .

Alternative Reading

From the writings of Max Picard (*Die Welt des Schweigens*, 24-25)

Speech and silence

Speech and silence go together. Speech without silence, the pause for reflection, would be like Shakespeare's clowns taken in isolation, without the contrasting sobriety of the more serious

roles; or like saints and martyrs in a somber medieval setting —
and no hint of their glorification. Whether it be speech or silence,
clown or hero, martyrdom or glorification, each complements the
other.

Spoken words must match the silence which they fill: and as
the words end, lapsing into silence, so a man's life itself sinks
finally into the abyss.

Truth is not the only quality words can possess: for there is
charity as well — no less part of the after-taste, in the silence
following the speech.

It is important that speech should match the pervading silence
in point of charity: for then charity is instilled into each word and
the speech embodies an inclination, a relation towards it. It is in
speech matched by the greatest silence that the greatest charity is
to be found.

Speech arising merely from some other speech is harsh and
aggressive. It is also lonely; and a great part of present-day melancholy arises from people making speeches really on their own,
soap-box fashion, separate from the needful silence, the pause for
reflection. This repudiation of silence (and repose) is a fault in a
man, the fault manifesting itself outwardly as melancholy; and it
is the dark frontier of melancholy that nowadays surrounds speech
— not any longer the interior border of silence.

Hence silence is there, present in speech, even after the speech
has arisen out of it. The world of speech is erected over the world
of silence. Speech is on a sure footing, confident to proceed in
sentences and ideas, always provided that the breadth and the
largesse inherent in silence extends beneath it, from which alone it
learns those qualities. Silence is to speech like the safety net beneath the man dancing on the high wires.

The mind behind the speech, yet somehow immense and intan-
gible within it, needs those unrestricted attributes of silence also,
to arch its own immensity over it. The mind may well indeed be
immense of itself; but the silence under it helps it move within its
own immensity. Silence is the natural basis for the immensity of
the mind, or spirit.

Silence is fundamentally the basis for spirit, the pedestal on
which it rests. What is unsayable and unsaid in the speech of some
mind links that mind with silence and makes it native to silence.

Speech has therefore a need to (moderate itself and) keep company with silence. The transparent, pervasive quality of silence makes the speech itself transparent, soaring aloft like a bright cloud over the sea of silence.

Responsory   *Ps 106:45; 89:34*
For their sake he remembered his covenant; † in his boundless love he relented.
V. I will never violate my covenant, nor go back on the promise I have made. † In his boundless . . .

FRIDAY   Year II

First Reading   Proverbs 15:8-9.16-17.25-26.29.33; 16:1-9; 17:5

Responsory   *Dt 6:12; Prv 15:33*
Never forget the Lord, who led you out of Egypt; † you shall fear the Lord, your God, and you shall serve him alone.
V. The fear of the Lord is a training in wisdom, and humility is the path to honors. † You shall fear . . .

Second Reading   From the writings of Julian of Norwich
                         (*Revelations of Divine Love* 74)

Reverent dread and humble love

Love and dread are brothers. They are rooted in us by the goodness of our Maker, and they will never be taken from us. We love by nature, and we love, too, by grace. We dread by nature, and, again, we dread by grace. It is right for the lordship and fatherhood of God to be feared, just as it is right for his goodness to be loved. And it is right for us, his servants and his children, to fear his lordship, and his fatherhood, just as it is right for us to love him for his goodness. Though this reverent dread and love may not be separated, they are not one but distinct, both in essence and in function. Yet neither can be had without the other. Hence my conviction that he who loves also dreads, even though he may be little aware of it.

All forms of dread other than the reverent one are not really holy though they sometimes seem to be. We can distinguish them in this way: the dread which makes us fly to our Lord, from all that is not good (the child to his mother's bosom), and fly with our whole heart; the same dread which knows our weakness and our need, and which knows too his everlasting, blessed love and goodness; the dread which finds its salvation in him alone, and clings to him in sure trust — the dread which does all that for us is kind and gracious, good and true. Anything contrary will be wrong, either wholly or in part. The solution is to recognize both states, and to reject the wrong one.

The effects which in this life naturally stem from reverent dread become, through the gracious working of the Holy Spirit, in heaven and before God, gentle, courteous, and delightful. There, through our love for him, we shall be near God and really at home; at the same time, through our dread, we shall be gentle before him, and courteous. Love and dread are both one in the end. It is our desire to fear our Lord God with all reverence, to love him in all humility, and to trust him with all our strength. When we dread and love him thus our trust is never in vain. The more we trust, and the more its strength, the more we please and honor the Lord we trust in. If we fail in this reverent dread and humble love (which God forbid!) our trust will be adversely affected at the same time. So there is much need to pray for grace from our Lord that he may give us this reverent dread and humble love both in our heart and in our work. For without this no one can please God.

Responsory   *Ps 113:4.6-7*

High above all nations is the Lord, yet he stoops from the heights to look down upon heaven and earth. † He lifts up the lowly from the dust, the needy from the dung-heap.
V. He has pulled down princes from their thrones and exalted the lowly. † He lifts up . . .

SATURDAY   Year II

First Reading   Proverbs 31:10-31

Responsory   *Jer 29:13-14; Mt 7:7*

You will seek me, and when you seek with your whole heart, you will find me; † I will let myself be found by you, says the Lord. I will restore your fortunes.
V. Seek, and you will find, knock on the door, and it will be opened to you. † I will let . . .

Second Reading   From a sermon by Adam of Perseigne
(Sermo, in Assumptione B. Mariae: PL 211, 734-736)

The woman of character

The *mulier fortis*, the woman of character, we can surely take to
be God's wisdom, in view of the rich abundance of all the blessings
that flow from it. For this it is which says: *I am the mother of tender
love, of fear, of due acknowledgment and sacred trust.* That wisdom
is the only true begetter of all things, the psalmist shows us when
he says: *You have created all things in wisdom* ("in" meaning "by,"
in Hebrew). Wisdom is regarded as a woman on account of its
fertility, and as being strong and full of character, because of its
omnipotence. Its strength and fortitude can be most clearly perceived in two ways: from its unlimited power and its unlimited
patience. Because it has no need of anything, its act of creating all
things was a sign of its pure power, just as its accepting every injury
from the unjust with equanimity and limitless patience shows its
complete innocence. Its fruitfulness likewise can be best considered under two heads: the fullness of wisdom and the fullness of
mercy. It is its wisdom whereby shape and order are given to the
universe, and the divine mercy whereby God has released the old
Adam in us from the death that was owing, by the grace flowing
from that death which was *not* owing and the price paid by Christ
in his own blood. What a unique combination of power and
fecundity! How strong in her weakness was this woman called
Wisdom! How fertile in her poverty!

The infirmity is manifest when the Lord of all things empties
himself out, taking the character of a servant, and the poverty,
when he has nowhere to rest his head, on the earth which he
created. But in truth that act of self-abasement accomplished the
salvation of humankind, and the state of poverty brought abundance to the poor. While the Lord of all, rich as he was, made
himself subject to the disadvantages of our needy condition, the
insecurity of our state of poverty grew into the security inseparable
from the Godhead. So fruitful was this emptying out that it added
glory to the angels, gave joy to the shepherds, faith to the magi,
and peace to those of good will. The weakness was so strong that
it cured paralytics and lepers, gave sight to the blind, hearing to

the deaf, the powers of walking to the lame and speaking to the dumb. Indeed, it raised the dead to life.

So strong, then, was this infirmity that when Christ died, according to his passible, suffering nature, the sun was darkened, the earth shook, the veil of the temple was torn asunder, rocks were split, tombs opened, and the bodies of holy men and women were brought to life again; hell was plundered, and in a wonderful manner (we see how) the stability of the established order was thoroughly disturbed, just at the moment when our Lady (Seat of Wisdom) was brought lowest in the estimation of men, for her seeming weakness. But then, where, or by whom, is the Lady found to be strong? The answer is: where small children, meaning the humble, treasure up wisdom: and no matter that wisdom has its abode in the heights, humility all the easier making its way thither. For the lower it abases itself, with all the more familiarity does the sublimest wisdom come without our grasp. It is the proud whom God rejects, bestowing his grace instead

Responsory   *Ps 104:30; Wis 1:7*

When you send forth your Spirit they are created, and † you renew the face of the earth.
V. The Spirit of the Lord has filled the whole world. † You renew . . .

Alternative Reading

From the writings of Luis de León (The Perfect Wife, 88-89)

The perfect wife

We know that everything, in which there is the least glimmer of good, is favorably regarded and appreciated, but no other good appears so patent to the eyes of beholders, nor arouses in the hearts of men such deep content as does a perfect wife. Nothing else is there concerning which men speak with such gladness or with such exalted expressions — either alone, in their intimate communings with themselves, or in conversation with others; either within their homes, or openly and in public.

For some will extol her housewifely capacities; other will laud her discretion; still others will exalt to the heavens her modesty, her purity, her sympathy, her sweet and sincere gentleness. They will comment on her shining countenance, the neatness of her dress, the labors of her hands, her watchings by night. They will mark the improvement in her serving-folk, the increasing value of her worldly property, her friendly and pacific intercourse with her neighbors. Her charities will not be overlooked. Men will recount how she has loved and how she has won her husband, praise the upbringing of her children, the fair treatment of all her dependents. Her deeds, her words, her looks will be magnified. They will make mention of her as holy in the sight of God, a source of bliss to her husband. They will call down blessings on her home, praise her kinsfolk, and count those happy who have been privileged to see and talk with her. She will be likened unto holy Judith, and called the glory of her race, the crown of her people. And for all that they say, they will find still more to say. Her fellow townsfolk sound her praises to the stranger within their gates. Pointing to her, parents take her as an example for their children, and the children for their children, and so her fame extends everywhere, and ever more and more. Her memory passes on from generation to generation, its voice clearly heard and external.

Years work no injury to her; time does not wither, rather does it cause her to blossom afresh. For she is as one planted by the watercourses, so that in her there will be no decay. Nor will age suffer her house, founded in the heavens, to fall. Therefore this only can come to pass: her praise is deathless whose entire span of life was an increasing homage to the goodness and grandeur of God, to whom alone is due eternal exaltation and glory. Amen.

Responsory   *Ps 104:30; Wis 1:7*
When you send forth your Spirit they are created, and † you renew the face of the earth.
V. The Spirit of the Lord has filled the whole world. † You renew the . . .

FIFTEENTH WEEK IN ORDINARY TIME

SUNDAY Year II

First Reading Job 1:1-22

Responsory *Jb 2:10; 1:21*

If we receive happiness from God, should we not accept sorrow also? † The Lord gives and the Lord takes away; may his will be done. Blessed be the name of the Lord.
V. Naked I came from my mother's womb, and naked I shall return. † The Lord gives . . .

Second Reading From the writings of Saint Gregory the Great
(Moralia in Job II, 17, 30—18, 31; SC 32bis, 203-205)

Job ends by praising God

When Job lost everything, at Almighty's God decree, to preserve his peace of mind he bethought himself of the time when he did not yet possess the things he had now lost; in that way, by realizing more and more clearly that once he had not had them, he would the more easily moderate his grief over their loss. For indeed whenever we lose something it can be a great consolation to call to mind the days when it so happened that we did not have it.

So, then, the blessed Job, wishing to cultivate patience as he bewails his losses, carefully considers to what state he is now reduced. To enhance his peace of mind he ponders yet more closely his origins, saying as he does so: *Naked I came from my mother's womb, naked I shall return whence I came.* In other words, the earth produced me naked, and naked will receive me back when I leave it. Since therefore the things I have lost were only what I had received and must perforce leave behind, what have I lost that really belonged to me? But then, because consolation derives not only from thinking about one's condition but also about the creator's uprightness, he is right to add: *The Lord has given, the Lord has taken away; as it has pleased the Lord, so has he wrought.*

He well says, *as it has pleased the Lord.* For since in this world we have to put up with things we do not like, it is needful that we should accommodate our best endeavors to him who cannot will anything that is unjust. Indeed, as regards whatever it is that displeases us, we have the consolation of knowing that we have it as his decree who takes pleasure only in what is just. If therefore we know that it is what is just and equitable that pleases the Lord, and that we can suffer nothing but what is pleasing to him, then all our sufferings must for that reason be justly and fairly imposed: and it would therefore be very unjust of us to grumble at suffering justly imposed.

We should note that, having got all that right, Job ends by praising God. This was so that his adversary might realize, overcome by shame at seeing Job's plight, that his own attitude, established in well-being as he is, is one of contempt for God, the same God to whom even this man, now fallen on evil times, can nevertheless sing a hymn of praise. We should realize that the enemy of our race can smite us with as many of his darts as there are temptations for him to afflict us with. For we do battle daily; and daily his onslaught of temptations rains down on us. But we in turn can fire our darts against him if, while buried in our tribulations, we will but react in humility. So it is that Job, albeit smitten by material afflictions, is after all a blessed and happy man.

We should not think that our champion merely receives wounds without inflicting any in return. Indeed, every prayer of patience offered by the sufferer in God's praise is a dart turned against the enemy's breast: and a much sharper blow is thereby struck than the one sustained. For the man in his afflictions loses only earthly goods, whereas in bearing humbly with his afflictions he has increased many times over his stock in heaven.

Responsory   *Sir 42:15-16; 43:28*

By the words of the Lord his works come into being, and all creation obeys his will. † As the sun as it shines looks upon all things, so the work of the Lord is full of his glory.

V. Where can we find the power to praise him, since he is greater than all his works? † As the sun . . .

MONDAY   Year II

First Reading   Job 2:1-13

Responsory   *Ps 38:2.3.4.12*
O God, do not chastise me in your anger, for your arrows have
pierced me through. † My body is sick because of your indignation.
V. My friends and neighbors avoid me in my sickness. † My body
is . . .

Second Reading   From a homily by Saint John Chrysostom
(Hom. in paralyticum demissum per tecta: PG 51, 62-63)

A steadfast example in Job

We can find ample consolation not only in the New Testament
but in the Old Testament as well. Consider the story of Job, and
how, after the loss of his wealth and the destruction of his herds,
not one, two or even three of his children were taken from him, but
all of them together in the very flower of their youth. When you
hear of his great spiritual courage, even if you are the weakest of
men, it is not so difficult to recover yourself and return to life.

For you, my friend, at least watched over your sick child as he
lay on his bed, you heard his last words and attended him as his
life came to an end, you shut his eyes and closed his mouth. But
Job was not present at his children's death, nor saw them dying in
the house where all were buried as in a single tomb. Yet after such
overwhelming disasters he neither grieved nor despaired, but said:
*The Lord gave, and the Lord has taken away; it has been done as the
Lord willed. Blessed be the name of the Lord for ever.*

Let us too utter these words in every misfortune that life brings
us, be it loss of wealth, bodily sickness, abuse, slander, or any other
human ill. Let us say: *The Lord gave, and the Lord has taken away;
it has been done as the Lord willed. Blessed be the name of the Lord for
ever.*

If we make this our philosophy, no misfortune will ever cause
us suffering, however many we endure. The gain will always be
greater then the loss, and the good will outweigh the bad, since
with these words you attract the favor of God and shake off the
tyranny of the devil. For as soon as you utter them, the devil at
once takes to flight, and when he has gone the cloud of dejection

lifts too and oppressive thoughts disappear in the company of their master; and besides all this you will have as your reward all the blessings both of earth and of heaven. You have a steadfast example in Job and also in the apostles, who scorned the terrors of this world for God's sake, and so gained the blessings of eternity. Let us then follow them, and in all that happens to us rejoice and give thanks to the benevolent God. So shall we pass this present life in contentment and gain the blessings to come, by the grace and kindness of our Lord Jesus Christ, to whom be glory, honor and power at all times, now and for ever and to endless ages. Amen.

Responsory   *Ps 118:33.34; Ps 18:8*
Teach me the demands of your statutes and I will keep them to the end. † Train me to observe your law, to keep it with my whole heart.
V. The precepts of the Lord are right, they gladden the heart. † Train me . . .

Alternative Reading

From the writings of Cardinal Jean Daniélou (*Holy Pagans of the Old Testament*, 89-90)

Job, once loaded with possessions, now a derelict

Did Job truly love God for himself or for the good things he had received from him? Was his religion without ulterior motive? Maybe he was unduly attached to his human happiness, to his family life, to the riches he possessed, to the esteem he enjoyed. More subtly still, perhaps he found a certain complacency in his very righteousness and in the privileges it earned him. That was precisely what Satan thought, not believing in Job's sincerity.

That is why it was necessary that Job's righteousness should be tested, and the essential theme, a new one, of the book of Job is this testing of righteousness. In order to discover whether Job loved God for himself or for what he received from God, he must be deprived of these good things, and this is what God allows Satan to do. It is important to note that it is a matter of permission. The law of the cosmic covenant, the temporal reward of virtue, is not abrogated, but only suspended. The proof of this is that Job will later recover his family, his herds and his good name. This is the primary meaning, at least, of what happened, the one we shall deal with first of all.

Here, then, is Job, once loaded with possessions, now a derelict. Everything he possessed has been taken away from him. Fire has consumed his sheep, the Chaldeans have stolen his camels, his children have been crushed to death. By a worse humiliation he is stricken with a repulsive leprosy, making him an object of loathing, to add to the suffering it inflicted on him. The esteem he had enjoyed disappears with his prosperity. Those who saw in his success a blessing from God now, quite logically, see in his downfall a divine condemnation and probe him to find out why. He becomes the laughing-stock of the young men, who make songs about him and spit in his face.

But the trial does not shake his righteousness. He does not hurl any curse at God, as his wife suggests. His integrity remains unshaken. He will accept unhappiness from God just as he had received happiness; *If we have received good things at the hand of God, why should we not receive evil?* Thus the spontaneity of his love is made evident. He is bound to God for himself and not for what he receives from him. His love was without ulterior motive; his righteousness was sincere; his fidelity in his unhappiness proves his fidelity in his happiness.

Responsory   *Ps 68:3; 1 Cor 2:9*

The righteous shall rejoice before God, † they shall exult and dance for joy.
V. Eye has not seen, nor ear heard, nor human heart conceived what God has prepared for those who love him. † They shall exult . . .

TUESDAY   Year II

First Reading   Job 3:1-26

Responsory   *Jb 3:24-26; 6:13*

My sighs have become my food, and my tears pour forth like flowing streams; whatever I fear happens, whatever I dread befalls me, † and trouble comes, O Lord.
V. I am a man without help, and aid is beyond my reach. † And trouble comes, O Lord.

Second Reading   From a letter by Saint John of the Cross
(Cartas 19)

The one who seeks nothing but God does not walk in darkness

When you are passing through that state of darkness and emptiness which belongs to spiritual poverty, you think that everyone and everything are lacking to you. That is not surprising, since at these times it also seems as if you have nothing to concern yourself with, indeed nothing at all that you either are aware of or will become so: for all that is groundless supposition.

He who seeks nothing but God does not walk in darkness, no matter how benighted or impoverished he may seem to be. And he who does not walk in presumption or in his own desire, desire neither for God nor for creatures, nor does his own will in this or in anything else, this man has nothing to stumble over or worry about. In that state, you are progressing well: do not fret but rejoice instead. Who are you, that you should worry about yourself? You would do well to stop it. Never have you been in a better state than you are now; for you have never been so humble, so submissive, taking so little account of yourself and of everything there is in the world; neither have you recognized yourself as being so evil hitherto, or God as so good, nor served God in such purity and disinterest as now, or gone into the flaws in your own motivation and integrity as perhaps you were accustomed to.

What is it that you want? What life, what way of going on do you picture yourself as pursuing in this life? What do you think it means, to serve God without doing evil, keeping his commandments? And to walk in the ways as best we can? If we do this, what need have we of other ideas or other delights or sweetness from other sources, where ordinarily there is no lack of pitfalls and dangers to the soul, which is prone to be deceived and enraptured with its notions and its desires, and with its own powers, which make it go astray? And so it is a great favor from God when the soul obscures and debilitates them, so that it cannot wander off with them. And since it cannot go astray, what is left over for it to do but to proceed along the straight road, the one laid down by the law of God and the Church, living only in faith that is obscure and true, certain hope, and flawless charity, and to hope for our good things there, while living here as pilgrims, poor people, exiles, orphans, waifs, and strays, out of the way and out of everything, hoping for all things there.

Rejoice and trust in God, who has given you signs of how well you can do, and indeed must do. If you do otherwise, it will not be surprising if he should be displeased at seeing you so foolish, having led you in the way most fitting for you and put you in so secure a place. Desire nothing but this way of progress and be tranquil in your soul: for all is well.

Responsory   *Ps 113:1.3.5*
When Israel came forth from Egypt, the house of Jacob from an alien people, † the sea fled at the sight; the Jordan turned back on its course.
V. Why was it, sea, that you fled, that you turned back, Jordan, on your course? † The sea fled . . .

WEDNESDAY   Year II

First Reading   Job 4:1-21

Responsory   *Dt 31:23.6; Prv 3:26*
Be strong and steadfast, for the Lord your God is going with you.
† He goes before you; there is nothing you need fear.
V. The Lord will be at your side to keep your foot from stumbling.
† He goes before . . .

Second Reading   From the writings of Meister Eckhart
                    (*The Book of Divine Comfort* 3, 90-91)

Pain and sorrow

You should know that it is impossible for all nature to break, destroy or even touch anything without intending betterment for that which is touched. Not content with doing equal good, she always wants to do something better. How is that? A wise physician never touches a man's bad finger so as to hurt him unless he can make the finger better, or make the man generally better, or give him relief. If he can make the man or the finger better, he does so. If he cannot, he cuts off the finger to benefit the man. And it is much better to lose the finger and save the man than to let both perish. One loss is preferable to two, especially when one is so much greater than the other. One should also realize that the finger, the hand, or any limb loves the person it belongs to far more dearly than itself, and will willingly, happily and without question endure pain for that person. I declare with assurance and in truth that such a member cares absolutely nothing for itself except for the sake of that, and in that, of which it is a member. Accordingly it would only be right and proper, and in conformity with our nature, if we loved ourselves solely for God's sake and in God. And if that were so, then everything would be easy and pleasant for us that God wanted from us and in us, especially if we realized that God could much less tolerate any lack or loss, if he did not know and intend a much greater advantage from it. Indeed, if a man has not trust in God on that score, it is quite right that he should have pain and sorrow.

Here is another consolation. Saint Paul says that God chastens all whom he accepts and receives as sons. Sonship involves suffering. Because God's Son could not suffer in the Godhead and in eternity, the heavenly Father sent him into time, to become man and suffer. So, if you want to be God's son and yet do not want to suffer, you are wrong. In the Book of Wisdom it says that God proves and tests to find out who is righteous, as we prove and test gold by fire in a furnace. It is a sign that a king or a prince trusts a knight when he sends him into battle. I have seen one lord who sometimes, when he had taken a man into his retinue, would send him out by night and then attack him and fight with him. And once it happened that he was nearly killed by a man he wanted to test in this way, and he was much fonder of that retainer afterwards than before.

Responsory   *Ps 43:3.2*

Their own sword did not win them the land, nor their own arm give them victory. † It was your right hand, your arm, and the light of your face, for you loved them.

V. Our fathers have told us the story of the deeds you did in their days. † It was your . . .

THURSDAY   Year II

First Reading   Job 5:1-27

Responsory   *Rom 8:17; 5:9*
We are God's heirs and coheirs with Christ, † if only we suffer with
him so that we may also be glorified with him.
V. Now that we have been justified in his blood, it is all the more
likely that he will save us from God's anger. † If only we . . .

Second Reading   From a sermon by Blessed Oger of Locedio
                      (PL 184, 927-928)

Job explains how it is that we can resist temptation

Those whom the Lord loves, he chastises: he chastises every
child he regards as his own. It is those people who are to be given
an eternity of rejoicing that feel the lash of his correction; but he
who grumbles of being beaten comes no nearer the taskmaster set
above him. Indeed, he will forgo his legacy of happiness in heaven
if he does not submit in patience and love to the scourge wielded
by God the Father. He who grumbles at the Lord's correction may
be sure of incurring the penalty reserved for grumblers.

Do not complain, then, beloved brethren, if you have to put up
with the Lord's correction; and do not feel frustrated when he
reproaches you. For all correction is bound to seem, in our present
state, a matter for grief, not for rejoicing; but later on, the serenity
resulting from it, in those who withstand the trial, restores the
needful balance. The grossness of bodily leisure is checked by the
Lord's scourges, and the soul is strengthened in virtue: and so the
unworthy impulses of our nature are checked and the soul is raised
on the wings of virtue to the contemplation of heavenly things. The
flesh forfeits what it has no further need of, and the spirit acquires
virtues which it did not have before. In this way, virtue is enhanced
by the Lord's correction and vice is cut back; what is mundane
comes to be despised, and heavenly things loved. If as we wait for
the rewards of eternity we are afflicted by some grave illness, or
strong temptation, even (it may be) some loss of temporal fortune,
we can and must draw strength from all of this. For when the battle
rages fiercest we need not doubt but that the victory which remains
ours will be all the more glorious. In this way we show how

ardently we long for God, going to him, not by the paths of tranquillity and comfort alone, but through hard, bitter experience as well. We cannot now return to the lost joys of paradise, except by way of temporal discomfort; and so with our hope of lasting happiness we must not underestimate the prospect of that which is inherent in our adversity. God's strictness never permits sin to go unpunished: but the anger of his judgment begins here and now with our chastisement; just as it will rest permanently on the reprobate, in their damnation.

Inside each of us is a doctor who cuts out the diseased, sinful parts which he finds ingrained in us: he cuts out the poison causing the rottenness by wielding the knife of tribulation. The *Truth Incarnate* has expressly told us that *every branch bearing fruit in me, God the Father will prune, to make it carry more fruit.* For when the mind experiencing temptation considers and realizes how much it has been displaced from the stability of its erstwhile virtue, it is in fear lest what it had just been about to gain should be utterly lost to it. Job explains how it is that we can resist temptation, and what power there is in us to fight it. He draws the sword of prayer, with the weeping of compunction and contrition: these weaken the force of temptation and Job's triumph is glorious. It is not Job himself, but the grace of Christ working through his prayer. And so it is that a mind which has been lazy and unfruitful in prosperity can rise up, to become stronger and more abundantly fruitful.

Responsory   *Ps 88:2.9; Ps:5:2*

Let my prayer come into your presence; incline your ear to my cry.
† I call to you, Lord, all the day long; to you I stretch out my hands.
V. Hearken to the sound of my cries, my king and my God. † I call to . . .

FRIDAY   Year II

First Reading   Job 6:1-30

Responsory   *Eph 4:15; Prv 4:18*
Let us speak the truth in love † so that in all things we may grow
into Christ who is our head.
V. The path of the just is like the passage of the dawn; it grows from
first light to the full splendor of day. † So that in . . .

Second Reading   From the writings of Saint Gregory the Great
                      (Moralia in Job XXIII, 2: PL 76, 251)

The allurement of fragrant leaves

It is because the ancient Fathers resemble trees bearing abundant fruit, being not merely attractive figures in themselves but
productive also of positive results, that their lives are so well worth
considering. For in so doing, we realize, as we wonder at the
freshness and originality of people in history, how much fecundity
there is in allegory, and how the sweetness of fruit to the taste can
be anticipated from the allurement of fragrant leaves. No one has
ever had the grace of supernatural adoption except through his
acknowledgment of the Only-begotten. And so it is fitting that he
who enlightens men and women that they may merit to shine forth
should himself be manifest in their lives and their words. For when
a lantern is lit in the darkness it is the lantern itself which is seen
before all the rest, everything else that it lights up. Hence if we
really wish to discern what has been made visible, we must try to
open the eyes of our minds to the light itself. This lesson shines
through the speeches of the blessed Job, like a fleeting twinkle,
even when those involved allegories are edited out and forgotten,
and the shadows of the darkest hours of night are as it were
removed. For he says: *I know that my Redeemer lives, and in my flesh
I shall see God.*

Indeed Saint Paul had found this same light in the night of
history, when he said: *All were baptized in the power of Moses, in
the cloud and in the sea, and all ate the same spiritual food and drank
the same spiritual drink. But they drank of the spiritual rock which
lay in their path: and the rock was Christ.* If, then, the rock was a type
or figure of the Redeemer, why should not the blessed Job apply

and use a figure of him whom he foretold and marked, indeed identified, with suffering? Wherefore Job is not without reason said to be grieving precisely because he bears in himself the likeness of him whom Isaiah had long ago announced as taking our sorrows on himself. Moreover our Redeemer showed himself to be one and the same person identified with his Holy Church which he took up and manifested. For of him it is said: *He is the head, Christ himself.* And again, of his Church it is written: *And the body of Christ, which is the Church.* Hence the blessed Job, who presented the type and bore the mark of the Mediator all the more faithfully for having prefigured his passion not merely in speech but even in suffering, since in his words and deeds he finds support in the idea of a redeemer, has lighted in a flash on the very significance of the body itself. Believing Christ and his Church to be one person, let us view it in the light of one person and everything he does, the body and its every act.

Responsory   *Ps 5:7; Is 6:3*

Through the greatness of your love I have access to your house. † I bow down before your holy temple, filled with awe.
V. Holy, holy, holy is the Lord of hosts; the whole earth is full of his glory. † I bow down . . .

SATURDAY   Year II

First Reading   Job 7:1-21

Responsory   *Rom 12:16; 1 Cor 3:18-19; 1:23.24*

Never allow yourself to be self-satisfied; if you pride yourself on your worldly wisdom, you will have to unlearn it all before you are truly wise; † worldly wisdom is foolishness in the eyes of God.
V. We preach a crucified Christ, and he is the power of God and the wisdom of God. † Worldly wisdom is . . .

Second Reading   From the writings of Saint John of the Cross
(The Ascent of Mount Carmel 1, 3)

Night for the soul

We shall call the absence of pleasure in the appetite for anything simply "night." For night is but the absence or privation of daylight, and for that reason also the privation of all the things that can be seen through the medium of light, whereby the power of vision remains in darkness and dispossessed of everything. So likewise the mortification of the appetite can be termed night for the soul, or (as we shall say) the night of the soul, since the state of being bereft of the pleasure of desiring anything is like remaining in the dark, with nothing there. For just as the power of vision makes use of the light to thrive and feed on the objects which can be seen, but are not seen when the light is extinguished, so also by using the appetites the soul is nourished and thrives on all those things which it can take pleasure in, according to its powers; whereas when the appetite is quenched, or rather mortified, the soul leaves off finding its nourishment in the pleasure it takes in all those things, and hence remains, as regards appetite and desire, in the dark, with nothing there.

For though it is true that it cannot leave off hearing and seeing and smelling and tasting and touching, yet it no longer does all that fortuitously, neither does the soul any longer embrace what it rejects or withstands without seeing or hearing or otherwise sensing it, just as he who wishes to close his eyes remains in the dark like a blind man lacking the power to see. As David says on this: *I am a poor man and a laborer from my youth*. He calls himself a poor man (though of course he was a *rich* man) because his heart was not in his being rich: and so it was as if he really were a poor man; whereas conversely if he had in sober truth been poor, but not reconciled to it, he would not then have been truly poor, spiritually poor, his soul being rich, indeed replete, with desires. For this reason we call this bareness the night of the soul, as we are not concerned here with mere lack of riches (which indeed will not lay bare the soul which nevertheless has the *desire* for riches) but with stripping the soul bare of all pleasure in or desire for them. It is this which leaves the soul free and, even though one may still possess riches, it is this which annuls them. For such mundane concerns are of no interest to the soul; neither can they harm it, since the only things that are of interest to it are the will and the desire for those riches which dwell in the soul itself.

Responsory   *Ps 37:1-3.16*

Do not fret because of the wicked, or envy those who do evil, for soon they will fade like the grass, and wither like green pasture. † Trust in the Lord and do good, and you will live in the land and be secure.

V. The few possessions of the righteous are better than the wealth of the wicked. † Trust in the . . .

SIXTEENTH WEEK IN ORDINARY TIME

SUNDAY   Year II

First Reading   Job 11:1-20

Responsory   *2 Cor 4:8-9.10*

We are afflicted in every way but never overwhelmed; we are
bewildered but never lose hope; † we suffer persecution, but have
not been abandoned.
V. At every moment we carry in our bodies the death of Jesus so
that in our bodies the life of Jesus may also be manifested. † We
suffer persecution . . .

Second Reading   From the writings of Jean-Pierre de Caussade
                        (Abandonment to Divine Providence I, 2)

God is revealing to us

All creatures that exist are in the hand of God. The action of the
creature can be perceived only by the senses, but faith sees in all
things the action of the Creator. It believes that in Jesus Christ all
things live, and that his divine operation continues to the end of
time, embracing the passing moment and the smallest atom in its
hidden life and mysterious action. The action of the creature is a
veil which covers the profound mysteries of the divine operation.

After the resurrection Jesus Christ took his disciples by surprise
in his various apparitions. He showed himself to them under
various disguises and, in the act of making himself known to them,
disappeared. This same Jesus, ever living, ever working, still takes
by surprise those souls whose faith is weak and wavering.

There is not a moment in which God does not present himself
under the cover of some pain to be endured, of some consolation
to be enjoyed, or of some duty to be performed. All that takes place
within us, around us, or through us contains and conceals his
divine action. If we were attentive and watchful God would continually reveal himself to us, and we should see his divine action
in everything that happened to us, and rejoice in it. At each
successive occurrence we should exclaim, *It is the Lord!* and we
should accept every fresh circumstance as a gift from God. We

should look upon creatures as feeble tools in the hands of an able workman, and we should discover easily that nothing was wanting to us, and that the constant providence of God disposed him to bestow upon us at every moment whatever we required.

Pursue then without ceasing, you faithful souls, this beloved one who with giant strides passes from one end of the heavens to the other. If you are content, nothing will hide him from you. He moves above the smallest blades of grass as above the mighty cedar. The grains of sand are under his feet as well as the huge mountains. Wherever you may turn, there you will find his footprints, and in following them perseveringly you will find him wherever you may be.

The present moment is the ambassador of God to declare his mandates. The heart listens and pronounces its *Fiat*. Thus the soul advances by all these things, and flows out from its center to its goal. It never stops but sails with every wind. Any and every direction leads equally to the shore of infinity. Everything is a help to it, and is, without exception, an instrument of sanctity.

To hallow the name of God is to know, to adore and to love his adorable will at every moment and in all its decrees. It was for this reason that Job blessed the name of God in his utter desolation. Instead of looking upon his condition as ruin, he called it the name of God, and by blessing it he protested that the divine will, under whatever form it might appear, even though expressed by the most terrible catastrophes, was holy.

Responsory   *1 Cor 10:11-12; Is 48:15*

These things happened as warnings and were written down for our instruction. Therefore † let those who think they are standing firm be careful or they may fall.

V. I myself have spoken and called him, brought him and prospered his plans. † Let those who . . .

MONDAY   Year II

First Reading   Job 12:1-25

Responsory   *Jb 12:13.14; 23:13*
   With God is all wisdom and power; in him are counsel and understanding. † When he destroys, there is no rebuilding; if he imprisons
   a man, no one can release him.
   V. Once he has decided, no one can change his mind; whatever he
   determines, he does. † When he destroys . . .

Second Reading   From the writings of Cardinal Jean Daniélou
                        (*Holy Pagans of the Old Testament*, 92-93)

*Suffering brings into the heart
something of the very mystery of existence*

   The cries which the insupportable character of suffering wrings
from Job are among the most vehement ever uttered. Against this
suffering he protests with his whole being. He will have not truck
with it. There is no trace of resignation in him either. The picture
of "Job the Patient" is a later elaboration; nothing could be less
patient than the true Job. He bears witness to the existence of
suffering and can do no other. Nothing can give him ease. Words
of consolation seem to him like derision. Only one course is possible in the face of it, either to fight it or to give way to it. Thus it
appears as an absolute, outside all discussion; and that is why the
discourses of Job's friends seem derisory. Suffering brings into the
heart something of the very mystery of existence.
   This is all the more striking in the case of Job because it is a
question of the suffering of a righteous man. This suffering is
therefore not susceptible of any explanation; it is wholly divorced
from reasoning; it derives from existence and not from logic. It
appears as a pure paradox, as the outcome of an irrational world.
But at the same time it brings us to the reality of existence; it lays
bare the roots of being. By depriving Job of everything that is not
essential, suffering makes him the pattern of sheer humanity. It
takes away from his righteousness everything that might possibly
disguise it, it loosens it from every compromise with happiness.

Responsory   Ps 55:22; 37:5
Entrust your cares to the Lord and he will support you. † He will
never allow the righteous to stumble.
V. Commit your life to the Lord; trust in him and he will act. † He
will never . . .

TUESDAY   Year II

First Reading   Job 13:13—14:6

Responsory   See Jb 13:20.21; see Jer 10:24
O Lord, do not hide your face from me; lift away from me the weight
of your hand, † and let not the fear of you terrify me.
V. O God, rebuke me with gentleness and not in anger, for your
anger will reduce me to nothing. † And let not . . .

Second Reading   From the writings of Thomas Merton
                        (*No Man Is an Island*, 69-72)

The saint is one so attuned to the spirit and heart of Christ

The saint is not one who accepts suffering because he likes it,
and confesses this preference before God and men in order to win
a great reward. He is one who may well hate suffering as much as
anybody else, but who so loves Christ, whom he does not see, that
he will allow his love to be proved by any suffering. And he does
this not because he thinks it is an achievement, but because the
charity of Christ in his heart demands that it be done.

The saint is one so attuned to the spirit and heart of Christ that
he is compelled to answer the demands of love by a love that
matches that of Christ. This is for him a need so deep and so
personal and so exacting that it becomes his whole destiny. The
more he answers the secret action of Christ's love in his own heart,
the more he comes to know love's inexorable demands.

But the life of the Christian soul must always be a thing whole
and simple and complete and incommunicable. The saints may
seem to desire suffering in a universal and abstract way. Actually,
the only sufferings anyone can validly desire are those precise,
particular trials that are demanded of us in the designs of divine
providence for our own lives.

Some men have been picked out to bear witness to Christ's love in lives overwhelmed by suffering. These have proclaimed that suffering was their vocation. But that should not lead us to believe that in order to be a saint one must go out for suffering in the same way that a college athlete goes out for football. No two men have to suffer exactly the same trials in exactly the same way. No one man is ever called to suffer merely for the sake of suffering.

What, after all, is more personal than suffering? The awful futility of our attempts to convey the reality of our sufferings to other people, and the tragic inadequacy of human sympathy, both prove how incommunicable a thing suffering really is.

Suffering, therefore, must make sense to us not as a vague universal necessity, but as something demanded by our own personal destiny. When I see my trials not as the collision of my life with a blind machine called fate, but as the sacramental gift of Christ's love, given to me by God the Father along with my identity and my very name, then I can consecrate them and myself with them to God. For then I realize that my suffering is not my own. It is the passion of Christ, stretching out its tendrils into my life in order to bear rich clusters of grapes, making my soul dizzy with the wine of Christ's love, and pouring that wine as strong as fire upon the whole world.

Responsory   *Ps 149:2-4*
Let Israel rejoice in its Maker; let the people of Zion exult in their king. † Let them praise his name with dancing, and sing psalms to him with timbrel and lyre.
V. For the Lord accepts the service of his people; he crowns the humble with victory. † Let them praise . . .

WEDNESDAY   Year II

First Reading   Job 18:1-21

Responsory   *Prv 3:11, 12; Heb 12:7*
Do not resent the Lord's correction, and take no offense when he
rebukes you; † for those whom he loves the Lord reproves, just as
a father chastises a favorite son.
V. God is treating you as his sons, for what son is there whom his
father does not discipline? † For those whom . . .

Second Reading   From a letter by Saint Fulgentius of Ruspe
                              (Epistola II, 9, 15-18: CCL 91, 203)

The good things of this life can be ours for good or evil

There are blessings in the temporal order which God may grant
here, but withhold or withdraw there: for instance, the blessings
of the married state, the procreation of children, abundance in
worldly goods, bodily health, and so forth. Such things can make
people happy — or make them miserable. The Lord bestows them
on the good and the wicked alike: and sometimes they are removed
by the same divine hand, whether from the good or the wicked.

Job was blessed, a happy man indeed, when living uprightly
amidst all his wealth; and yet he was more blessed in his even more
upright and irreproachable condition of poverty. He was blessed
when surrounded by his ten children, but more blessed when,
smitten with the loss of all of them at once, he nevertheless remained unshakable in his love for God. He was blessed in his
bodily health, but rendered more so by the wounds and injuries,
the ulcers and sores that he received: more blessed on his dung
heap than in a palace adorned with marble.

We observe the difference, the contrast: one man is well endowed with riches and good health, yet miserable; another, destitute and plagued by ill-health, is a genuinely happy man even so.
The rich man who dressed in purple and fine linen and fared
sumptuously every day lived such a pointless life, for all his
feasting. How impoverished he really was, despite the vast wealth!
How naked despite the fine apparel, how sick for all his bodily
fitness, how famished for all the unstinted fare, how wretched in
his merry-making, how lonely amidst the conversation of friends,

how downcast for all the pampering by the menials! How different from Lazarus, made rich in his poverty, blessed in his wretchedness, happy in his misfortune, made sound again despite his sores, homeless indeed, yet making himself at home; without clothing but not without faith; without the strength of bodily health, yet strong in charity; without food yet not without Christ; exposed to dogs, but the companion of angels; not offered even the very crumbs from the rich man's table, yet regaled with the bread of heaven.

The good things of this life can be ours for good or evil; they are to be rated accordingly. Temporal blessings, then, it is sometimes good to enjoy, but sometimes not; sometimes it is good to despise them, but sometimes it is not. It is good indeed to have them when they conduce to the fear of God; but equally it can be good to despise them, when that is done for the sake of the glory that comes from Almighty God himself, and not from human beings.

Responsory   *Ps 91:11-12; Heb 12:1*

He will charge his angels to guard you wherever you go; † they will bear you upon their hands that you may not strike your foot against a stone.
V. Since we are surrounded by so great a cloud of witnesses, let us run with resolution the race that lies before us, our eyes fixed on Jesus, the pioneer and perfecter of our faith. † They will bear . . .

THURSDAY   Year II

First Reading   Job 19:1-29

Responsory   *Ps 37:30.31; 112:6.7*

The mouth of the just man utters wisdom, and his tongue speaks what is right. † The law of God is in his heart.
V. The just man will be remembered for ever; he shall have no fear of evil news. † The law of . . .

Second Reading   From the writings of Cardinal Jean Daniélou
(*Holy Pagans of the Old Testament*, 99-101)

Job and Christ

The comparison between Job and Christ bears not only upon some particular aspect, such as temptation, patience, suffering. It bears upon the human condition as such in terms of suffering, that is to say as a question mark. It goes further than merely to prefigure Judaism; it touches humanity as a whole. When Jesus, stripped of his garments, covered with bruises, encompassed with shame, stands before the judgment seat of Pilate, the Roman judge, it is not Isaac or Moses or David that is recalled to mind. He transcends the prefiguration of Judaism. Pilate is right in saying: *Ecce homo*. He is mankind itself reduced to the nakedness of its tragic condition; and Job was its most perfect prefiguration.

Thus there is a real and mysterious link between Job and Jesus. Job is the question, Jesus the answer.

Jesus is the immediate answer to Job because he shares his suffering and is the only one to do so. Suffering encloses a man in solitude, puts him outside communion with his fellow men. Between Job and his friends an abyss was cleft. They regarded him with astonishment as a strange being, as the sudden appearance of the unprecedented in the midst of the very ordinary, as one marked with a sacred sign. But they could no longer get to him. Only Jesus could cross this abyss, descend into the abyss of misery, plunge into the deepest hell. And it is only because he has first shared the suffering of everyone who suffers that in him and by him every man who suffers can find communion with other men.

Jesus is furthermore the answer to Job because he gives a meaning to suffering. Not that he explains it, for it does not come within the sphere of explanation. But he puts it into the world of the supernatural. Suffering is the means whereby the righteous man may be reunited with the sinner. It exists in a sinful universe. But the suffering of the righteous shatters the logic of suffering and sin. It allows suffering to exist where sin does not exist; and because it is bound up with sin, by this very fact it allows the righteous man to take the load of sin upon himself and so to destroy sin. It allows the righteous man to enter into communion with sinners. Thus

Jesus unveils the hidden meaning of Job's suffering, a suffering which remained a mystery to Job himself.

Finally, Jesus is the answer to Job because he does away with his suffering. Suffering cannot be accepted any more than it can be explained. If love can cause someone to take suffering upon himself, it is the love therein alone that is lovable and its final purpose is to do away with suffering. The book of Job is in fine a book of hope. The Septuagint did well to make the dawn of resurrection rise above the suffering of the righteous Idumean. But this resurrection finds its justification in Christ alone. He took suffering upon himself in order to do away with suffering. More still, he descended into the lower region to reach the very root of evil, so that those who had been grafted thereon might be freed from evil. Thus the resurrection of Christ is the supreme answer to the heart-rending cry of Job and justified his protestation.

Responsory   *Is 55:8-9; Heb 11:2*
My thoughts are not your thoughts, nor are your ways my ways, says the Lord. † For as the heavens are high above the earth, so are my ways above your ways, and my thoughts above your thoughts.
V. It was for their faith that the people of former times won God's approval. † For as the . . .

FRIDAY   Year II

First Reading   Job 22:1-30

Responsory   *1 Cor 1:30-31; Jn 1:16*
God has given us Christ Jesus to be our wisdom, our strength, our holiness and our redemption; † this is why Scripture tells us: Let him who would boast, boast in the Lord.
V. Of his fullness we have all received, grace upon grace. † This is why . . .

Second Reading   From the writings of Meister Eckhart
                        (Book of Divine Comfort Part II)

Learn not to love that you may learn to love

No vessel can hold two separate kinds of drink. If it is to contain wine, we must pour out the water; the vessel must be bare and empty. And so, if you would receive divine joy and God, you must pour away creatures. Saint Augustine says: "Pour out, that you may be filled. Learn not to love that you may learn to love. Turn away that you may be turned toward." In short, to take in, to be receptive, a thing must be empty. The masters say that if the eye had any color in it in perceiving, it would perceive neither the color it had nor those it had not. But since it is free of all color, it perceives all colors. The wall has color in it, and so perceives neither its own color nor any other; it cares naught for color, no more for gold and azure than for coal-black. The eye has no color, and yet truly has it, for it rejoices in color with pleasure and delight. And the more perfect and pure the powers of the soul are, the more perfectly and extensively they take in what they perceive, and receive the more widely and have the greater delight in, and become the more one with what they receive, so much so that the highest power of the soul, which is bare of all things and has nothing in common with things, receives nothing less than God himself in the extent and fullness of his being. And the masters show that nothing can equal this union, this fusion and bliss for joy and delight. Therefore our Lord says in striking words: *Blessed are the poor in spirit*. He is poor who has nothing. *Poor in spirit* means: as the eye is "poor" and bare of color yet receptive of all colors, so is he poor in spirit who is receptive of all spirit, and the spirit of all spirits is God. The fruit of the spirit is love, joy and peace. Bareness, and poverty, having nothing and being empty transforms nature; emptiness makes water run upwards and performs many other miracles of which it is not the place to speak now.

So, if you would seek and find perfect joy and comfort in God, see to it that you are free of all creatures and of all comfort from creatures; for assuredly, as long as you are or can be comforted by creatures, you will never find true comfort. But when nothing can comfort you but God, then God *will* comfort you, and with him and in him all that is bliss, while what is not God comforts you, you will have no comfort here or hereafter, but when creatures give you no comfort and you have no taste for them, *then* you will find comfort both here and hereafter.

Responsory   *Ps 145:4-5.14*

One age shall proclaim your works to another, shall declare your mighty deeds. † People will speak of your splendor and glory, and tell of your wonderful works.
V. The Lord supports all who stumble and raises all who are bowed down. † People will speak . . .

SATURDAY   Year II

First Reading   Job 23:1—24:12

Responsory   *Dt 6:12; Prv 15:33*

Never forget the Lord, who led you out of Egypt; † you shall fear the Lord, your God, and you shall serve him alone.
V. The fear of the Lord is a training in wisdom, and humility is the path to honors. † You shall fear . . .

Second Reading   From a sermon by Cardinal John Henry Newman *(Parochial and Plain Sermons* VI, 114-115)

We walk by faith, not by sight

Faith only can introduce us to the unseen presence of God; let us venture to believe, let us make trial before we see, and the evidence which others demand before believing, we shall gain more abundantly by believing. Almighty God is hidden from us; the world does not discover him to us; we may go to the right hand and the left, but we find him not. The utmost we can do in the way of nature is to feel after him, who, though we see him not, yet is not far from every one of us. *Behold he goes by me,* says Job, *and I see him not; he passes on also, and I perceive him not. Oh that I knew where I might find him! that I might come even to his seat. Behold, I go forward, and he is not there; and backward, but I cannot perceive him. On the left hand where he works, but I cannot behold him; he hides himself on the right hand, that I cannot see him.*

This is the veil that is cast over all nations: the want of intercourse or communion between the soul and him who made it. We can speak to his creatures, we cannot speak to him. Once it was not so; man was created upright, and then he saw God; he fell, and lost God's image and God's presence. How must he regain his privilege, but by becoming what he once was? He lost it by sinning, he must regain it by pureness. And till this recovery he must accept it on faith; he is allowed to apprehend and enjoy it by faith. He begins with faith, that he may end with holiness; he is allowed to begin with faith, because faith is itself of a holy nature, and the first fruits and earnest of holiness to come. Faith is the religion of sinners beginning to purify themselves for God, and in every age, and under every dispensation, the just have lived by faith. "By faith" Moses "endured, as seeing him who is invisible"; for lack of faith Balaam met an angel in the way and discerned him not. Thus *we walk by faith, not by sight; we look not at the things which are seen, but at the things which are not seen*. We set him on our right hand, *whom having not seen, we love: in whom, though now we see him not, yet believing, we rejoice with joy unspeakable and full of glory, receiving the end of our faith, even the salvation of our souls.*

Responsory   *Phil 2:12-13; Eph 3:20*

Work out your salvation with fear and trembling, for † God is at work in you, inspiring both the will and the deed for his own chosen purpose.
V. Glory be to him whose power, working in us, can do immeasurably more than we can ask or imagine. † God is at work . . .

Alternative Reading

From the writings of Yves Congar (*God, Man and the Universe*, 412-413)

God's final answer to Job's questions

It is because God wishes to bring Job to live out his religious convictions, to resolve the problem of life existentially, that after the speeches of Job's friends, and Job's own answers as he continues to protest, he intervenes himself. For poetic beauty the passage is perhaps unsurpassed in the bible. The answer given is philosophical; but it is not this that is remarkable about it, for in all essentials what is said in this respect can already be found in the speech of Elihu. Apart from any answer to the problem, it is to question Job himself that God addresses him: Strip then, and enter the lists; it is my turn to ask questions now, yours to answer them. The parts are reversed. Job was for arguing with God, for calling him to account and seeking his reasons; but here he is, directly and personally questioned himself. You, says God, would have put me to the question; now it is you who must make a reply. What do you know? What do you know even of the simplest things that take place at your side every day? What causes the movement of the sea, how come the birds to be made? Come, tell me!

Will he who would criticize God venture to make any answer? God's own answer, in theory, is simple. How, he asks Job, can you question and judge me? You know nothing. Every being, everything created, is a mystery: and so are the evils that come about. This appeal to mystery, Job had heard already and rejected. After all, it may be precisely the mystery that gives scandal — scandal that is, in the etymological sense, the thing that causes us to trip and fall down. But it may also, as Pascal said, be something to be reverenced. The parting of the ways between revolt and worship lies very deep down, at the secret center of the heart, where we make the choice either to be ourselves the supreme arbiters or frankly to admit that God infinitely transcends us. What it comes to, ultimately, is that our frank acceptance of our condition as creatures must be more than intellectual, it must also be lived out. As in the creator's partners by virtue of our freedom, we have to realize our condition as unequal partners of the living God and so voluntarily submit to be led where he wills.

For this it is necessary that we encounter him personally, not to argue with him any more, but to be ourselves questioned and freely submit. God's whole treatment of souls that he seeks to draw to him aims at getting them to say "yes" at an even deeper level: first by conversion and faith, then by entering upon the successive stages of the spiritual life. But conversion is effected by putting oneself in the presence of the living God at an existential point, a point where there is nothing but him and our true selves, from which he has brushed away, as it were, the various "havings" that serve us as alibis and lead us to evade the decisive issues of "being." It is the point when Job says: I acknowledge it, you can do all you will, and no thought is too difficult for you. Here indeed is one that clouds over the truth with his ignorance! I have spoken as fools speak, of things far beyond my ken. I have heard your voice now; nay, more, I have had sight of you.

Responsory   *Phil 2:12-13; Eph 3:20*

Work out your salvation with fear and trembling, for † God is at
work in you, inspiring both the will and the deed for his own chosen
purpose.

V. Glory be to him whose power, working in us, can do immeasurably more than we can ask or imagine. † God is at . . .

SEVENTEENTH WEEK IN ORDINARY TIME

SUNDAY   Year II

First Reading   Job 28:1-28

Responsory   *1 Cor 2:7; 1:30*

I speak of God's secret wisdom, hidden from men, † which, before
time began, God planned for our glory.
V. God has made us one with Christ Jesus, and given us Christ to
be our wisdom. † Which, before time . . .

Second Reading   From a commentary by Saint Hilary of
                       Poitiers (In Ps. 127, 2-6: CSEL 22, 629-632)

Set your feet in the ways of the Lord

In treating of the fear of the Lord scripture says: *Come and listen
to me, my children: I will teach you the fear of the Lord.* We have to
learn the lesson which is taught, since this kind of fear does not
originate in terror, but is based on learnings; it has nothing to do
with natural timidity, but is gained by observing the commandments, following the prescriptions of a blameless life and by acquiring knowledge of the truth. For, if God is feared merely because of the numerous fires caused by lightning and the havoc
wrought by thunderbolts, or because of the widespread destruction occasioned by earthquakes, when gaping chasms swallow
everything up, that fear is in no way related to faith, since it is
prompted by the fear of misfortune. Our fear of God, on the other
hand, is wholly rooted in love; in fact, the perfect love of God puts
an end to terror. This love of ours for God, moreover, is fully
expressed by our obedience to his commands, our compliance with
his statutes and our confidence in his promises. Let us listen to the
words of Scripture: *Now, Israel, what is it that the Lord, your God,
demands of you? He demands that you fear the Lord, your God, and
walk in all his ways; that you love him and keep his statutes with all
your heart and soul. Thus will you prosper.* The prophet also spoke
in the same vein, using similar words, when he said: *Blessed are all
who fear the Lord and walk in his ways.* He is pointing out the fact
that "those who fear" are not blessed on account of their natural

timidity, which engenders fear in other men as well, nor on account of the awe they feel before the One who can rightly command their awe; rather their blessing results from their walking in the ways of the Lord. Fear produces obedience, not panic; submission is the hallmark of fear.

Many indeed are the ways of the Lord, yet he himself is the Way. He called himself the Way and then explained his meaning by saying: *No one can come to the Father except through me.* The present discourse, however, is concerned with the prophets and their writings, by which men are brought to Christ. So many ways there are, converging from every side into the one, true way! Now, both these points are illustrated in one and the same passage from the prophet, Jeremiah, which runs: *Set your feet in the ways of the Lord; inquire after God's eternal paths. Search out the good way and walk in it.*

How many paths we must inquire into if we would discover the one way that is good! How many ways we must walk if we would find with the help of numerous guides the only way which leads to everlasting life! Some of these ways are set before us in the law and the prophets, others in the gospels and apostolic writings, while further ways are to be found in the works of various masters. Blessed are they who walk in them in the fear of God.

The prophet is not dealing here with our present, earthly life; his words are concerned with the blessing which awaits those who fear the Lord and walk in his way, for all who walk in the ways of the Lord will eat "fruit-bearing labors." This kind of eating is not a bodily activity, because the food to be eaten is incorporeal; this is, on the contrary, a reference to the spiritual food, which gives life to our souls, by which I mean good works. Such are goodness, chastity, compassion, patience, and serenity, with whose help we must labor to overcome the vices which assail our bodies. And the fruit of these labors is eternal life: but first we must feed upon the labor which will produce these eternal fruits, and we must nourish our souls on it as long as we live in the body. Thus through the food, which these labors provide, we shall obtain the living bread, the bread of heaven, from the hands of him who said: *I am the living bread from heaven.*

Responsory   *Lv 20:7.26*
  Consecrate yourselves and be holy, for I am the Lord your God.
  Keep my laws and obey them, for † it is I, the Lord, who make you
  holy.
  V. You must be holy to me, because I, the Lord, am holy. † It is I . . .

MONDAY   Year II

First Reading   Job 29:1-10; 30:1.9-23

Responsory   *Jb 30:17.19; 7:16*
  All night long my bones are racked with pain, a gnawing pain that
  never sleeps. † God has cast me into the mire, where I am like dust
  and ashes.
  V. Spare me, Lord, for my days are but a breath. † God has cast . . .

Second Reading   From a sermon by Saint Zeno of Verona
                         (Tract. II, XV: PL 11, 441-443)

Job symbolized Christ

   We are given to understand, brethren, that Job somehow exem-
plified, or symbolized, Christ. We can approach this truth by way
of a comparison. For Job was called a just man by God: God who
is that fountain of justice of which all who are blessed taste. For of
him it is said: *The sun of justice shall rise on you.*
   Job is called truthful. But the authentic truth itself is the Lord,
who says in the gospel: *I am the way and the truth.* Job was a rich
man. But who could be richer than the Lord himself in whose sight
all rich people are but servants and slaves? To him the earth
belongs, and all nature, as blessed David says: *The earth is the
Lord's and the fullness thereof, the world and all who dwell therein.*
Job is thrice tempted by the devil. Likewise, as the gospel narrates,
the Lord also was assailed three times by the tempter. Job lost the
advantages he had enjoyed. The Lord also set aside his riches in
heaven for the love of us, making himself a poor man so as to enrich
us. A raging devil killed off Job's sons; and the prophets, the Lord's
sons likewise, the ravening brood of the Pharisees put to death. Job
was pitted with ulcers, just as the Lord, by assuming the flesh of
the human race, was polluted with the squalor of sinful humanity.

Job's very wife exhorted him to sin, just as the synagogue itself pressed the Lord to conform to the corrupt ways of the elders. Job's friends taunted him, we are told; and the priests of the Lord, worshiping themselves, taunted him no less. Job sits on a dungheap alive with worms: and the Lord likewise, in the veritable dungheap of this world, a banquet whereat he associated with people seething with the entire range of vice and depravity, people who in sober truth are but worms. But Job recovered his health and his wealth. So also the risen Lord offered not merely health but immortality to those who believe in him; and he retrieved the mastery over all of nature, as he himself testified, saying: *All things are made over to me by my Father.* Job raised children not of his own getting; and the Lord likewise had the holy apostles as his spiritual children, after the prophets. The blessed Job rested in peace. But the Lord remains eternally blessed, before all ages and from age to age everlasting.

Responsory   *Jn 8:12; Rm 13:12*
I am the light of the world. † Anyone who follows me will not walk in darkness, but will have the light of life.
V. Let us cast off the deeds of darkness and put on the armor of light. † Anyone who follows . . .

TUESDAY   Year II

First Reading   Job 31:1-8.13-23.35-37

Responsory   *Jb 31:3; Prv 15:3; Jb 31:4*
Does not calamity befall the wicked and disaster the evildoers? † The eyes of the Lord are everywhere observing the evil and the good.
V. Does he not see my ways, and count all my steps? † The eyes of . . .

Second Reading   From the writings of Saint Gregory the Great
(Moralia in Job 22, 17: PL 76, 237-238)

Job seeks a helper

After revealing his sublime feats of heroism the saintly Job seeks a helper, knowing as he does that his own merits do not avail for him to reach the highest peak. And on whom indeed does he rest his gaze but the only-begotten Son of God, who took a human nature, laboring in mortality, and in so doing brought nature his saving help? For he it was who, once made man, brought us men his help so that, since the way back to God did not lie open to man, left to himself, it might become so through God-made-man. We are a long way from being just and immortal, unjust and mortal as we are. But between him who is immortal and just and us, who are neither the one nor the other, the Mediator of God and man has appeared: and he is both mortal and just, having death in common with men and justice with God. And because through our baseness we are far from the heights he occupies, he joins in his own person the lowest with the highest, to make a way for us back to God, so combining the highest with the lowest.

The blessed Job, then, seeks this Mediator, speaking as it were for the whole Church, when having said: *Who will grant me a helper?* he aptly goes on, *that the Almighty one may hear my petition.* For he knew that men's prayers for the repose of eternal freedom can only be heard through their advocate. Of him, we are told through John the apostle that: *If anyone has sinned we have Christ the just man as advocate with the Father; and he is the propitiation for our sins, not for ours alone but also for those of the whole world.* And Paul the apostle speaks of him as: *The Christ who died for us, and indeed who rose again, who is at the right hand of God, and who intercedes for us.* It is for the only-begotten Son of God to intercede with his co-eternal Father, presenting himself as man; and then his having made intercession on behalf of human nature amounts to taking up that nature to the level of his own divine nature.

The Lord intercedes for us not in words, but in mercy; for what he did not wish to see condemned or lost in his chosen ones, that he set free by taking it on himself. A helper is therefore sought, that our petition might be heard: for unless some mediator intercedes for us our prayers would undoubtedly remain as if unspoken, in the ears of Almighty God.

Responsory   *1 Jn 4:9.16b; Jn 3:16*

God's love for us was revealed when he sent his only Son into the world so that we might have life through him. † God is love, and whoever lives in love lives in God and God lives in him.

V. God loved the world so much that he gave his only Son, so that whoever believes in him should not perish but have eternal life. † God is love . . .

WEDNESDAY   Year II

First Reading   Job 32:1-6; 33:1-22

Responsory   Rom 11:33-34
How deep are the riches and wisdom and knowledge of God! † How unsearchable his judgments!
V. Who has known the mind of the Lord? Who has been his counselor? † How unsearchable his judgments!

Second Reading   From a sermon by Saint Bernard of Clairvaux
                      (Sermo VII, 3-4: PL 183, 560-561)

Whom does God commend in this world?

Do not judge before the time, Saint Paul says, *when the Lord shall come to shed his light on what lies hidden in the darkness.* For the celebration then will be perfectly in order and in no way premature, each one receiving his praise from Almighty God himself. Even now, though not unreservedly and not without fear and much solicitude, we nevertheless glory in the Lord, with the Holy Spirit bearing witness to us internally that we are God's children. Hence we may well boast of having so great a Father and of being a concern to him whose majesty it is beyond words to express. So the prophet says: *Lord, what is man that you should exalt him? or why should he be so close to your heart?* Whoever is to boast, then, let it not be in his own merits. For what has he that he has not received? And if he has received, why should he boast as though he had not? Let him therefore boast of him from whom he has received, not to suggest that he himself is a great one but that the God is who made him great: he should make his boast, that is to say, not as though he had not received, but like one who had. For the apostle does not say: Why boast, if you have received? but: Why boast *as though* you had *not* received? The point is not to forbid boasting, but to teach how it should be done.

But what does he mean when he says: *It is not the man who commends himself who is credit-worthy, but he whom God commends?* Whom does God commend in this world? How can Truth itself commend someone who is still found to be reprehensible? He himself says: *Those whom I love I admonish and chastise.* Can the commendation be wholehearted? Utterly so, I think. For what could be a better or a stronger recommendation than the pledge of divine love toward us? There is no more credible, no more certain testimony, in this life, of his love than the prophet's yearning desire: *Oh that he who is just in his mercy will admonish me in his mercy and reproach me for my sins.*

Now this reproach, whereby the Spirit of truth is continually giving us hints in secret about where we fail, keeps at bay our pride, negligence, and ingratitude. It is from this threefold vice that almost every kind of religious is at risk, to the extent that they become less attentive to the promptings of the heart, to perceive what the Spirit of truth who touches no one outwardly may nevertheless say inwardly to them. Unless I am mistaken, this is because those desirous of their own glory can take no repose anywhere, finding inside themselves nothing to glory in, not even a little. Nevertheless we trust and indeed glory in the Lord whose mercy is so great over us that he protects us from the graver sins, those which lead to spiritual death, and so kindly deigns to manifest to us the shortcomings of our imperfection and the grossness of our behavior, pardoning what is acknowledged, to the extent that once firmly rooted in humility and solicitude and gratitude, we glory no longer in ourselves but in the Lord alone.

Responsory   *Mi 6:8; Acts 17:28*

The Lord has shown us what is good; † what he requires of us is only this: to act justly, to love tenderly and to walk humbly with our God.

V. He is not far from any one of us, for in him we live and move and have our being. † What he requires . . .

THURSDAY   Year II

First Reading   Job 38:1-30; 40:1-5

Responsory   *Rm 9:20; Jb 38:3*
Who are you, a man, to dare argue with God? † The pot has no right
to say to the potter: Why did you make this shape?
V. Brace yourself like a man; I will question you, and you shall
answer what I ask. † The pot has . . .

Second Reading   From the writings of Saint Gregory the Great
(Moralia in Job XXVIII, Praefatio: PL 76, 445-446)

Proved not to be mighty

After the loss of his goods, the death of his children, the wounds
of his body, the words of his wife inciting him to evil, the insulting
language of his comforters and the spear thrusts of so many
sorrows bravely received, Job ought to have been praised by his
judge for the strength of his constancy — but Job is not now going
to be called out of this world. He is about to receive back twofold,
he is about to be restored to his former health, to enjoy his restored
possessions longer, so Almighty God is obliged to reprove him
whom he preserves with strict justice in case Job's very victory
should lay him low with the sword of pride.

There is nothing, is there, that so commonly slays people than
consciousness of their own virtue. It puffs them up with self-satis-
faction and at the same time empties them of the truth; it suggests
that they are sufficient unto themselves to achieve their rewards
and at the same time diverts them from the will to amend. Job, then,
was just before his scourges, but he remained more so after them;
before them he was praised by the mouth of God; after them and
because of them he grew in stature. As a pipe of ductile metal is
lengthened by hammering, so Job rose in God's esteem the more
he was chastised. But he who stood so firm in virtue when struck
down needed to be humbled. He needed to be humbled so that the
arrows of pride should not pierce that sturdy beast which the
wounds already received had certainly failed to pierce. It was
necessary to search out someone who surpassed Job — but what
about God's words: *Have you seen my servant Job, that there is no
one like him in all the earth?* How then could Job be humbled by

comparison with another when God himself had attested that there was no one like him? What, then, was left but for the Lord himself to describe his own accomplishments? So he asks: *Can you bind the chains of the Pleiades or loose the cords of Orion?* And again: *Have the gates of death been revealed to you, or have you seen the gates of deep darkness?* Or: *Have you commanded the morning ever since your days began and caused the dawn to know its place?*

Who can do these things but the Lord? Yet a human being is asked so that he may learn that he is unable to do these things, so that a man who has grown limitless in virtue and is surpassed by no other man may know he is surpassed by God and so avoid elation. But how highly is he exalted who is so sublimely humbled! How great is the victory of the man who has been brought low by comparison with God! How much greater than a man is he who is shown by the witness of creation to be less than God! He is very mighty who is proved by such questioning to be not at all mighty.

Responsory   *1 Jn 4:9.16b; Jn 3:16*

God's love for us was revealed when he sent his only Son into the world so that we might have life through him. † God is love, and whoever lives in love lives in God and God lives in him.

V. God loved the world so much that he gave his only Son, so that whoever believes in him should not perish but have eternal life. † God is love . . .

FRIDAY   Year II

First Reading   Job 40:6-24; 42:1-6

Responsory   *Jb 42:5-6; 40:5.4*

I have heard of you by word of mouth, O Lord, but now that I have seen you for myself I disown all that I have said, † and I repent in dust and ashes.

V. Though I have spoken once, I will not speak again; though twice, I will do so no more. I shall put my finger against my lips. † And I repent . . .

Second Reading   From the writings of Saint Hilary of Poitiers
(De Trinitate XII: PL 10, 467-468)

I am in your debt for the awareness

There are many instances from everyday life where the cause itself is unknown, but the effect decidedly not so. And there is need for faith truly in the religious, supernatural sense wherever there is the ignorance due to my nature itself. For when I raise to your heaven those weak eyes that are my light I believe myself to see nothing other than your heaven. When surveying those circles and spheres carrying the stars, the yearly returns and vigils, the north star, the morning star, all these being given their differing tasks to perform, I perceive you to be at work in matters of which my perception is even so very incomplete. When I see the wonderful rise and fall of the sea, it is not the origin of the waters alone nor yet the motion of this vast swirling mass that I pursue and ponder, but rather, on apprehending the ground for belief in the cause which I cannot even so observe, that I am mindful, in things my mind does not grasp, of you also.

When I turn my mind's eye to the earth, what is sown by hidden forces breaks free of what it had received, springs to life, multiplies and flourishes. There is really nothing here that I could understand properly by the light of nature; but then my ignorance itself contributes to my dim understanding of you, as long as I understand clearly that, being unfamiliar and baffled by the nature that serves me, I understand, as I say, that you alone can properly be of advantage or benefit to me. Not knowing or understanding myself either, I feel that all the more for that I am in awe of the fact that I am even a mystery to myself. For aware of, yet not comprehending, the movement of my mind in the act of passing judgment, or its way of functioning, or its life, I am in your debt for the awareness, for your communicating that awareness of nature delighting me, beyond the perception of natural origins. And when I come to understand you, albeit in ignorance of myself, may I respect you with my understanding and not lose hold of my faith in your omnipotence at the thought of my ignorance of your ways: that my mind may be taken up with the origin of your only-begotten and so have something left over of itself, that I may further strive after my Creator and my God.

Responsory   *Ps 11:4-5.7*
The eyes of the Lord look down upon the world; his gaze tests
humankind. † The Lord tests the just and the unjust; he hates all
who love violence.
V. The Lord is just and loves justice; the upright shall see his face.
† The Lord tests . . .

SATURDAY   Year II

First Reading   Job 42:7-17

Responsory   *See Jb 42:7.8*
The Lord said to Eliphaz: you and your friends have not spoken
truthfully of me as has my servant Job; † he will pray for you.
V. I shall hear his prayer and forgive you your foolishness in
speaking against me. † He will pray . . .

Second Reading   From the writings of Saint Gregory the Great
(Moralia in Job, Praefatio 13: SC 32bis, 135-136)

The Lord had to be foretold without cease

Among the wonderful works of divine dispensation it is pleasing to note how every star in turn appears on the face of heaven to
illuminate the night of this present life, until at the end of that night
there rises like a true morning star the Redeemer of the human race.
For the interval of night, lit up by the rising and setting of the stars
in their courses, is shot through with the great beauty of heaven.
Then so that the light of the stars should shine out in turn, each in
its own time, to pierce the darkness of our night, Abel came to
represent innocence; Enoch, to teach moral purity; Noah, the patience to work in hope; Abraham, to show obedience; Isaac, chastity in marriage; Jacob, to teach us to endure toil; Joseph, to repay
evil with good; Moses, to represent gentleness; Joshua, to teach us
confidence in adversity; Job, to show us patience in the midst of
misfortune. Those are the stars we see shining in the heavens, to
light our steps on our laborious way through the darkness of our
night. For the divine dispensation presented to the human mind
as many examples of righteousness as if sending so many stars into
the dark sky above sinners, until the true morning star rose, to

announce the eternal dawn to us, and because of his divine nature shining more brilliantly than the other stars.

All the elect who lived a holy life before the Lord foretold his coming in prophetic words and deeds. Not one of the righteous failed to announce him symbolically. It was obviously right that all should represent the good, by which all were good, and which they knew was useful to all. The Lord had to be foretold without cease, since he was given to us to be received without measure and possessed without end: so that all the ages might say together what the end of the ages showed in the universal redemption. That is why it was also inevitable that even blessed Job, who revealed so great a mystery as the Lord's incarnation, should symbolize in his own life the one whom he described in words, and through his own suffering show what the Lord would suffer, foretelling the sacrament of his passion all the more truly because he prophesied it not only in words but in actual suffering.

Responsory   *Ps 16:7-8; Mt 19:17*

I will bless the Lord who gives me counsel, who even at night directs my heart. I keep the Lord always before me: † since he is at my right hand, I shall stand firm.

V. If you wish to enter into life, keep the commandments. † Since he is . . .

Alternative Reading

From a homily by Origen of Alexandria (In Gen. Hom. VIII, 10: SC 7bis, 232-235)

Blessed be the name of the Lord

A clear way of spiritual understanding is opened for those who know how to hear these words. For everything which has been done reaches to the vision, for it is said that *the Lord saw*. But the vision which *the Lord saw* is in the spirit so that you too might see these things in the spirit which are written and, just as there is nothing corporeal in God, so also you might perceive nothing corporeal in all these things, but you too might beget a son Isaac in the spirit, when you begin to have *the fruit of the Spirit, joy, peace*. Which son, however, you will at length so beget if, as it is written of Sarah: "It ceased to be with Sara after the manner of women," and then she bore Isaac, so the things after the manner of women should cease also in your soul, so that you no longer have anything womanish or effeminate in your soul, but "you act manfully" and manfully gird your loins. You will beget such a son if your breast is "protected with the breastplate of justice; if you are armed with the helmet of salvation and the sword of the Spirit." If, therefore, the things after the manner of women cease to be in your soul, you beget joy and gladness as a son from your wife, virtue and wisdom. Now you beget joy if "you count it all joy when you fall into various temptations" and you offer that joy in sacrifice to God.

For when you have approached God joyfully, God again gives back to you what you have offered and says to you: *You will see me again, and your heart shall rejoice, and no one shall take your joy from you.* So, therefore, what you have offered to God you shall receive back multiplied. Something like this, although in another figure, is related in the gospels when in a parable someone is said to have received a pound that he might engage in business, and the master of the house demanded the money. But if you have caused five to be multiplied to ten, they themselves are given to you, they are granted to you. For hear what scripture says: *Take his pound and give it to him who has ten pounds.*

So, therefore, we appear at least to engage in business for the Lord, but the profits of the business go to us. And we appear to offer victims to the Lord, but the things we offer are given back to us. For God needs nothing, but God wishes us to be rich, and desires our progress through each individual thing.

This figure is shown to us also in these things which happened to Job. For he too, although he was rich, lost everything because of God. But he bore well the struggles with patience and was magnanimous in everything which he suffered and said: *The Lord gave, the Lord has taken away; as it has pleased the Lord so is it done. Blessed be the name of the Lord.* Because of this, behold what finally is written about him: *He received back twice as much,* Scripture says, *as he had lost.*

Do you see what it means to lose something for God? It means to receive it back multiplied. But the gospels promise you something even more, *a hundredfold* is offered you besides also *life eternal* in Christ Jesus our Lord *to whom belongs glory and sovereignty forever and ever. Amen.*

Responsory   *Ps 16:7-8; Mt 19:17*

I will bless the Lord who gives me counsel, who even at night directs
my heart. I keep the Lord always before me: † since he is at my right
hand, I shall stand firm.

V. If you wish to enter into life, keep the commandments. † Since
he is . . .

BIOGRAPHICAL SKETCHES

Abhishiktananda (1910-1973), born in Brittany, Henri le Saux entered the monastery of Saint Anne de Kergonan in 1929. Quite early in his monastic life he felt drawn to India, and in 1945, he was allowed to approach Indian bishops. In 1947 he received a favorable reply from the Bishop of Tirnchirappali, and together with a secular priest, Jules Monchanin who was already in the diocese, started an ashram called Shantivanam, integrating elements of Indian sannyasa with Christian monasticism. Dom Henri, who adopted the Indian name Abhishiktananda (Bliss of the Anointed One), was at this time profoundly influenced by a contemporary holy man, Sri Ramana Maharshi, and through him was initiated into the Hindu tradition of "advaita" or non-duality. The rest of his life was a struggle to integrate this experience into his Christianity. In the end he achieved it, not on the conceptual level but in the inner peace of his own prayer. His chief works are *Prayer, Saccidananda, Hindu-Christian Meeting Point*, and *The Further Shore*.

Adam of Perseigne (c.1138-1221), a Cistercian monk of Potigny, in 1138, was placed at the head of the monastery of Perseigne in the diocese of Mans. As in the case of St. Bernard, abbot Adam was given several important missions by Pope Innocent III. He even took part in preaching the Fourth Crusade. These functions did not prevent him from watching over the spiritual welfare of his community, as is witnessed by the imposing number of sermons he has left us. His work preserves the characteristics of the Cistercian school with a predilection for the Virgin Mary whom he is fond of presenting as co-redemptrix. He died about 1221.

Ambrose (339-397), born in Trier, was the son of a praetorian prefect of Gaul. On the death of Auxentius, the Arian bishop of Milan, Ambrose, while still a catechumen, was elected to the see by acclamation. We know from Saint Augustine that as bishop he was accessible to everyone. Although Ambrose was influenced by the Greek Fathers, especially Origen, his preaching had the practical bent characteristic of Western theological writers.

Angela of Foligno (1248-1309) was born into a wealthy family in Foligno where she spent most of her life. She became a Franciscan tertiary devoting her life to prayer after the death of her husband. She experienced many religious visions of Christ's crucifixion. These visions were later recorded by Brother Arnold and came to be known as the *Liber Visionum et Instructionum*. She was canonized by Pope Innocent XII in 1693.

Aphraates of Persia (280-345), surnamed the Wise Man of Persia, was first a monk and then a bishop, perhaps at Mar-Mattai, to the north of Mosul. He has left a work containing 23 documents called variously *Letters, Sermons, Discourses*, but more usually *Demonstrations*. These seem to have been written in reply to requests for explanations concerning the faith.

Aphraates responds by treating various subjects which range from the Christian truth about Christ to works of piety, the monastic life, and the final resurrection. His literary production is of the greatest importance for the understanding of the Syrian language and the monasticism of his day; though he is not original as a theologian, he serves as an excellent witness to a tradition which is clearly apostolical.

Athanasius (c.296-373) was born at Alexandria and probably attended Alexandria's famous catechetical school. As a deacon and secretary to Alexander, bishop of Alexandria, he attended the Council of Nicaea (325). In 328 he himself became bishop of Alexandria, and for the next forty-five years was the principal defender against the Arians of faith in the divinity of Christ. In consequence he suffered repeated exile and many other trials.

Augustine (354-430) was born at Thagaste in Africa and received a Christian education, although he was not baptized until 387. In 391 he was obtained priest and in 395 he became coadjutor bishop to Valerius of Hippo, whom he succeeded in 396. Augustine's theology was formulated in the course of his struggle with three heresies: Manichaeism, Donatism, and Pelagianism. His writings are voluminous and his influence on subsequent theology immense. He molded the thought of the Middle Ages down to the thirteenth century. Yet he was above all a pastor and a great spiritual writer.

Bede (c.673-735), who received the title of Venerable less than a century after his death, was placed at the age of seven in the monastery of Wearmouth, then ruled by Saint Benet Biscop. From there he was sent to Jarrow, probably at the time of its foundation in about 681. At the age of 30 he was ordained priest. His whole life was devoted to the study of scripture, to teaching, writing, and the prayer of the Divine Office. He was famous for his learning, although he never went beyond the bounds of his native Northumbria. Bede is best known for his historical works, which earned him the title "Father of English History." His *Historia Ecclesiastica Gentis Anglorum is* a primary source for early English history, especially valuable because of the care he took to give his authorities, and to separate historical fact from hearsay and tradition. In 1899 Bede was proclaimed a Doctor of the Church.

Bernard (1090-1153), entered the monastery of Citeaux with thirty companions in 1112. He received his monastic training under the abbot, Saint Stephen Harding, who sent him in 1115 to make a foundation at Clairvaux in France. Soon one of the most influential religious forces in Europe, Bernard was instrumental in founding the Knights Templar and in the election of Pope Innocent I in 1130. He was a strenuous opponent of writers such as Abelard, Gilbert de la Porrée, and Henry of Lausanne. Above all, Bernard was a monk; his sermons and theological writings show an intimate knowledge of scripture, a fine eloquence, and an extraordinarily sublime mysticism.

Berulle, Pierre de (1575-1629) was a seventeenth century French cardinal and founder of the Carmelite Order in France. He also considered the first to discover Descartes and encouraged the philosopher to write his great works.

Bossuet, Jacques Benigne (1627-1704), outstanding Churchmen and orator, was born at Dijon. As the fifth son of the family he was destined for the Church from an early age and educated at Dijon, Metz, and at the College de Navarre in Paris. Saint Vincent de Paul prepared him for his ordination to the priesthood in 1652. Seven years later he took up residence in Paris where his fame as a preacher spread rapidly; his funeral orations evoked especial admiration. In 1669 he was appointed bishop of Condom, and in the following year was entrusted with the education of the Dauphin for whom, amongst other works, his *Discours sur l'histoire universelle* was written. In 1681 he was transferred to the see of Metz: it was for the religious in his charge that the *Méditations sur l'Évangile* and the *Élévations sur les mysteres* were written. Amongst his voluminous writings 137 sermons have been preserved.

Caesarius of Arles (c.470-543), born in Chalon on the Saone, entered as a monk at Lerins in 489. He was so outstanding in the perfection of his life and in his sense of justice that he was eventually made archbishop of Arles. He legislated for both nuns and monks, his Rule for Virgins being written for his sister Saint Caesaria, superior of a community of nuns. Influenced by Saint Augustine's teaching on grace, he successfully combatted semi-pelagianism at the Council of Orange in 529. He was a celebrated preacher; his practical charity was such that he melted down church plate to relieve prisoners, and the quality of his prayer is reflected in his challenging statement: "A man worships that on which his mind is intent during prayer."

Catherine of Siena (1347-1380) Caterina di Giacomo di Benincasa, took a vow of virginity at the age of 7. At 18 she received the Dominican habit, when she began to live in solitude and silence in her room. After her "mystical espousal" to Christ in 1368 she rejoined her family and devoted herself to the service of the poor and sick, but continued her life of contemplation. In Pisa in 1373 she began her prolific letter writing career. Through this, and her many travels, she sought to influence public affairs, to bring about a reform of the clergy, and the return of the papacy to Rome from Avignon. Possessed of exceptional apostolic powers, especially in the reconciliation of sinners, she became the center of a group which regarded her as teacher and spiritual guide. As well as her *Dialogue*, a spiritual work of considerable importance, we still have many of Catherine's letters. She was canonized in 1461, and declared a doctor of the Church in 1970.

Caussade, Jean-Pierre de (1675-1751), born at Toulouse, entered the Jesuit novitiate there at the age of 18. From 1694 to 1702 he taught classics and, after completing his theology in 1706, was ordained priest. He then taught grammar, physics and logic until 1714, after which he was moved about as a preacher and confessor to at least seven places. It was at Perpignan that his *Instruction on Prayer* was written, but his most famous work was compiled from letters and notes kept by Visitation nuns and published after his death under the title of *Abandon*. English translations are usually published under the title of *Abandonment to Divine Providence*.

Chardin, Pierre Teilhard de (1881-1955), a priest of the Society of Jesus, was a scientist and theologian of unparalleled insight. Enlightened by a passionate love of God immanent in all things, and taught by a life time's meticulous study of geology, biology and paleontology, he was brought to a vision of the universe's evolution towards its rebirth and transformation in a union of love with Christ, its "Omega-Point". This he explored in many of his writings, notably *Le Milieu Divin* and *The Phenomenon of Man*. His life was one with his teaching, absorbed in adoration, deeply aware of God's presence at all times.

Chromatius (c.335/340-407), born in Aquileia in Northern Italy, was an influential member of the presbyterium by 368, and in 388 succeeded Valerian in the see of Aquileia. A friend of Saint John Chrysostom and Saint Ambrose, Chromatius was a zealous pastor, whose teaching is not systematic, but centered on the liturgical year, the mystery of Christ and his Church. His works have been published in *Corpus Christianorum*.

Clement of Alexandria (c.150-215) was born at Athens of pagan parents. Nothing is known of his early life nor of the reasons for his conversion. He was the pupil and the assistant of Pantaenus, the director of the catechetical school of Alexandria, whom he succeeded in about the year 200. In 202 Clement left Alexandria because of the persecution of Septimus Severus, and resided in Cappadocia with is pupil, Alexander, later bishop of Jerusalem. Clement may be considered the founder of speculative theology. He strove to protect and deepen faith by the use of Greek philosophy. Central in his teaching is his doctrine of the Logos, who as divine reason is the teacher of the world and its lawgiver. Clement's chief work is the trilogy, *Exhortation to the Greeks*, *The Teacher*, and *Miscellaneous Studies*.

Clement of Rome (c.96), the third successor of Saint Peter, was pope from 92 to 101. He had known both Saint Peter and Saint Paul. His letter to the Corinthians, written in 95 or 96, is the earliest Christian writing apart from the New Testament of which the name, position, and date of the author are historically attested. The occasion of the letter was the outbreak of factious disputes similar to those condemned by Saint Paul forty years earlier. Clement's intervention seems to have been successful, as his letter was so highly esteemed at Corinth that it was still being read in the Church in about 170. It is important for the history of dogma and of liturgy.

Columban (563-615), an Irish monk of the sixth century, born in the province of Leinster in 563, has remained famous as a result of the numerous monasteries he established in Gaul, Switzerland, and Italy. He died at Bobbio in 615 in the abbey that he had founded the previous year and that went on to become one of the centers of western monasticism. The monastic reform which he undertook with success can be seen in the rigors of his own penances, and in his *Rule*, which was less balanced than that of Saint Basil, and did not meet with the same longevity.

Congar, Yves (1904-), a French Dominican, born in Sedan in 1904, was one of the most respected modern theologians of the Church. For the last thirty years he has played a leading role in theological studies, especially in the fields of ecclesiology and ecumenism, and was one of the most heeded experts at the Second Vatican Council. Father Congar classified himself as a reformist rather than a revolutionary as regards change in the Church, seeking a change that is progressive and desiring to find the answers to the present situation in the tradition of the Fathers of the Church. He is a member of the Vatican's International Theological Commission.

Cyprian (d.258) was converted to Christianity in 246, and two years later was elected bishop of Carthage. His extant writings comprise a number of short treatises and letters. Cyprian was a man of prayer, who drew his strength from his faith in Christ and in the Holy Spirit dwelling in the Church. He had a keen sense of the unity of the Church, even though his position on certain questions undermined the unity he sought to defend.

Cyril of Alexandria (d.444) succeeded his uncle Theophilus as patriarch in 412. Until 428 the pen of this brilliant theologian was employed in exegesis and polemics against the Arians; after that date it was devoted almost entirely to refuting the Nestorian heresy. The teaching of Nestorius was condemned in 431 by the Council of Ephesus at which Cyril presided, and Mary's title, Mother of God, was solemnly recognized. The incarnation is central to Cyril's theology. Only if Christ is consubstantial with the Father and with us can he save us, for the meeting ground between God and ourselves is the flesh of Christ Through our kinship with Christ, the Word made flesh, we become children of God, and share in the filial relation of the Son with the Father.

Danielou, Jean (1905-1974), born into a privileged family, his father being a politician and his mother an educationalist, did brilliantly at his studies, and in 1929 entered the Society of Jesus. He came under the influence of de Lubac and got to know Teilhard de Chardin. In 1940 he was chaplain to students in Paris and committed to the cause of resistance. Widely ecumenical in his views, he was a peritus at Vatican II under Pope John XXIII, and was made a cardinal by Pope Paul VI. As an author he was at home in many fields of erudition, including scripture, patristics, theology, and spirituality.

Ephrem (c.306-373), the only Syrian Father who is honored as a doctor of the Church, was ordained deacon at Edessa in 363, and gave an outstanding example of a deacon's life and work. Most of his exegetical dogmatic, controversial and ascetical writings are in verse. They provide a rich mine of information regarding the faith and practice of the early Syrian Church. The poetry of Ephrem greatly influenced the development of Syriac and Greek hymnography.

Francis of Sales (1567-1622), born on the family estate of Sales in Savoy, was educated at Annecy, Paris, and Padua. In 1593 he was ordained priest and in the following year courageously set out to win back the people of the Chablais from Calvinism to Catholicism. Thanks to his ardent zeal and habitual gentleness he made eight thousand converts within two years. He was appointed coadjutor to the bishop of Geneva and in 1602 succeeded to the see. Together with Saint Jane Frances de Chantal he founded the Order of the Visitation. He died at Lyons when returning from Avignon. His best known writings are the *Introduction to a Devout Life* and the *Treatise on the Love of God*. In 1877 he was declared to be a doctor of the Church.

Fulgentis of Ruspe (468-533) left the Roman civil service for the monastic life at the age of twenty-one. In 508 he became bishop of Ruspe in North Africa. A faithful disciple of Saint Augustine, he was the best theologian of his time, and possessed a fluent knowledge of Greek. Many of his writings were directed against the Arians, from whom he suffered constant persecution.

Gregory Nazianzen (329-389) was one of the three great Cappadocian Fathers. Desiring a retired, contemplative life, he became a monk, but in 362 his father, the bishop of Nazianzas, ordained him priest against his will, and ten years later he was raised to the episcopate by his friend Saint Basil. In 379 Gregory was called to Constantinople, where his preaching helped to restore the Nicene faith and led to its final acceptance by the Council of Constantinople in 381. To the "Five Theological Orations" preached at Constantinople Gregory owes his title, "The Theologian."

Gregory of Nyssa (c.330-395), the younger brother of Basil the Great, chose a secular career and married. Reluctantly, however, in 371, he received episcopal ordination and became bishop of Nyssa, an unimportant town in Basil's metropolitan district of Caesarea. Gregory was the greatest speculative theologian of the three Cappadocian Fathers and the first after Origen to attempt a systematic presentation of the Christian faith Gifted spiritually as well as intellectually, he has been called "the father of Christian mysticism." His spiritual interpretation of Scripture shows the influence of Origen.

Gregory Palamas (1296-1359) was born at Constantinople, and prepared by the piety of his parents for a monastic vocation. Gregory became a monk of Mount Athos at the age of about 20. In 1347 he was made bishop of Thessalonica. Gregory stressed the biblical teaching that the human body and soul form a single united whole. On this basis he defended the physical exercises used by the Hesychasts in prayer, although he saw these only as a means to an end for those who found them helpful. He followed Saint Basil the Great and Saint Gregory of Nyssa in teaching that although no created intelligence can ever comprehend God in his essence, he can be directly experienced through his uncreated "energies," through which he manifests himself to and is present in the world. God's substance and his energies are distinct from one another, but they are also inseparable. One of these energies is the uncreated divine light, which was seen by the apostles on Mount Tabor. At times this is an inward illumination; at other times it is outwardly manifested.

Gregory the Great, Saint (c.540-604), a Roman by birth, is one of the four great doctors of the Western Church. His great grandfather was Pope Felix III (483-492). After a brilliant secular career he became a monk, having turned his own house on the Clivus Scauri into a monastery dedicated to Saint Andrew. From c.578 to 585 he was in Constantinople as "apocrisiarius", or papal nuncio, at the imperial court. His *Morals on Job* were conferences given at their request to the small band of monks who accompanied him there. In 590 he was elevated to the see of Peter in succession to Pelagius II. Apart from Saint Leo the Great, Gregory is the only pope who has left examples of his preaching to the Roman people. These are his homilies on the gospels, and on Ezekiel. His *Book of Pastoral Rule* became the textbook of medieval bishops. Gregory is known as the apostle of the English because he sent the monk, Saint Augustine of Canterbury, to evangelize England. He died on 12 March, but his feast is kept on 3 September, the date of his elevation to the papacy.

Griffiths, Bede (1906-1993), born Alan Richard Griffiths in London, England, he took the name Bede in 1932 and was ordained a Catholic priest in 1940. He was sent to Farnborough in 1947 where he was the prior first. During this time at Farnborough, he met Father Alapatt and together in 1955, they started a Benedictine house in India. Father Bede was a prolific writer and scholar all his life. He wrote his autobiography, *The Golden String*, in 1954. His other writings include numerous articles and books on Hinduism and Christian theology. In 1993, Father Bede died from complications due to a stroke.

Guerric of Igny (c.1070/1080-1157), about whose early life little is known, probably received his education at the cathedral school of Tournai (1087-1092), perhaps under the influence of Odo of Cambrai (1087-1092). He seems to have lived a retired life of prayer and study near the cathedral of Tournai. He paid a visit to Clairvaux to consult Saint Bernard, and is mentioned by him as a novice in a letter to Ogerius in 1125-1126. He became abbot of the Cistercian abbey of Igny, in the diocese of Reims in 1138. A collection of 54 authentic sermons preached in chapter on Sundays and feast days have been edited. Guerric's spirituality was influenced by Origen.

Henry of Friemar (d.1340), an Augustinian, was influenced by Giles of Rome. He passed on to the Augustinian Order valuable historical data, but he likewise wrote treatises on the spiritual life, especially on discernment.

Hilary of Poitiers (315-367) was elected bishop of Poitiers in 353. Because of his struggles with the Arians and his treatise on the Trinity, for which he was exiled, he has been called "the Athanasius of the West." He also wrote a commentary on Saint Matthew's gospel and another on a selection of the psalms. His style is difficult and obscure and he makes much use of allegory.

Hildegard of Bingen (1098-1179), was a German nun, mystic, and scholar. Having entered religious life as a child, Hildegard founded the Benedictine convent of Rupertsberg near Bingen in 1147. Renowned for her visions, related in the *Scivias*, Hildegard was a theologian, physician, and composer as well as an energetic reformer.

Hilton, Walter was a doctor of canon law, probably at Cambridge, in the fourteenth century. For approximately the last ten years of his life he was a canon regular of Thurgarton Priory in Nottinghamshire, where he died in 1396. He is best known as a spiritual theologian and the author of *The Scale of Perfection*.

Ildefonsus of Toledo (607-667), monk and abbot, served the church in Spain as archbishop of Toledo. He composed a prayer which echoes the *Sub tuum praesidium* of the third century.

Irenaeus, Saint (c.140-200), born in Asia Minor and in his youth a disciple of Saint Polycarp, became bishop of Lyons. He wrote his principal work, *Against the Heresies*, to combat Gnostic dualism. At the heart of his theology is a vision of the unity, the recapitulation of all things in Christ. Just as all have sinned in one man, Adam, so all are offered salvation in Christ, the second Adam.

Isaac of Stella, born in Great Britain, is a Cistercian spiritual writer of the first rank. He studied in France under the most famous teachers of his age. Later, he entered the abbey of Stella in Poitou and became its abbot in 1147. Some twenty years later, at the head of a small group, he went to establish the monastic life in the Isle of Re near La Rochelle. In his sermons, Isaac harmoniously combined the theological vigor of patriotic traditions, the new demands of rigorous intellectual depth, and the human sensitivity characteristic of the Cistercian school of the 12th century.

Jacob of Sarugh (451-521) was a Syriac ecclesiastical writer and was educated at Edessa. He became Bishop of Batnae in 519 and died shortly thereafter. His writing consisted mainly of homilies with biblical themes written in a dodecasyllabic metre. Referred to as "The Flute of the Holy Spirit," Jacob also wrote some hymns, three anaphoras and several letters.

Most of his homilies have not been published and only a few have been translated. His feast day in the Syrian Orthodox Church is November 29.

Jerome (c.342-420) was born at Strido near Aquileia, and studied at Rome, where he was baptized. After travels and a period of solitude in the Syrian desert, he was ordained priest by Paulinus of Antioch, and became secretary to Pope Damasus I in 382. He settled finally at Bethlehem in 386, where he served as superior of a monastic community and devoted himself to study. Outspoken in many of the controversies of his day, Jerome's greatest achievement was his translation of the Bible into Latin from the original languages.

John Chrysostom (c.347-407) was born at Antioch and studied under Diodore of Tarsus, the leader of the Antiochene school of theology. After a period of great austerity as a hermit, he resumed to Antioch where he was ordained deacon in 381 and priest in 386. From 386 to 397 it was his duty to preach in the principal church of the city, and his best homilies, which earned him the title "Chrysostomos" or "the golden-mouthed": were preached at this time. In 397 Chrysostom became patriarch of Constantinople, where his efforts to reform the court clergy, and people led to his exile in 404 and finally to his death from the hardships imposed on him. Chrysostom stressed the divinity of Christ against the Arians and his full humanity against the Apollinarians, but he had no speculative bent He was above all a pastor of soul and was one of the most attractive personalities of the early Church.

John Climacus, called Climacus from his book *The Ladder* (Climax) *of Paradise* or *Divine Ascent*, lived during the sixth century but we know very little about him. He entered the religious state at the age of sixteen and lived for forty years as a solitary in a hermitage at the foot of Mount Sinai. He ultimately became superior-general of all the monks and hermits in that country. So widespread did his reputation become that St. Gregory the Great who was then pope asked for his prayers and sent gifts for his hospital near Mount Sinai. His book was a celebrated ascetic treatise dealing with the monastic virtues and vices, the anchoritic and cenobitic life, and the nature of total dispassionateness which is held up as the ideal of Christian perfection.

John of the Cross, Saint (1542-1591), co-founder with Saint Teresa of Avila of the Discalced Carmelites, was born of a poor family at Fontiveros in Old Castille. In 1563 he entered the Carmelite Order at Medina del Campo, and studied at Salamanca before his ordination to the priesthood in 1567. At this time he met Saint Teresa and became an ardent supporter of her movement of reform, for which he suffered greatly. John of the Cross is considered one of the greatest lyric poets of Spanish literature. His mystical teaching rests on his own experience, the study of the scriptures, and the discipline of Thomistic philosophy.

Julian of Norwich (c.1342-1413) was an anchoress whose *Revelations of Divine Love* are the fruit of her reflection on sixteen "showings" centered on our Lord's Passion, which she experienced while lying gravely ill. Her meditation on the mysteries she saw led her to a profound insight into the problem of sin and evil. She saw all things enfolded in God's love, all kept in him, who shall make "all things well."

Landsberg, John Justus (1489/90-1539) is perhaps better known by the Latin form of his name, Lanspergius, which he took from the place of his birth in Bavaria. After receiving the degree of Bachelor of Arts in Cologne, he entered Saint Barbara's, the celebrated charterhouse there. He made his profession in 1509, and in due course was ordained a priest. From 1530 to 1534/35 he was prior of the charterhouse of Vogelsang, and at the same time preacher at the court of John III, duke of Juliers, Cleves, and Berg, an unusual function for a Carthusian. Landsberg was one of the best spiritual writers of his day, the chief characteristic of his spirituality being the contemplation of Christ, the man-God, in his life, and in his passion and death. Landsberg was the editor of the works of Saint Gertrude, the great apostle in the middle ages of devotion to the heart of Jesus, and he himself was one of the earliest promoters of this devotion.

Leander of Seville (540-600) was bishop of Seville from 577 to 578. During 580 and 585, Leander traveled several times to Constantinople where he met Gregory the Great. It is believed that he influenced Gregory's *Moralia in Iob*. He supported Catholic orthodoxy in Spain and opposed the Arianism of the Visigoths. He was responsible for converting Prince Hermenegild in 579 and was involved in the Third Council of Toledo in 589. His surviving works include a homily presented at the Council of Toledo and a manual for nuns entitled *De Institutione Virginum*.

Leo the Great (c.400-461) was elected pope in 440. At a time of general disorder he did much to strengthen the influence of the Roman see. Although he was not a profound theologian, Leo's teaching is clear and forceful. His Tome was accepted as a statement of Christological orthodoxy at the Council of Chalcedon (451). One hundred and forty-three of his letters and ninety-six sermons have survived. The latter, which cover the whole of the liturgical year, have been published in a critical edition.

León, Luis de (1528-1591), in 1543, after his education in Madrid and Valladolid, became an Augustinian friar in Salamanca. He was a great linguist and scholar, and held various chairs at the university there. His understanding of Hebrew led him to question the accuracy of the Vulgate, which made him suspect to the Inquisition. His translation of the *Song of Songs* from the Hebrew into Spanish led to his imprisonment for four years. He was eventually absolved and restored to his chair in the University. He wrote much poetry, but his best known prose work was *The Names of Christ*. Made up of commentaries on the different names of Christ —

Shepherd, Prince of Peace, etc. — it is a beautifully written manual of Christianity.

Meister Eckhart (c.1260-c.1327), the Dominican master of theology, used daring paradox to make people aware of the limitations of the human mind, and thus receptive to a higher kind of knowledge without sense-impressions, images, or ideas. Though misunderstanding resulted in his dying under a cloud, Eckhart's reputation was saved by Tauler and Suso. Scholarly opinion now vindicates his orthodoxy, and Pope John Paul II has quoted him approvingly. His mystical insights appeal to members of other faiths. Eckhart acquired his mystical knowledge while living a busy, practical life during a period of unrest and violence: he can speak to our age.

Merton, Thomas (1915-1968), born in France, was educated in England, became a Catholic in Rome, and found peace with God at the Cistercian abbey of Gethsemane, U.S.A., which he entered three years after his baptism in 1941. His many writings were based on his experience of the monastic life, both in community and, in his last three years, as a hermit. His thought developed from explorations of the life itself to a realization of its universal significance in society and its affinities with Eastern monasticism, especially Zen Buddhism. It was this latter interest that led him to Thailand, where he died as the result of an accident.

Newman, John Henry (1801-1890) was born in London and brought up in the Church of England. He went up to Trinity College, Oxford, in 1817, became a Fellow of Oriel five years later, was ordained deacon in 1824 and appointed Vicar of Saint Mary's, Oxford, in 1832. The impact of his sermons was tremendous. He was the leading spirit in the Tractarian Movement (1833-1841) and the condemnation of "Tract 90" led to his resignation from Saint Mary's in 1843. Two years later he was received into the Catholic Church. He was ordained in Rome and founded a house of Oratorians in Birmingham. Newman's *Essay on the Development Christian Doctrine* throws light on his withdrawal of previous objections to Roman Catholicism; his *Apologia* reveals the deepest motives underlying his outward attitudes, and the *Grammar of Assent* clarifies the subjective content of commitment to faith. In 1879 he was made a cardinal.

Nicholas Cabasilas (b.1322/23) was a native of Thessalonica. After receiving an excellent education, first at Thessalonica and then in Constantinople, he entered the imperial service, in which for ten years he played a prominent part. After the deposition in 1354 of his friend, the emperor John VI Cantacuzenos, Cabasilas entered the Manganon monastery near Constantinople, and probably became a priest. This was the period of his greatest literary output, his two principal works being *The Life in Christ* end A *Commentary on the Divine Liturgy*, both of which were written for lay people. The kernel of Cabasilas' teaching, which was praised by the Council of Trent and by Bossuet, is the Christian's deification by means of the sacraments. Cabasilas died some time after the capture of Thessalonica by the Turks in 1387.

Novatian was a Roman theologian who later converted to Catholicism. He is best known for his work *De Trinitate* which was written in Latin. Novatian died during the Valerian persecution (253 to 260).

Ogerius (c.1205-1214), a disciple of Saint Bernard of Clairvaux, was abbot of Locedio in Piedmont. Little is known about his life, but the veneration in which he was held is shown by the dedication to him of the parish church of Locedio in 1653. Some of his sermons to his monastic community are found among the works of Saint Bernard.

Origen (185-253) One of the greatest thinkers of ancient times, Origen became head of the catechetical school of Alexandria at the age of eighteen. In 230 he was ordained priest by the bishop of Caesarea. His life was entirely devoted to the study of scripture and he was also a great master of the spiritual life. His book *On First Principles* was the first great theological synthesis. Many of his works are extant only in Latin as a result of his posthumous condemnation for heterodox teaching. Nevertheless, in intention he was always a loyal son of the Church.

Paul VI (1897-1978), born Giovanni Battista Montini, was ordained priest in 1920 and in 1925 entered the Vatican Secretariat of State. In this service of the Church he filled several important posts until he was named archbishop of Milan by Pius XII on 1 November 1954. Montini was made a cardinal in December 1958, and elected pope on 21 June 1963. During his long pontificate he showed himself to be an intrepid pastor and a determined promoter of the decrees of the Second Vatican Council In spite of opposition he firmly held the bark of Peter on its course into a new age.

Paulinus of Nola (353/354-431), the son of a noble family of Bordeaux, seems to have received a good education, for he sat at the feet of the famous Ausonius. After a brief public career he was baptized, and in agreement with his wife Therasia retired from the world, after dividing his fortune between the Church and the poor. He was ordained priest at Barcelona in 394. Shortly afterward he settled at Nola, near the tomb of Saint Felix, and with his wife opened a home for monks and the poor. In 409 he was ordained bishop. Paulinus was the foremost Christian Latin poet of this period, and the friend of Martin of Tours, Ambrose, and Augustine. Many of his letters survive. They are filled with Christian hope and charity and reflect the Church's understanding of the mystery of salvation.

Philoxenus of Mabbug (440-523) was born in 440 and was considered one of the leading thinkers of the Syrian Orthodox Church. Philoxenus was a prolific writer whose works were written in Syriac. His works include *Discourses on the Christian Life*, as well as works that dealt with the Incarnation. He was appointed the bishop of Mabbug by Peter the Fuller in 485 and later died in 523.

Picard, Max (1888-1965), philosopher and writer. He is best known for his works *Flight from God* and *The World of Silence*. He died at age 77 in Sorengo/Tessin.

Primasius of Hadrumetum (6ᵗʰ century), was the bishop of Hadrumetum in Northern Africa. He is best known for his commentary on the Book of Revelations.

Procopius of Gaza (c.475-c.538), was a rhetorician and biblical scholar. He was an important figure of the School of Gaza. He commented extensively on 1 and 2 Samuel, 1 and 2 Kings, 1 and 2 Chronicles, and on Isaac. His commentary on Octateuch the Shorter was preserved in the Codex Monac and was later translated into Latin and Greek. He is best known for the style of his epistles; approximately 166 of his epistles exist.

Prosper Gueranger (1805-1875), was ordained a priest in 1827 and later became a Benedictine monk. He purchased the priory of Solesmes in 1832 which opened a year later, and in 1837, was made its first abbot by Gregory XVI. He was a prolific writer and was greatly interested in liturgical matters. His best known works include the three-volume *Institutions liturgiques* (1840-1851) and the nine-volume *L'Année liturgiques* (1841-1866). He died in Solesmes in 1875.

Quodvultdeus of Carthage, friend and disciple of Saint Augustine, became bishop of Carthage about 437. But he was cast out by Geneseric in 539 and retired to Compania where he died about 453. It is highly probable that twelve sermons composed during the years 437-439 have been falsely attributed to Saint Augustine and should rather be attributed to Quodvultdeus. The same is true of six or seven other sermons which were in part handed down in Augustine's time.

Ralph the Fervent (d.1101) was a conscientious, erudite curé in the former diocese of Poitiers, who earned the sobriquet "ardens" by the ardor of his parochial sermons of which more than two hundred survive. They show a methodical treatment of the epistles and gospels of Sundays and greater feasts, emphasizing points of dogma and morals with frequent illustration from scripture and drawing widely on the Fathers and a variety of other authors. Although he was no respecter of persons and did not hesitate to reprove the great, the dissolute troubadour Count William IX of Poitiers, Duke of Aquitaine, included him in his court because of his great reputation. Ralph died in the Holy Land while on a crusade with the Count. Two books of letters and a history of crusading have not survived, but three manuscript copies of a theological summa have been preserved.

Rolle of Hampole, Richard (c.1300-1349), born in Yorkshire, went to Oxford, England, but broke off his studies at the age of eighteen to become a hermit. His last years were spent near the monastery of Cistercian nuns at Hampole, where he died and was buried. His prolific writings on mystical and ascetical topics contain references to his own experiences, "heat", "sweetness" and "song" being characteristic terms. He was commemorated in martyrologies of 1608 and 1672.

Rupert of Deutz (1070-1129) was born at Liege and entered the Benedictine monastery of Saint Laurence in that town. He died as abbot of Deutz, near Cologne. The author of several commentaries and treatises on holy scripture, Rupert is a typical representative of the monastic training he had received. He defended the mystical theology of the Benedictine tradition against the dialectic methods introduced into theology by Anselm of Laon and William of Champeaux.

Stuhlmueller, Carroll (1923-1994), member of the Congregation of the Passion since 1943, was professor of Old Testament studies at The Catholic Theological Union in Chicago and the only male member of the steering committee of the Women's Ordination Conference. A past president of the Catholic Biblical Association, he served as general editor of *The Bible Today*, as editor of *Old Testament Message*, a twenty-three-volume international commentary series, and on the editorial boards of the *Journal of Biblical Literature* and the *Catholic Biblical Quarterly*. He was the author of twenty-three books and many scholarly and popular articles on the Bible.

Symeon the New Theologian (949-1022), born in Galata in Paphlagonia, Symeon was educated in Constantinople, where in 977 he entered the famous monastery of Studios. Soon afterward he transferred to the nearby monastery of Saint Mamas, was ordained priest in 980, and about three years later became abbot. During his twenty-five years of office he instilled a new fervor into his community, but opposition to his teaching forced him to resign in 1005 and in 1009 he was exiled to Palonkiton on the other side of the Bosphorus. He turned the ruined oratory of Saint Marina into another monastery, and although he was soon pardoned, chose to remain there until his death rather than compromise his teaching. The greatest of Byzantine mystical writers, Symeon combined the contemplative tradition of Mount Sinai with the cenobitic tradition of Saint Basil and Saint Theodore of Studios. Symeon was much influenced by the homilies attributed to Macarius of Egypt, and taught that mystical experience of God is a normal part of a truly Christian life. For him this meant having a personal relationship with Christ dwelling in us through the Spirit. Symeon is called the "new" theologian to distinguish him from Saint Gregory Nazianzen, who has the title of "the theologian."

Tertullian (c.160-225), a native of Carthage, was bon of pagan parents. He gained a reputation at Rome as an expert in law, but after becoming a Christian in 195 he returned to Carthage and became a priest. After Augustine he is the most important and original early Latin theologian. Tertullian has been called the creator of ecclesiastical Latin, because many of the new terms he coined found a permanent place in theological vocabulary. His rigorist views led him to become a Montanist in 207.

Theodoret of Cyrus (c.393-466) was born in Antioch and educated there in the monastic schools. In about 416 he entered the monastery of Nicerte. He became bishop of Cyrrhus in 423 and for thirty five years governed his diocese with great wisdom and zeal. Soon after his election, however, he became involved in the christological controversy between Nestorius and Cyril of Alexandria, and sided with his friend Nestorius. Theodoret seems to have held Nestorian views at least until 434-435. At the council of Chalcedon, however, he was prevailed upon to anathematize Nestorius. Theodoret was the last great theologian of Antioch. His exegetical works are among the finest of the Antiochene school, and he made a contribution to almost every field of sacred science.

Thomas More (1477/8-1535) was born in London. After spending four years in the London Charterhouse without taking vows, he followed his father into the legal profession, eventually becoming Lord Chancellor of England. His wit and learning made his house in Chelsea the meeting piece for scholars such as Erasmus, Colet, and Grocyn. By the integrity of his public life, his virtues as husband and father, and his piety, More gave a shining example of what a Christian layman should be. His writings include many letters, refutations of the heresies of the time, and devotional works, but the book that made him famous all over Europe was his Utopia. More refused to sign an oath accepting the Act of Succession because it would have involved the repudiation of papal supremacy. For this he was imprisoned in the Tower of London for fifteen months and finally died a martyr's death.

Walter of Saint Victor (d.1180) was prior of the Augustinian Canons of Saint Victor. He wrote approximately 21 sermons covering various feast days. He is noted for his *Contra Quator Labyrinthos Franciae*, a highly controversial work which attacked the dialectical method espoused by Abelard, Peter Lombard, Peter of Poitiers, and Gilbert de la Porree.

Zeno of Verona (d.375) was bishop of Verona from 362. He was African by birth and his sermons, *Tractatus*, were similar in scope to writers like Tertullian and Cyprian. His sermons were not in circulation until the early Middle Ages. In art, Zeno of Verona is usually represented with a fish.

BIBLICAL CURSUS

Ordinary Time, Year II
Weeks 1-17

First Week

Monday	Genesis 1:1—2:4
Tuesday	Genesis 2:4-9.15.25
Wednesday	Genesis 3:1-24
Thursday	Genesis 4:1-24
Friday	Genesis 6:5-22; 7:17-24
Saturday	Genesis 8:1-22

Second Week

Sunday	Genesis 9:1-17
Monday	Genesis 11:1-26
Tuesday	Genesis 12:1-9; 13:2-18
Wednesday	Genesis 14:1-24
Thursday	Genesis15:1-21
Friday	Genesis 16:1-16
Saturday	Genesis 17:1-27

Third Week

Sunday	Genesis 18:1-33
Monday	Genesis 19:1-17.23-29
Tuesday	Genesis 21:1-21
Wednesday	Genesis 22:1-19
Thursday	Genesis 24:1-27
Friday	Genesis 24:33-41.49-67
Saturday	Genesis 25:7-11.19-34

Fourth Week

Sunday	Genesis 27:1-29
Monday	Genesis 27:30-45
Tuesday	Genesis 28:10—29:14
Wednesday	Genesis 31:1-18
Thursday	Genesis 32:4-31
Friday	Genesis 35:1-29
Saturday	Genesis 37:2-4.12-26

Fifth Week

Sunday	Genesis 39:1-23
Monday	Genesis 41:1-7.25-43
Tuesday	Genesis 41:56—42:26
Wednesday	Genesis 43:1-11.13-17.26-34
Thursday	Genesis 44:1-20.30-34
Friday	Genesis 45:1-15.21-28; 46:1-7
Saturday	Genesis 49:1-28.33

Sixth Week

Sunday	1 Thessalonians 1:10—2:12
Monday	1 Thessalonians 2:13—3:13
Tuesday	1 Thessalonians 4:5-18
Wednesday	1 Thessalonians 5:1-28
Thursday	2 Thessalonians 1:1-12
Friday	2 Thessalonians 2:1-17
Saturday	2 Thessalonians 3:1-18

Seventh Week

Sunday	2 Corinthians 1:1-14
Monday	2 Corinthians 1:15—2:11
Tuesday	2 Corinthians 2:12—3:6
Wednesday	2 Corinthians 3:7—4:4
Thursday	2 Corinthians 4:5-18
Friday	2 Corinthians 5:1-21
Saturday	2 Corinthians 6:1—7:1

Eighth Week

Sunday	2 Corinthians 7:2-16
Monday	2 Corinthians 8:1-24
Tuesday	2 Corinthians 9:1-15
Wednesday	2 Corinthians 10:1—11:6
Thursday	2 Corinthians 11:7-29
Friday	2 Corinthians 11:30—12:13
Saturday	2 Corinthians 12:14—13:13

Ninth Week

Sunday	Galatians 1:1-12
Monday	Galatians 1:13—2:10
Tuesday	Galatians 2:11—3:14
Wednesday	Galatians 3:15—4:7
Thursday	Galatians 4:8-31
Friday	Galatians 5:1-25
Saturday	Galatians 5:25—6:18

Tenth Week

Sunday	Philippians 1:1-11
Monday	Philippians 1:12-26
Tuesday	Philippians 1:27—2:11
Wednesday	Philippians 2:12-30
Thursday	Philippians 3:1-16
Friday	Philippians 3:17—4:9
Saturday	Philippians 4:10-23

Eleventh Week

Sunday	Isaiah 44:21—45:3
Monday	Ezra 1:1-8; 2:68—3:8
Tuesday	Ezra 4:1-5.24—5:5
Wednesday	Haggai 1:1—2:10
Thursday	Haggai 2:11-24
Friday	Zechariah 1:1—2:4
Saturday	Zechariah 2:5-17

Twelfth Week

Sunday	Zechariah 3:1—4:14
Monday	Zechariah 8:1017.20-23
Tuesday	Ezra 6:1-5.14-22
Wednesday	Ezra 7:6-28
Thursday	Ezra 9:1—10:5
Friday	Nehemiah 1:1—2:8
Saturday	Nehemiah 2:9-20

Thirteenth Week

Sunday	Nehemiah 3:33—4:17
Monday	Nehemiah 5:1-19
Tuesday	Nehemiah 7:72—8:18
Wednesday	Nehemiah 9:1-2.5-21
Thursday	Nehemiah 9:22-37
Friday	Nehemiah 12:27-47
Saturday	Isaiah 59:1-14

Fourteenth Week

Sunday	Proverbs 1:1-7.20-33
Monday	Proverbs 3:1-20
Tuesday	Proverbs 8:1-5.12-26
Wednesday	Proverbs 9:1-18
Thursday	Proverbs 10:6-32
Friday	Proverbs 15:8-9.16-17.25-26.29.33; 16:1-9; 17:5
Saturday	Proverbs 31:10-31

Fifteenth Week

Sunday	Job 1:1-22
Monday	Job 2:1-13
Tuesday	Job 3:1-26
Wednesday	Job 4:1-21
Thursday	Job 5:1-27
Friday	Job 6:1-30
Saturday	Job 7:1-21

Sixteenth Week

Sunday	Job 11:1-20
Monday	Job 12:1-25
Tuesday	Job 13:13—14:6
Wednesday	Job 18:1-21
Thursday	Job 19:1-29
Friday	Job 22:1-30
Saturday	Job 23:1—24:12

Seventeenth Week

Sunday	Job 28:1-28
Monday	Job 29:1-10; 30:1.9-23
Tuesday	Job 31:1-8.13-23.35-37
Wednesday	Job 32:1-6; 33:1-22
Thursday	Job 36:1-30; 40:1-5
Friday	Job 40:6-24; 42:1-6
Saturday	Job 42:7-10

INDEX OF AUTHORS

Abhishiktananda, Swam 5, 14
Adam of Perseigne 249
Ambrose of Milan 15
Angela of Foligno 234
Aphraates of Persia 73
Athanasius of Alexandria 239
Augustine of Hippo 22, 25, 53, 69, 107, 126, 127, 172, 184, 186, 216,
. . . . 224, 240
Bede of England 82, 193, 210, 212, 217
Bernard of Clairvaux 66, 285
Bérulle, Pierre de 9
Bossuet, Jacques 197
Cabasilas, Nicolas 226
Caesarius of Arles 85
Catherine of Siena 12
Caussade, Jean Pierre de 109, 266
Chardin, Pierre Teilhard de 112
Chromatius of Aquileia 17, 87
Clement of Alexandria 228
Clement of Rome 40, 46
Columban 158, 177
Congar, Yves 277
Cyprian of Carthage 103, 223
Cyril of Alexandria 83, 94, 118, 203, 205, 208, 219
Daniélou, Jean 20, 24, 32, 39, 48, 60, 148, 198, 255, 268, 273
Eckhart, Meister 72, 163, 190, 258, 274
Ephem of Syria 18
Francis of Sales 58
Fulgentius of Ruspe 104, 271
Gregory the Great 78, 200, 252, 262, 283, 287, 290
Gregory Nazianzen 169
Gregory of Nyssa 29, 211
Gregory Palamas 2
Griffiths, Bede 31
Guéranger, Prosper 242
Guerric of Igny 80, 181, 221, 238
Henry of Friemar 136
Hilary of Poitiers 7, 68, 195, 280, 289
Hildegard of Bingen 4, 36
Hilton, Walter 207
Ildefonsus of Toledo 160
Irenaeus of Lyons 35
Isaac of Stella 174
Jacob of Sarugh 54
Jerome of Bethlehem 164
John Chrysostom 28, 43, 51, 100, 102, 121, 140, 151, 155,
. . . . 176, 178, 192, 230, 254
John Climacus 76
John of the Cross 257, 263
John Justus Landsberg 244
John the Solitary 166
Julian of Norwich 8, 231, 247

Leander of Seville 115
Leo the Great 138, 214
Luis de León 250
More, Thomas 145
Merton, Thomas 156, 170, 269
Newman, John Henry . . . 10, 37, 45, 97, 111, 116, 122, 132, 147, 188, 236, 276
Novatian 88
Ogerius of Locedio 260
Origen of Alexandria 1, 49, 55, 63, 291
Paul VI 133
Paulinus of Nola 135
Philoxenus of Mabbug 61
Picard, Max 246
Procopius of Gaza 91
Quodvultdeus of Carthage 89, 92, 95
Ralph the Fervent 119, 130, 142
Rolle, Richard 180
Rupert of Deutz 62, 75, 98
Stuhlmueller, Carroll 202
Symeon the New Theologian 106, 124
Tertullian of Carthage 152
Theodoret of Cyrus 56, 162
Walter of Saint Victor 143
Zeno of Verona 282